Study Skills

for

Psychology Students

Study Skills

for

Psychology Students

A PRACTICAL GUIDE

SYLVIE C. COLLINS

Lecturer in Applied Social Psychology, University of Leeds

PAULINE E. KNEALE

Senior Lecturer in Geography, University of Leeds

HODDER
ARNOLD
AN HACHETTE UK COMPANY

For Sam and Jacob, Emma, Alice and Clara

First published in Great Britain in 2000
This impression reprinted in 2008 by
Hodder Education, an Hachette UK Company,
338 Euston Road, London NW1 3BH

www.hoddereducation.co.uk

The advice and information in this book are believed to be true and accurate at the date of
going to press, but neither the authors nor the publisher can accept any legal responsibility
or liability for any errors or omissions.

British Library Cataloguing in Publication Data
A catalogue record for this book is available from the British Library

Library of Congress Cataloging-in-Publication Data
A catalog record for this book is available from the Library of Congress

ISBN 978 0 340 76218 9

9 10

Typeset in Palatino and Gill Sans by Phoenix Photosetting, Chatham, kent
Printed and bound in India by Replika Press Pvt. Ltd.

What do you think about this book? Or any other Hodder Education title?
Please send your comments to www.hoddereducation.co.uk

CONTENTS

PREFACE

This book is for psychology students who want information about research and study in Higher Education, and is designed to defuse confusion and build confidence. It assumes that most psychologists would rather spend their extra time in hostelries, analysing the psyches of consumers, than in the library. Most people using self-help books or on training courses find that 90+ per cent of the material is already familiar, but the few new elements make it worthwhile. The 90 per cent increases your confidence that you are on the right track, and the remainder, we hope, sparks some rethinking, reassessment and refining. The trick with university study is to find a combination of ideas that suits you, promotes your research and learning, and adds self-confidence. As with all texts, not all the answers are here, but who said study would be a doddle? This text is intended for reference throughout your degree; some items will seem irrelevant at first but may be important later. There is a real difference between reading about a skill and applying the ideas in your degree. The **Try this** activities are designed to make the link between skills and their practical application, and to give you an opportunity to practise either mentally, or mentally and physically.

We hope you will enjoy some of the humour; this is not meant to be a solemn book, but it has serious points to make. The four crosswords follow the style familiar to readers of UK broadsheet newspapers, two quick crosswords and two cryptic; all the answers have vaguely psychological connections. Keep remembering you should be enjoying studying psychology at university; it is supposed to be exciting and it can be fun as well as a challenge.

KEEP SMILING!

ACKNOWLEDGEMENTS

Many thanks to all the Leeds psychology and geography undergraduates and postgraduates who helped to shape this text. Also to members of the School of Geography who previewed and commented on *Study Skills for Geography Students*, which this text builds on. Thanks are especially due to Mark Newcombe for the graphics, and to colleagues at Leeds in the Staff and Departmental Development Unit, Learning and Support Office and Careers Service, especially Chris Butcher, Maggie Boyle, Val Butcher and Sue Hawksworth.

Short extracts from book reviews are reproduced with permission from the *British Journal of Educational Psychology* and the *British Journal of Developmental Psychology*, © The British Psychological Society.

What's the difference between a psychologist and a magician?

A psychologist pulls habits out of rats.

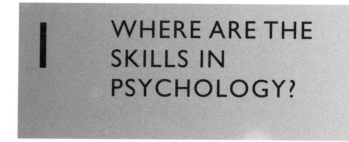

WHERE ARE THE SKILLS IN PSYCHOLOGY?

Be careful not to let education get in the way of your learning.

Studying psychology at university is about being an independent learner. You get to organise your own activities and to set your own agenda. This text is designed to help you get a grasp on what is expected, and provide helpful ideas on how to study. There is a tendency to assume that one already knows about studying, having done a bit at school. However, university education is different, and it may be useful to be offered a shortcut to understanding what learning at university involves, so that you can more quickly get to grips with psychology – which is (possibly) one of the reasons why you are studying it. It also aims to build your self-confidence by giving practical hints, advice and examples. If you are asked to compile a bibliography, present a seminar or refine an argument DON'T worry about how to do it; look it up, get the job done and go clubbing. You already have lots of study skills: reading, note-making and exams are normal activities. This book suggests ways to review and refine what you do and offers some new ideas that will make the study side of life less hassle.

Unlike many psychology texts, this one aims to be cheerful and adds some games to divert you. There are some terrible jokes; writing them down inevitably diminishes humour, but smile as you groan. Light relief is vital in study. If you find deep thinking leads to deep kipping, have a coffee, solve a crossword clue or tackle a wordsearch to refresh your brain, but remember to go back to thinking after your break!

A psychology degree has two elements:

- **The psychological knowledge element**, including all the current theories from biological and social psychology, the dopamine pathways, the consequences of child abuse, the relationship between food and exercise, the psychological implications of the development of Artificial Intelligence. The scope is universal because, of course, 'psychologists do it everywhere with everyone they meet'.

- **The skills element**. Often called transferable skills, they allow psychologists to be efficient researchers and are of longer-term benefit in the workplace. Most psychology graduates will acquire practical experience of the skills and attributes shown in Figure 1.1. Some will be picked up by osmosis, others will be taught at varying levels of detail.

In the last years of the twentieth century, UK student numbers expanded and the emphasis switched from lecturers teaching to students learning. Self-motivated

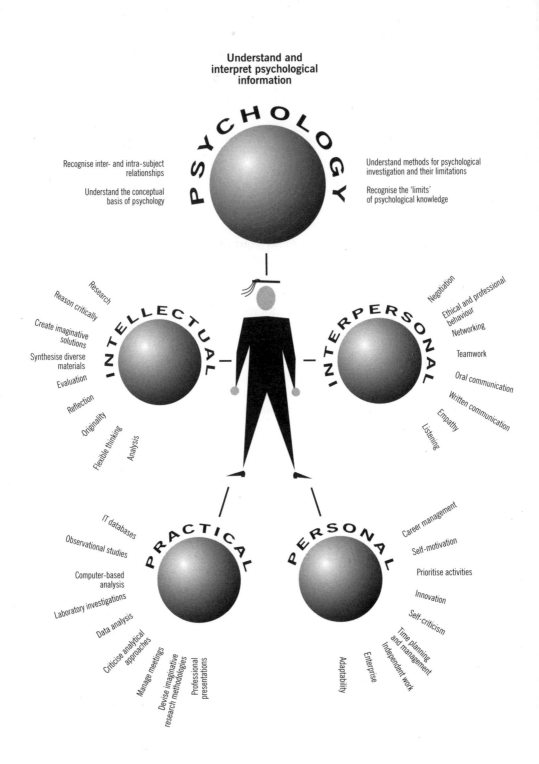

Figure 1:1 Skills and attributes of a psychology student

learning is vital in life, enabling you to keep abreast of developments and initiatives. Employment is unpredictable. Job market and company requirements change rapidly. Employers need individuals who are flexible about their careers. An efficient graduate is someone who sees their career as a process of work and learning, mixing them to extend skills and experience. This is the essence of lifelong learning.

In the jargon of career management and personal development, the phrase 'transferable skills' is readily quoted. To add value to your degree, you need to recognise and reflect on what you do every day in your course (see Chapter 2), and understand where these skills have market value. Employers claim to be happy with the academic skills students acquire, but they also want graduates with skills such as listening, negotiating and presenting. Any strengthening of your skills and experience of skill-based activities should add to your self-confidence and improve your performance as a psychologist and as a potential employee.

In addition to traditional psychology skills, your degree will give you the opportunity to experience some of the latest electronic trends, tele-working, surfing the world wide web (www), electronic journals, video-conferencing, e-mail, bulletin boards, databases and spreadsheets, and video. University encourages you to get wired, get trained and build your own electronic resource base. The technology may seem daunting but it is fun too. (And if some 5-year-old proto-anorak wearer can manage, so can you!)

The importance of graduates acquiring 'skills' as well as knowledge is well established and was reinforced in the Dearing Report (NCIHE, 1997), which defined four key graduate skills – happily psychology degrees are awash with them (see Table 1.1) However, these four need some unpacking to show what is involved. AGCAS (1997) lists the self-reliance skills that organisations and companies desire. Most elements involve Communication, IT and Learning how to learn:

✔ Communication skills, both written and oral, and the ability to listen to others.

✔ Interpersonal or social skills, the capacity to establish good, professional working relationships with clients and colleagues.

✔ Organisational skills, planning ahead, meeting deadlines, managing yourself and co-ordinating others.

✔ Problem analysis and solution, the ability to identify key issues, reconcile conflicts, devise workable solutions, be clear and logical in thinking, prioritise and work under pressure.

✔ Intellect, judged by how effectively you translate your ideas into action.

✔ Leadership – many psychology graduates eventually reach senior positions managing and leading people.

✔ Teamwork, working effectively in formal and informal teams.

✔ Adaptability, being able to initiate and respond to changing circumstances, and to continue to develop your knowledge, interests and attitudes to adapt to changing demands.

Graduate skills	In psychology degrees
Communication	All modules. Oral and written communication in seminars, tutorials, workshops, debates, group work, practical classes.
Numeracy	All modules using statistics, computing, databases, data handling; calculations in practicals, projects and dissertations.
Use of Information Technology	Word processing. Modules using graphics, statistics, databases, programming and SPSS (Statistical Package for the Social Sciences).
Learning how to learn	Taking personal responsibility for learning as an individual, and in group research, field work, projects and dissertations.

Table 1:1 Where to find NCIHE (1997) skills in action

✔ Technical capability, the capacity to acquire appropriate technical skills including scheduling, IT, statistics, computing and data analysis, and to update these as appropriate.

✔ Achievement, the ability to set and achieve goals for yourself and for others, to keep an organisation developing.

Most psychologists can expect to finish a degree with a sound knowledge of a number of parts of the subject, and to have developed graduate skills in synthesising information while researching psychological issues from different perspectives. While academic content varies from university to university, most psychology graduates will have gained practical experience of the skills and attributes shown in Figure 1.1. By graduation you should feel confident in listing these skills on a curriculum vitae (CV), and be able to explain where in the degree these abilities were practised and demonstrated.

1.1 LEARNING ACTIVITIES AT UNIVERSITY: WHAT TO EXPECT, AND SPOTTING THE SKILLS!

Psychology degrees are traditionally divided into three years called either Years 1, 2 and 3, or Levels 1–3. There may be an additional year intercalated for an industrial placement or a year abroad. A typical year is divided into 10 or 12 teaching blocks called modules or units, addressing psychological or related topics. Psychology degrees are usually progressive, which means that standards and difficulty increase each year, and modules in later years build on experience and learning in earlier years. This section outlines the main activities at university and some of the skills that can be practised during them.

Lectures

Believing any of the following statements will seriously damage your learning from lectures:

✘ In good lectures the lecturer speaks, the audience takes very rapid notes and silence reigns.

✘ The success of a lecture is all down to the lecturer.

✘ A great lecturer speaks slowly so students can take beautifully written, verbatim notes.

✘ Everything you need to know to get a first class degree will be mentioned in a lecture.

✘ Lectures are attended by students who work alone.

Lectures are the traditional teaching method, usually about 50 minutes long, with one lecturer and loads of students. If your lectures involve 300+ students they may seem impersonal and asking questions is difficult. Good wheezes to manage lectures include:

✔ Get there early, find a seat where you can see and hear.

✔ Have a supply of paper, pens and pencils ready.

✔ Get your brain in gear by thinking, 'I know I will enjoy this lecture, it will be good, I really want to know about . . .', 'Last week we discussed . . ., now I want to find out about . . .'!

✔ Before the lecture read through the notes from the last session, and maybe some library material too. Even 5 minutes' worth gets the old brain in gear.

✔ Look at handouts carefully. Many lecturers give summary sheets with lecture outlines, main points, diagrams and reading. Use these to plan reading, revision and preparation for the next session.

✔ Think critically about the material presented.

✔ Revise and summarise notes soon after a lecture; it will help in recalling material later. Decide what follow-up reading is required.

Skills acquired in lectures include understanding psychological issues and recognising research frontiers and subject limitations.

Tutorials: What are they? What do you do?

Usually a tutorial is a 50-minute discussion meeting, with an academic or postgraduate acting as the chairperson, and 6–12 students. The style of tutorials varies between departments, but there is normally a set topic, involving preparation. You might be asked to prepare a short talk, write an essay, write outline essays, prepare material for a debate, review a paper, and to share your information with the group. The aim is to discuss and evaluate issues in a group that is small enough for everyone to take part. Other jolly tutorial activities include brainstorming examination answers, comparing note styles, creating a poster, planning a research strategy, discussing the practicalities of a research proposal, evaluating dissertation possibilities, and the list goes on.

The tutor's role is NOT to talk all the time, is NOT to teach, and is NOT to dominate the discussion. A good tutor will set the topic and style for the session well in advance so everyone knows what they are doing, and will let a discussion flow, watch the time, make sure everyone gets a fair share of the conversation, assist when the group is stuck and sum up if there is no summariser to do so as part of the assignment. A good tutor will give comments on your activity, but tutorials are YOUR time.

Some tutors will ask you to run a couple of tutorials in their absence, and to report a summary of the outcomes. This is not because tutors are lazy, but because generating independence is an important part of university training. Student-led and student-managed tutorials demonstrate skills in the management of group and personal work. When a tutor is ill, continuing unsupervised uses the time effectively. A tutor may assign, or ask for, volunteer chairpersons, timekeepers and reporters to manage and document discussions.

Your role is to arrive at the session fully prepared to discuss the topic NO MATTER HOW UNINTERESTED YOU ARE. Use tutorials to develop listening and discussion skills, to become familiar with talking about psychological issues and to build up experience of arguing about ideas.

Top Tips

✔ Taking time to prepare for tutorials will stop (or lessen) nerves, and you will learn more by understanding a little about the topic in advance.

✔ Reviewing notes, and reading related material, will increase your confidence in discussions.

✔ Asking questions is a good way of saying something without having to know the answer.

✔ Have a couple of questions or points prepared in advance, and use them early on. Get stuck in!

✔ Taking notes in tutorials is vital. Other people's views, especially when different to your own, broaden your ideas about a topic, but they are impossible to recall later unless noted at the time. Tutorial notes make good revision material.

Tutorial skills include listening, communication, presentation, critical reasoning, analysis, synthesis, networking and negotiation.

Seminars

Seminars are a slightly more formal version of a tutorial, with 12–30 people. One person (or more than one) makes a presentation for about half the allotted period, leaving ample time for group discussion. Seminars provide a great opportunity to brainstorm and note the ideas and attitudes of colleagues. Spot extra examples and approaches to consider later. Take notes.

Even if you are not a main speaker, you need to prepare in advance. In the week when you speak you will be enormously grateful to everyone who contributes to the discussion. To benefit from this kind of co-operation you need to prepare and make contributions in the weeks when you are not the main presenter.

ONLY TO BE READ BY THE NERVOUS. (Thank you.) If you are nervous, alarmed or just plain terrified, then volunteer to do an early seminar. It gets it out of the way before someone else does something brilliant (well, moderately reasonable) and upsets you! Acquiring and strengthening skills builds your confidence so seminars appear less of a nightmare. By the third week you will know people and be positively blasé.

Seminar skills include discussion, listening, analysis, teamwork, giving a professional performance and networking to more connections than are available through Orange.

Workshops or large-group tutorials

Workshops are classes with 20–40 students that support lecture and practical modules. They have varied formats. They may be called large-group tutorials, support classes or revision classes. There will usually be preparation work and a group activity. Tutors act as facilitators, not as teachers. Expect a tutor to break large groups into sub-groups for brainstorming and discussion. These sessions present a great opportunity to widen your circle of friends and to find colleagues with similar and diverse views.

Workshop skills are the same as for tutorials and seminars with wider networking and listening opportunities.

Computer and laboratory practicals

Practical classes are the 'hands-on' element of a psychology degree. Many departments assign practical class time, when tutor support is available, BUT completing exercises and developing your proficiency in IT, computing and measuring skills will take additional time. Check out the opening hours of computer laboratories on campus.

Assessment

Assessment comes like Christmas presents, regularly and in all sorts of shapes. Assessments should be regarded as helpful because they develop your understanding. There are two forms:

- Within-module assessment of progress, where the marks do not count (formative), and usually involve some feedback.

- Assessments where the marks do count (summative). Feedback may or may not happen, depending on the test and system. The results eventually appear on your degree result notification for the edification of your first employer who wants written confirmation of your university prowess.

There is a slight tendency for the average student to pay less attention to formative, within-module assessments, where the marks do not count. Staff design formative tests because they know 99 per cent (± 1 per cent) of students need an opportunity to 'have a go', to get an insight into procedures and expected standards, when marks are not an issue.

Assessments are very varied: examinations, essays, oral presentations, seminars, posters, discussion contributions, debates, reports, reviews of books and papers, project designs, critical learning logs, laboratory competence, computer-based practicals, multiple choice tests . . . It is a matter of time management to organise your life and them (Chapter 3). You should know in advance exactly how each module is assessed and what each element is worth. Many modules have mixed assessments, so those who do very well in examinations or essay writing are not consistently advantaged. Many departments have standard assessment criteria. Get hold of your own departmental versions or see examples for essays (Chapter 9), oral presentations (Chapter 13), practical reports (Chapter 15), dissertations (Chapter 18) and poster presentations (Chapter 21). If you cover all the criteria then the marks come rolling in.

Amongst the many skills enhanced by assessments are thinking, synthesis, evaluation, originality and communication.

Non-academic experience

Do not underestimate what you know! In your years at university you also acquire loads of personal skills, like negotiating with landlords, debt crisis management, charming bank staff, juggling time to keep a term-time job and deliver essays to deadline, being flexible over who does the washing up and handling flatmates and tutors. Add evidence of these skills to your CV and job application forms.

1.2 THE RESEARCH PROCESS

All psychology students are 'reading' for a degree, finding out for themselves – the research process. Taught activities involve 20–50 per cent of the timetable,

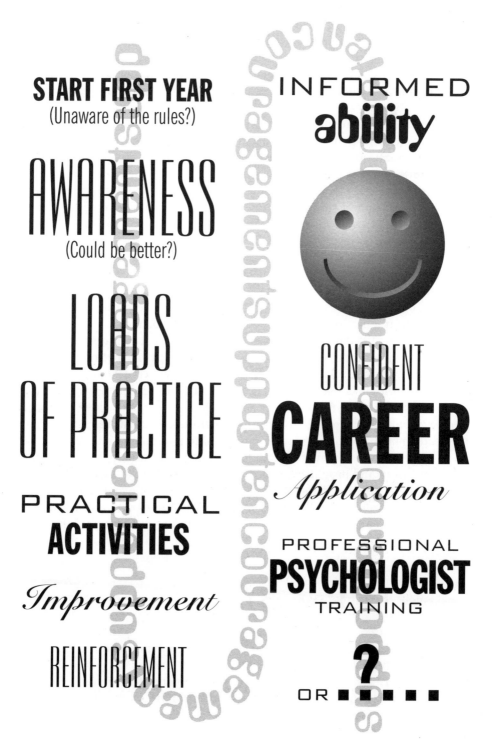

Figure 1:2 The skills route

leaving plenty of time for personal research into different sub-topics, and study activities that reinforce understanding. The scope of psychology is vast. Covering all aspects is impossible. Every psychologist is aiming to maximise their own research activities, to expand their psychological knowledge within the constraints of time, facilities and energy. Consequently, working in a group can be seriously beneficial.

Psychological issues are not simple. Lecturers will indicate what is already well understood, discuss areas of the subject where we are less sure about what happens and point out where knowledge is missing, provisional, uncertain and worthy of further investigation. Most psychological issues are highly interlocking and multidimensional. Psychologists' greatest strength is their ability to take complex, unclear and at times contradictory information from a wide range of sources and to synthesise it to make sense of the picture on a range of different levels.

By the time you graduate you should have an enhanced ability to recognise both the boundaries of knowledge of psychology, what is known and what is not known, and what you as an individual know and do not know. Recognising the boundaries of one's own expertise is a relevant life skill. Someone who does not understand the implications of their actions in making changes to procedures, for example, is a potential danger to themselves and the wider community. University learning is not about recalling a full set of lecture notes. It is about understanding issues and being able to relate and apply them in different contexts.

Recognising the links between psychology and other disciplines will enhance your research ability. Large numbers of psychology students have no formal school psychology background. If you are one of these students remember this is not a disadvantage; you are obviously interested in psychology, and all topics are fresh and not confused by half-remembered notes. Psychology draws on many subjects for theory and insights; it is likely that a number of your lecturers did not do psychology at university. Use the background information and skills you have from other subjects to strengthen your psychological research. Mature students with longer experience of life, politics, social conditions and general knowledge have an extensive skill base to build on.

1.3 HOW TO USE THIS BOOK

No single idea is going to make a magical difference to your learning, but taking time to think about the way you approach tasks like reading and thinking, listening and writing, researching and presenting should help your efficiency. Studying is a personal activity. There are no 'right' ways, but there are tips, techniques, shortcuts and long-cuts.

If you attempt to read the whole book in one go you are likely to feel got at and preached at. *This is not the idea*. Have a look through the chapter headings and index. If you are concerned or stuck then we hope you will find a section that will help. Use the book as a handbook throughout your degree. Some parts are relevant for Year 1, others like the dissertation and project advice (Chapter 18) will matter more in the last year. When you have an essay or book review to write, then look at the relevant chapters. No one expects you to know the whole of the Greek alphabet or all the acronyms used in psychology, but if someone mentions either there is a bit of this book (pp. 241 and 249) which can act as a reference. The key is to view this as encouragement (Figure 1.2). Build on your existing skills and follow the skills route. There are lots of **Try This** opportunities, suggesting ways of practising or applying your skills. Adapt them to your needs. Treat them as part of your psychology learning rather than as isolated skill exercises. You build experience by doing things, not by watching them.

The aim of the book is to encourage you, to help build your self-confidence in your skills, and to show where they are transferable and marketable. Your task is to decide to what extent you agree with the ideas in this book and apply them for your own purposes. In some ways this is like a cookery book: many of the **Try This** activities are recipes, BUT adapt, garnish, modify and extend them. University research is a creative activity, like cooking. Some statements are deliberately controversial, designed to encourage thinking. Most of the figures and examples are deliberately 'less than perfect'. You are asked to consider how they can be improved, and what needs changing, as a way into active criticism. Universities provide IT facilities and gymnasiums, but getting more skilled means 'working out'. The first year is a good time to practise and enhance study skills, but it is important to keep practising and reflecting throughout your degree.

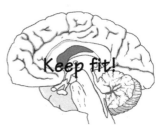

1.4 REFERENCES AND FURTHER READING

For a background on what psychology involves see:

Hartley, J. (1998). *Learning and Studying: A Research Perspective.* London: Routledge. (Reviews some really interesting research on students' study skills.)

Heffernan, T.M. (1997). *A Student's Guide to Studying Psychology.* Hove: Psychology Press.

The British Psychological Society website at http://www.bps.org.uk. Accessed 14 April 2000.

For skills try:

AGCAS (1997). *Making Applications.* Graduate Careers Information, Association of Graduate Careers Advisory Services.

Bucknall, K. (1996). *Studying at University: How to Make a Success of Your University Course.* Plymouth: How To Books.

Buzan, T. (1995). *Use Your Head.* London: BBC Books.

Buzan, T. & Buzan, B. (1993). *The Mind Map Book.* London: BBC Books.

Drew, S. & Bingham, R. (eds) (1997). *The Student Skills Guide.* Aldershot: Gower.

NCIHE (1997). *Higher Education in the Learning Society.* Report of the National Committee of Inquiry into Higher Education. London: HMSO.

Northedge, A., Thomas, J., Lane, A. & Peasgood, A. (1997). *The Sciences Good Study Guide.* Buckingham: Open University.

Payne, E. & Whittaker, L. (2000). *Developing Essential Study Skills.* Harlow: Prentice Hall.

Weinstein, C.E. & Hume, L.M. (1998). *Study Strategies for Lifelong Learning.* Washington, DC: American Psychological Association.

Psychograms I

Try these psychological anagrams. Answers on p. 253.

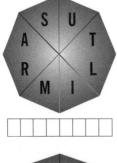

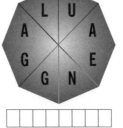

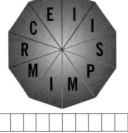

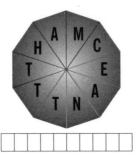

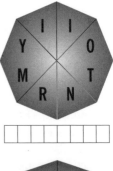

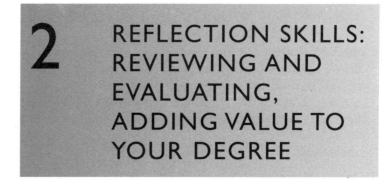

2 REFLECTION SKILLS: REVIEWING AND EVALUATING, ADDING VALUE TO YOUR DEGREE

All my real skills are undervalued.

Psychology students can be described as autonomous lifelong learners who take responsibility for planning their own learning, deciding what to research and how to operate. This is a complicated way of saying it is up to you decide what to do and when to do it. Degrees involve personal decisions about what to read, research, ignore, practise, panic over. . . . Regularly reviewing your schedule, work plans and achievements reduces associated worries and provides some sensible options when there is a choice (although many decisions are motivated by a looming deadline). Taking control and responsibility for your work can seem scary, and the lack of guidance about academic work is one reason why many new university students feel disoriented, chucked in at the deep end without a *Baywatch* lifeguard in sight.

This chapter discusses why evaluation and reflection are useful skills, and how reflection techniques can give you a framework to help your decision-making in your studies. There is a variety of **Try This** activities because everyone has their own needs and priorities, and different activities will be relevant at different times of year and in different years of your degree. Most activities will benefit from a 'mental and physical (pen in hand)' approach. The knack is to develop this style of thinking so that it becomes automatic; reviewing becomes a process you can do while waiting for the bus or cleaning out the gerbil.

The skill benefits from this chapter are thinking, evaluation, reviewing and reflection. Reflection skills are not easily taught, or acquired overnight. They develop with experience and maturity. They are the outcome of thinking actively and often about experiences and placing them in a personal context, an iterative process.

2.1 WHY REFLECT?

Adding value to your degree
Some students find it hard to see how parts of their degree course interconnect; this is demotivating. One quote from a final-year student encapsulates this:

I had a great time in the first two years at university and I enjoyed the different psychology modules but I had no idea why the lecturers seemed so keen on statistics or why we had to do psychophysics. It seemed like a lot of different things until somewhere in the final year when I could begin to see the relevance of different sections. I think I would have understood it and got more interested a bit sooner if I had done some more reading, psychology as a whole might have gelled sooner.

Taking a little time to think about interconnections between modules – for example, why principles of perception are important for developmental psychologists, or which statistical tests can be used in your project – can help give your modules more cohesion and can therefore be motivating.

Increasing employability

Many employers look for enthusiastic graduates with skills of articulation and reflection, those who can explain, with examples, and evaluate their experience and qualities. Recruiters want to identify people with the awareness and self-motivation to be proactive about their learning. The ability to teach oneself, to be aware of the need to update one's personal and professional expertise, and to retrain, is vital for effective company or organisational performance and competition (Boud, Cohen and Walker, 1993; Harvey, Moon, Geall and Bower, 1997; Hawkins and Winter, 1995).

Your academic background may be of little interest to an employer. Whether you are expert in neuropsychological assessment, have researched the aetiology of eating disorders or the phenomenon of synaesthesia is not important. What is relevant is that faced with the task of researching the market for a new type of furbie you can apply the associated skills and experience gained through researching 'attitudes towards smoking among adolescents' (thinking, reading, researching, presentation, making connections) to the marketing of large-eyed furry toys. It is your ability to use the skills acquired through school and university in a workplace role that an employer will value.

Remember that an employer is looking for a mix of skills: evidence of your intellectual, operational or practical and interpersonal skills (look back at Figure 1.1). Your psychological nous is demonstrated by your degree certificate. You need also to include your practical, transferable and 'hands-on' skills on your CV. Keeping a record of your thoughts on forms like those in the **Try This** activities here, or in a diary or journal-style log, will pay off when filling in application forms. They will remind you of what you did and of the skills involved.

If you plan to work in very large multinational companies where skills training is a big budget item and there are many training courses, your lifelong learning will be enhanced by company policy. If you want to establish your own business, or to join small and medium-sized enterprises (SMEs) with small numbers of employees and modest budgets, then your university skills will be directly beneficial. Psychologists with 'skills' are valuable employees.

2.2 Getting started

Some businesses require graduate trainees to keep a daily log in their early years of employment. This encourages staff to assess the relative importance of tasks and to be efficient managers of their time. It is a reflective exercise where at 4.50 p.m. each day, you complete a statement like:

I have contributed to the organisation's success/profits today by ....

....

I was fully skilled to do...

I was less capable at ....

Other comments..

At the end of the week or month these statements are used to prioritise business planning and one's Continuing Professional Development (CPD). It is an activity that most new employees hate. However, most will admit, later, that it taught them an enormous amount about their time and personal management style, and they wished they had started sooner. In time, this type of structured self-reflection becomes automatic; individuals continually evaluate their personal performance and respond accordingly.

The psychology student equivalent:

I contributed to my psychology degree today by ....

....

I could have been more efficient at doing this if ....

Tomorrow I am going to ....

Reviewing the whole day may seem too much of a drag. It may be easier to start by responding to statements like:

What I have learned from this paper/lecture is ....

It fits with ....

It has a methodology that could be used for..

In future I will..

There are six **Try This** activities in this chapter, each suited to different stages of a degree course. These kinds of forms can be used to build up a learning log, recording your university experience. A learning log can act simply as a diary, somewhere to note activities and skills, but a reflective log asks for a more detailed, reasoned response.

2.3 REFLECTING ON YOUR DEGREE EXPERIENCE

Try This 2.1 asks you to articulate your feelings about your current, personal approach to learning and your degree course. If you then evaluate your response and decide to do something in response to your reflection, you are taking charge.

TRY THIS 2.1 – Personal reflection

This is a random list of degree skills. For those relevant to you now, make a self-assessment of your current position and a reflective explanatory comment (see examples here). Expand the list to suit your own position.

Skill	Current skill level High	Low	Comment
Delivering essays on time.		*	I've had two extensions this semester. I need to sort out the technical problems ahead of the deadline, instead of on the day.
Speaking in tutorials and seminars.			
Listening carefully to discussions and responding.	*		I can do this. Maybe I am still too concerned about whether people agree or not.
Being efficient in library research.		*	I spend hours going from one building to the next chasing up materials. I could try looking for alternative books in the same place.
Knowing when to stop reading.	*		I read to the last minute, and then rush the writing. Some reading deadlines would help.
Making notes.	.		
Using standard grammar, spelling and punctuation in writing.	*		Pretty confident about my spelling. Need to find out how grammar check on the computer works.
Using diagrams to illustrate points.			

Skill	Current skill level High Low	Comment
Organising ideas coherently.		
Including relevant information in essays.	*	I try to include everything in an essay, to show I have done some reading!
Including accurate information in reports and essays.		
Drawing the threads of an argument together and so developing a logical conclusion.	*	I've had 'weak concluding section' feedback on two essays. I haven't worked out how to address this yet.
Summarising information from different sources.		
Putting ideas into my own words.		
Negotiating.	*	Managed a tricky situation in the group practical this week – feeling pretty good about it.
Disagreeing in discussion without causing upset or being upset.	*	Ditto.
Using databases to extract psychological information.	*	Am fine on PsychLit. Haven't tried Web of Science yet.
Being more open to new ideas.		
Identifying the important points.	*	Underlining or highlighting bits in notes would help and wouldn't take as long as rewriting things.
Being organised and systematic.	*	My files are OK. If I used a diary it might help.
Trying out new ideas.		
Making time to sit down and think about different ideas.	*	This seems really odd, because you sort of do thinking all the time. It's not really a cool activity. Could try when no one knows – in bed maybe.
Using IT for word processing.		
Reading appropriate material.		

Try This 2.2 is a self-assessment exercise you might want to repeat after a term or semester. Please note that when people self-assess a skill before and after an activity, the assessment at the end is frequently lower than that at the start. Although the skill has been used and improved during the activity, by the end it is possible to see how further practice and experience will lead to a higher skill or competence level. Now look at **Try This 2.2**. In thinking about your strengths and weaknesses talk to family and friends, ask what skills you have and what you do well.

TRY THIS 2.2 – Being pro-active about skill development

Having completed **Try This 2.1** go back to the list and highlight three skills you would like to be proactive about in the next three months. Now make some notes about how to be active about these three issues. Like New Year's resolutions, this activity can bear revisiting.

Top Tip

✔ Reflection is reinforced when you write down your thoughts or speak them aloud.

2.4 WITHIN-MODULE REFLECTION

Some modules will have a learning log as part of the assessment process. As part of a skills module or as part of a practical or dissertation it serves the dual purpose of a diary and a reflective statement. Practise by answering some of the questions in **Try This 2.3**. With a little thought you can adapt most of them for most modules, or for your degree as a whole.

TRY THIS 2.3 – Reflecting on a class or module

Pick a module, or part of it, and answer the questions that are appropriate. Some sample answers from psychology students are included on p 253.

- What I want to get out of attending this module is ....
- In what ways has this module/session helped me to develop a clearer idea of myself, my strengths and weaknesses?
- Record your current thinking about the skills you *can* acquire from this module. Tick those you want to develop and make a plan.
- I have discovered the following about myself with respect to: decision-making . . . ; research . . . ; thinking . . ..
- How efficiently did I (my group) work?
- What skills did I use well? What skills did other members of the group use well?

- How did preparation for my (the group) presentation progress? What were my concerns?
- What skills were lacking in me (the group) and caused things to go badly?
- How did I (the group) make decisions?
- What have I learned about interview technique? / asking questions? / planning laboratory work? / observing in the field?
- What did I enjoy most about the exercise / session / module / degree course?
- What did I enjoy least about the exercise / session / module / degree course?
- What was the biggest challenge to me in this exercise / session / module / psychology degree?
- Give personal examples that illustrate two of the skills and attributes you have gained from this module.

The last four questions in **Try This 2.3** are frequently asked in interviews. Thinking of an answer in advance gives you more chance to enthuse and be positive. You may not have had much experience of some skills, but some experience is better than none.

TRY THIS 2.4 – Reflecting on a day

Brainstorm a list of things that happened (5 minutes maximum, just a back-of-an-envelope list), e.g.:
- *Played a game of squash.*
- *Went to rehearsal.*
- *Went to Dr Alien's lecture.*
- *Talked to Colin.*

Then brainstorm a list of things that made the class / day unsatisfactory, e.g.:

✗ *Colin went on for hours.*
✗ *Bus was late.*
✗ *I didn't understand what Dr Alien was going on about.*
✗ *Printer queues were hours long.*

Leave the two lists on one side for a couple of hours. Then grab a cup of coffee and a pen, reread your lists and make a note of where you might have saved time or done something differently. Consider what might make life more satisfactory if these situations happen again:

✔ *Natter to Colin for an hour MAXIMUM! over coffee and leave.*
✔ *Take a book on the bus.*
✔ *Have a look at Dr Alien's last three lectures. If it still doesn't make sense ask my tutor or Dr Alien.*
✔ *Need to take something to read, or do on-line www searches, while printouts are chugging through.*

Sometimes one recognises that a particular lecture, laboratory class or day has passed without being of any real benefit to one's degree. Try to identify why; **Try This 2.4** and **Try This 2.5** contain some ideas.

TRY THIS 2.5 – Reflecting on a class

The seminar was: very useful / useful / OK / boring / not worth going to

The good things about it were..

The things that weakened it were..

To make it useful in retrospect I will .... (read ...., check out .... on the www, talk to ....)...

In order to get more from the next seminar I will...

By analysing and reflecting on what is happening in a structured manner you will feel more in control. Following up one in ten of the ideas you have will be an improvement on the present. It is possible to review in your head (the bus stop might be a good location) but writing down your list is likely to be more beneficial. It will develop your reflective skills and prompt action on those reflections if you put the lists somewhere where you will see them again.

2.5 WHAT TO DO FIRST?

There are many competing demands on your time, and it is not always obvious whether the next priority is to finish a practical report, browse the library shelf for next week's essay or read another paper. Reflect on who or what takes most of your time. Some tasks do take longer than others, but the proportions should be roughly right. Questions that encourage prioritising tasks include:

? Why am I doing this now, is it an urgent task? (see also Table 3.1)

? Is the time allocated to a task matched by the reward? For example, it is worth considering whether a module essay worth 33 per cent deserves five times the time devoted to a tutorial essay worth 20 per cent?

? When and where do I work best? Am I taking advantage of times when my brain is in gear?

? How long have I spent on this web search, seminar preparation, statistics worksheet, communication essay? Were these times in proportion? Which elements deserve more time?

? Am I being interrupted when I am working? If I worked somewhere else would that help?

? Who causes me to take time out? Are there ways of limiting this by say an hour a week?

2.6 START ON YOUR CV NOW

Use reflective material to amplify your CV. The thought of leaving university, applying for jobs and starting a career is probably as far from your mind as the problem of primate acquisition of language. Nevertheless, for those desperate for money and applying for summer jobs, having a focused CV could significantly increase the chance of selection for that highly paid shelf-filler or checkout job. Building up a CV as your degree course progresses can save time in the last year. An electronic CV designer may be available on-line; the university careers service should be able to advise you. Reflecting on your skills at an early stage may highlight the absence of a particular skill while there is time to get involved in something that will demonstrate that you have acquired it before the end of your degree. Have a go at **Try This 2.6**.

If you have forgotten what skills your modules involved, look back at the course outline. It is likely to include a statement like: 'On completion of the module students will be able to . . .'. Use this kind of statement to amplify your CV and jog your memory.

TRY THIS 2.6 – Skills from my psychology degree

Expand and tailor this list for your degree, from your university. Be explicit in articulating the skills and the evidence. Update it each semester. There are a few starter suggestions in the second column.

Skills acquired from my degree to date	
Numeracy	*Statistics modules in Years 1 and 2. Calculations for laboratory practicals. I completed multivariate analyses of variance for my project.*
Able to meet deadlines – essays, reports, practical write-ups etc.	*All essays completed in time.* *Organised group project and planned the mini-deadlines that kept our team on track.*
Teamwork skills – workshop, group work	
Communication and presentation skills, tutorials, seminars and presentations	*Used OHPs and video in tutorial and workshop presentations in Level 2 and PowerPoint in the Finalists' Conference.*

TRY THIS 2.6 – *Continued*

Skills acquired from my degree to date – *continued*	
Computing skills	
IT skills	*Word processing of essays and 10,000-word dissertation. Included Excel diagrams, PowerPoint graphics and output from SPSS packages.*
Able to put ideas across	
Able to work individually	
Time management skills	
Organisational skills	*Final-year dissertation, interview study at local hospital, required co-ordination with GPs, ward staff and patients.*
Self-motivated	
Able to prioritise tasks	
Problem-solving	

Try This 2.6 does not include skills acquired through leisure pursuits or work experience. Compile a second list from those experiences. Driving, shorthand, stocktaking, flying, language skills, writing for a newspaper or magazine, acting as treasurer, secretary or chair of a society – all these involve skills like time management, negotiation, listening, writing reports. Work experience does not have to be paid; voluntary activities can give you valuable experience that pays dividends on a CV.

2.7 REFERENCES AND FURTHER READING

On the changing nature of work and the importance of skills, see the following:

Boud, D., Cohen, R. & Walker, D. (1993). *Using Experience for Learning.* Buckingham: Society for Research in Higher Education and Open University Press.

Harvey, L., Moon, S., Geall, V. & Bower, R. (1997). *Graduates' Work: Organisational Change and Students' Attributes.* Birmingham: Centre for Research into Quality and Association of Graduate Recruiters.

Hawkins, P. & Winter, J. (1995). *Skills for Graduates in the 21st Century.* Birmingham: Association of Graduate Recruiters.

Purcell, K. & Pitcher, J. (1996). *Great Expectations: The New Diversity of Graduate Skills and Aspirations*. Manchester: Higher Education Careers Services Unit, Careers Service Trust, Institute for Employment Research.

If these are unavailable in your library or careers service offices, do a library keyword search (see p. 35) using career, lifelong learning, graduate skills and career development.

People Links?

By changing one letter at a time, and keeping to real words, can you make connections between these people's names? Answers on p. 254.

JUNG	WEST	BECK	GALE
ROSE	HULL	WALL	BURT

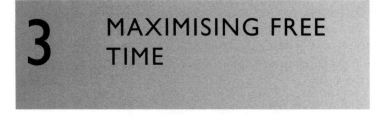

3 MAXIMISING FREE TIME

Found it, photocopied it, time for coffee.

University is different from school life and employment. There is lots of free time for snowboarding, street luge, ballroom dancing, being elected Ski Club Secretary, playing the banjo and socialising, but many students find meeting coursework deadlines difficult. Time management techniques are especially vital for those with a heavy sport or social programme, a part-time job in term-time, and for part-time and mature students with jobs running in parallel with the degree. Developing your time management skills should allow you to do all the boring tasks efficiently, like laundry and essays, leaving free time for other activities. It is unlikely that any one idea will change your life overnight, but a few time-saving shortcuts can relieve pressure. Try something. Use your reflection and evaluation skills to identify what to do next and to assign time to your studies.

Ideally, one can envisage research, whether for an essay or a dissertation, moving linearly from inception to final report or presentation (Figure 3.1a). Regrettably, the research process is rarely this simple. The normal elements of life intervene, and the way you view and treat any topic usually changes as research progresses. This means that a linear research model is not realistic. The reality of normal progress (Figure 3.1b) requires plenty of time for the research process to evolve. Half-way through your research you may have to go back almost to the start, reconsider your approach and execute a revised programme. Your ability to manage time, and recognising and adjusting to changing goalposts, are vital skills improved by university life.

3.1 IS THERE A SPARE MINUTE?

Start by working out what time is available for research and study by filling out your timetable using **Try This 3.1**. Assume social and sport activities will fill every night and all weekend, and that arriving at university before 10 is impossible. The remaining time is available for research, reading, thinking, planning and writing without touching the weekend or evenings. If you add a couple of evening sessions to the plan it will save money, due to temporary absence from bar or club, and get essays written. Divide this total research time by the number of modules to get a rough target of the hours available for support work per module.

PLANNING RESEARCH ANALYSIS INTERPRETATION COMMUNICATION

REPORT OR ORAL

The Optimist

The Realist

Figure 3:1a Ideal process   *Figure 3:1b Realistic process*

TRY THIS 3.1 – What spare / research time?

Fill in your timetable: lectures, practicals, ... the works. Block out an hour for lunch and a couple of 30-minute coffee breaks each day. Add up the free hours between 10 and 5 to find your Total Research Time.

	Morning		Afternoon		Evening	
Monday						
Tuesday						
Wednesday						
Thursday						
Friday						
Saturday						
Sunday						

3.2 WHAT DO I DO NOW?

Confused? You will be.

Diaries and timetables

University timetables can be complex, with classes in different places from week to week. So diaries are vital. A weekly skeleton timetable will locate blocks of time for study (**Try This 3.1**). Use it to allocate longer free sessions for tasks that take more concentration, like writing, reading and preparing for a tutorial or seminar. Use shorter one-hour sessions to do quick jobs, like tidying files, sorting lecture notes, summarising the main points from a lecture, reading a paper photocopied for later, highlighting urgent reading, on-line searches, thinking through an issue and making a list of points that you need to be clearer about. Don't be tempted to timetable every hour. Leave time for catching up when plans have slipped.

Lists

Sort out what you need to do under four headings: Urgent now, Urgent next week, Weekly and Fun (Table 3.1). If you tackle part of the non-urgent task list

Urgent now	Urgent next week	Weekly	Fun
Essay: *Animal communication* By Friday Worksheet 3 for *Stats* prac.	Read for tutorial: *Drugs and behaviour* (Carlson, 1991) Find out about *Primary and secondary appraisal* (Lazarus)	Cliff-diving Ironing Supper	Friday: Bowling Party: Jim's birthday, get card and bottles

Table 3:1 Keeping track of essentials

each week, you will be less overwhelmed by Urgent Now tasks at a later date. Have a go at **Try This 3.2**.

Photocopying a diary template with your regular commitments marked – lectures, tutorials, sport sessions, club and society meetings – gives a weekly skeleton for planning. If weekly planning is too tedious, go for the 30-second, breakfast-time, back-of-an-envelope version. It can really assist on chaotic days when one-hour classes spread across the day, encouraging time to disappear. There are free hours but 'no time to do anything properly'. Completing short jobs will avoid breaking up days when there is more time. Try to set your day out something like this:

9 Lecture	10 *Coffee Siobhàn and Ed*	11 Lab. SPSS practical	12 *Finish SPSS worksheet. Lunch*	2 Tutorial	3 *Sort file. Read last week's Working Memory seminar notes*	4 Semantic Memory seminar	5–9 *Shop. Night out*

Even on average days which are easier to manage, 2 or more free hours give more research time for concentrated activities. Set out your average day like this:

10–12 *Notes for tutorial essay Substance Abuse*	12 Lecture	1 *Lunch. e-mail*	2 Practical	3–5 *Notes tutorial essay Substance Abuse*	5–9 *Telly and phone calls*

Knowing what you want to do in your research slots saves time. Deciding in advance to go to the library after a lecture should ensure you head off to the right floor with the notes and reading lists you need. Otherwise you emerge from a lecture, take 10 minutes to decide you would rather read about the aetiology of anxiety and depression than cognitive behaviour therapy, discover you haven't got the anxiety and depression reading list, so look at the cognitive behaviour therapy list to decide which library and floor to visit. All this takes 45 minutes and the time has gone.

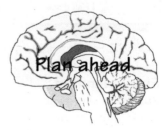

3.3 TRACKING DEADLINES

Deadlines are easily forgotten. For some people a term or semester chart will highlight deadlines that initially seem far away. Figure 3.2 shows two chart styles. Which would suit you? The first is essentially a list, whereas the second one shows where pressure points build up. In this example Weeks 10 and 11 already look full. The computer report due on Friday needs finishing before the Ball on Thursday! This second style highlights weeks where personal research time is limited by other commitments.

Module	Assessment	Due date	Personal deadlines
PSYCi218 Effective Living	Essay: Intimacy and Sexuality	10 Dec.	*Check out a couple of background texts and case studies by November 25. Draft by Dec. 1, figures and revise for Dec. 10*
PSYC1030 Statistics	Practical	16 Nov.	*Sort out the data set and run SPSS by 12 Nov. Write up by 15 Nov.*

Week No./ Date	Social	Seminars	Computing	Tutorial	Essays	Laboratory
1 Sept. 29			Report 1 Fri.			
2 Oct. 6			Report 2 Fri.			
3 Oct. 13		PSYC1030 Tues. Worksheet	Report 3 Fri.			Report Thurs.
10 Dec. 1	Psych Soc. Ball Thurs.	PSYC1030 Worksheet Mon.	Report 10 Fri.	Tues. Oral Presentation: Attributions		
11 Dec. 8	End of term. Xmas shop. Hall dinner.	PSYC1030 Summary Test Tues.	Report 11 Fri.		Interpersonal Attraction essay: Fri.	Language practical Thurs.

Figure 3:2 Sample semester planners

Essay planning

Run your plan past yourself, backwards. Assuming your essay is due in seven weeks' time, allow:

(a) Week 7: slippage, the worst flu ever, final checking and completing references and diagrams. (This is generous, unless you get flu.)

(b) Week 6: Finish final version.

(c) Weeks 4 and 5: Read and draft sections, review and revise, repeat library and electronic searches.

(d) Week 2–3: Brainstorm keywords, do library and Internet search, decide on main focus, highlight lecture notes and references, browse for additional information, start writing.

(e) Week 1: Put the main jobs and deadline dates on your Semester plan and Urgent list (Table 3.1).

OK, the chances of 1:1000 students doing this are small, but it is a good idea!

Projects and dissertations

See the section on dissertations (Chapter 18). Starting to plan dissertations in Year 1 is a good idea!, though not essential.

3.4 WHAT NEXT?

Get into the habit of reviewing what you have to do and look at the relative importance of different activities, so you don't miss a deadline. Have a go at **Try This 3.3** as practice in prioritising.

TRY THIS 3.3 – Priorities?

Using yesterday as the example, jot down the time devoted to each task, amending the list to suit your activities.

Real life	Hours	Priority	Psychology degree	Hours	Priority
Eating			Reading		
Sleeping			Browsing in the library		
Washing/dressing			Lecture attendance		
Exercise			Sorting lecture notes		
Travelling			Writing		
TV			Thinking		
Other leisure			Computer practicals		
Reading for fun			Laboratory practicals		
Housework			Planning time		
Washing/ironing			On-line searches		

Then reflect on where you could re-jig things to release two lots of 20 minutes. What should have priority? Twenty minutes may not seem much, but if you grab a couple of slots to sort notes, reread last week's lecture notes or skim an article, that's 40 minutes more work than you would have done.

Tackling **Try This 3.3** might encourage you to use a day planner to organise your time better, similar to the one shown in Table 3.2. To have a go, write a 'to do' list for tomorrow, then order your activities (2 = indicates an intention to be double tasking, in this case reading while the washing tumbles around). Put some times against the activities. Ticking off jobs as they are done feels good!

Priority	MUST DO!	When
1	Post Mother's Day card	On way to university
2 =	Read chaps 3–5 of *Memory Recovery* by Knott Quite	10–12
3	Look at bio-psych notes for seminar	12–1
2 =	Launderette visit	3–5
4 =	Check e-mail	After Lunch 1.30ish
4 =	Spell check tutorial essay	After supper
6	Lecture 2.00 in psychology lecture theatre	2.00
5	Sort out practical notes	After supper
7	Make a list of jobs for tomorrow	After supper

Table 3.2 An organiser like this?

If you can do a task immediately and easily, that may be the most efficient approach. Generally it helps to allocate larger tasks to longer time chunks and leave little tasks for days that are broken up. Do not procrastinate: 'I cannot write this essay until I have read . . .' is a lousy excuse. No one can ever read *all* the psychological literature, so set a reading limit, then write, then go clubbing.

Top Tips

☺ Get an alarm clock / buzzer watch / timetable / diary.

☺ If the psychology library is full of your best mates wanting to chat, head to the music or theology library. Do tasks requiring total concentration in comfortable conditions where the lighting is good, the atmosphere is conducive to study and no one will interrupt you.

☺ Plan weekends well ahead; sport, socialising and shopping are critical. Having worked hard all week, you need and deserve time off. Following a distracting, socially rich week, maybe there is time for some study. Sunday can be a good time to draft a report, and a great time for reading and thinking: very few people interrupt.

☺ Filing systems: 'so many modules, so many handouts, my room could be a recycling depot'. Take 10 minutes each week to sort out notes and papers. Supermarkets let you have strong boxes free. Indexing files will help.

☺ Investigate the use of bibliographic databases to organise your references. Are you exploiting your IT skills to save you time? Computers and especially the Internet encourage a positive feeling of hours spent diligently communicating with the universe. It also takes hours. Are you being side-tracked? Ask 'Am I wasting good living time?'

☺ Good (OK, some or any) organisation can save on stress later. Being stressed usually wastes time. Not all assignments are easy. Recognise that the difficult ones, and especially those everyone dislikes, will take longer – plan more time for them. Divide the tasks into manageable chunks and tackle them separately. Finishing parts of a task ahead of time gives you more opportunity to think about the psychological interpretations.

☺ Vacations. Recover from term. Have a really good holiday. Consider taking a typing course, look at a speed-reading guide, or follow an on-line tutorial to improve word processing and spreadsheet skills. Think about project and dissertation possibilities.

☺ Time has a habit of drifting away very pleasantly. Can you spot and limit lost time when the pressure is on? Minimise walking across campus. Photocopy at lunchtime when you are in the Union anyway. Pick up mail while in the department. Ask yourself, 'Is this a trip I need to make?', 'Could I be more time efficient?' Make an agreement with a friend to do something in a certain time and reward yourselves for success afterwards.

☺ View apparently 'dead time', when walking to university or cleaning the bathroom, as a 'thinking opportunity'. Use it to plan an essay, mentally review lecture ideas, and so on.

☺ Be realistic. Most days do not map out as planned, things (people) happen, but a plan can make you a little more efficient some of the time.

If you decide to investigate some of these ideas, give them a real go for three weeks. Then reread this chapter, consider what helped and what did not, and, where necessary, try something else. Find a routine that suits you and recognise that a routine adopted in your first year will evolve in following years. A realistic study timetable has a balance of social and fitness activities. Don't be too ambitious. If there was no reading time last week, finding 30 minutes to read one article this week is a step forward.

3.5 REFERENCES AND FURTHER READING

Rudd, S. (1989). *Time Manage Your Reading*. Aldershot: Gower.

Trueman, M. & Hartley, J. (1996). A comparison between the time-management skills and academic performance of mature and traditional entry students. *Higher Education*, **32**, 199–215.

Hey, you don't have to suffer from insanity . . .

You could enjoy every minute of it.

4 LIBRARY AND ELECTRONIC RESOURCES

A library serves no purpose unless someone is using it.

Once you discover that all the lecture notes you took so conscientiously are completely unintelligible, or you did not quite make it to a lecture, using the library might be a good wheeze. Inconveniently, many libraries have texts that psychologists need catalogued under sociology, biology, philosophy, computing and medicine. This usually means psychology texts are found at many locations and sometimes in different buildings. Some psychology departments have their own collections, and those in other departments, in linguistics or education, for example, may be useful. Then there are all the electronic resources. Material can be accessed world-wide. Such fun. There is a maze of information, but finding the way is not always obvious. While it may be beyond Mulder and Scully or Randall and Hopkirk, you CAN DO THIS. The skills include researching, evaluating, information retrieval, IT, flexible thinking and scheduling.

University libraries can seem scary and confusing. Most people feel very lost for the first few visits. This chapter gives information about library resources and research strategies, tips and hints that will, we hope, reduce the mystery.

4.1 LIBRARY RESOURCES

For most library visits you need a library card to get in and out, funds for photocopying, paper for notes. Watch your bags – the opportunist thief finds a library attractive; people leave bags while searching the shelves. A few minutes with guided tours, watching videos and on-line explanations of your library's resources, tips on accessing library and on-line documents will save hours of inefficient searching. Use the library staff. Ask them to show you how the catalogues and search engines work. It is probably harder for psychologists than medics or musicians to find their way to the right material. Find out where the

newspapers, the collections for biology, sociology, languages, politics, education
. . . and your option subjects are kept.

Books and journals

There is an emphasis, at university, on reading academic journals. Journals
contain collections of articles written by experts, published in every area of
academic study. They are the way in which academics communicate their
thoughts, ideas, theories and results. The considerable advantage of a journal over
a book is that its publication time is usually six months to two years. Recent
journals contain the most recent research results. Check the location of:

- Recent issues of journals or periodicals. These may be stored in a different area
  of the library. At the end of the year they will be bound and join the rest of the
  collection. Reading recent issues can give a real feel for the subject and topics
  of current interest.

- Government publications with statistics and bills and papers relevant to
  applied psychologists.

- Oversized books. These do not readily fit on shelves and are often filed as
  Quartos – at the end of a subject section. They are easy to miss.

- Stack collections containing less commonly used books and journals.

Catalogues

Cataloguing systems are exclusive to particular universities. Happily, every
library has handouts on how to retrieve material. Library information is accessed
either via an on-line computer catalogue, which shows where the book should be
shelved and whether copies are on loan or not, or from a card index. Before
searching, highlight the papers and books on the reading list that you want to
read, so search time is quick. If the books are out, check at the shelf references for
other texts that will substitute. If the on-line catalogue is accessible from any
networked campus computer, you can do bibliographic searches and mark up
reading lists while the library is shut. Traditional card index catalogues locate
texts by author and title, but a keyword search is not possible.

How do you know which items on a reading list are journals
and which are books?

There is a convention in citing references, used in most texts and articles, that
distinguishes journal articles from books, and from chapters in edited books.
Traditionally, a book has its *TITLE* in italics (or underlined in handwritten text), a
journal article has the title of the *JOURNAL* in italics, and where the article is a
chapter in an edited book the *BOOK TITLE* is in italics:

Allport, G.W. (1954). *The Nature of Prejudice*. Wokingham: Addison-Wesley.

Boden, M.A. (1999). Computer models of creativity. In R.J. Sternberg (Ed.), *Handbook of
Creativity*. Cambridge: Cambridge University Press.

Cook, T. and Emler, N. (1999). Bottom-up versus top-down evaluations of candidates' managerial potential: An experimental study. *Journal of Occupational and Organizational Psychology*, **72**, 423–40.

To find the Boden article, you search for Sternberg (1999). This convention eases library searches because, as a rule of thumb, you search for the italicised item first. You will never find the title of a journal article in a library main catalogue, but you will find the journal title and its library shelf location. In spotting journals look for numbers, as here 72, 423–40, indicating volume 72 and pages 423–40; books do not have this clue. Where there are no italics to help the game is more fun; you have to work out whether it is a journal or book you are chasing. (All students play this game, it's a university tradition.)

Unfortunately you cannot take out all the books at the beginning of term and keep them for the whole term. Find out what you can borrow and for how long, and what is available at other local libraries, the city or town library. If a university library does not hold the article or book you want, you can borrow it from the British Library via the interlibrary loan service. There is likely to be a charge for this service, so be sure it is a book or article you really need. Many university libraries offer short-loan arrangements for material that staff have indicated everyone will want to read. Check out the system, especially the time restrictions on a loan. Return your books on time. *Fines are serious*, especially for restricted loans, and a real waste of good drinking money. When you need to get your hands on texts that are out, RECALL them. It encourages other people, especially staff, to return them.

On-line searches can be made using the title, author or keywords linked by Boolean operators. The three main Boolean operators are used either in words or symbol form: **+** , **–** or **AND OR NOT**. 'Child, infant' should pick up entries for both. 'Abuse or maltreatment AND gender NOT sex*' should locate material on the relationship between gender and non-sexual child abuse. Use OR when there are synonyms, and NOT to exclude topics. The introduction or Help information for each electronic database should explain which symbols can be used for searches.

Before searching make a list of keywords, and decide if you need to search for English and American spellings. Typically a short string of words will be taken as a phrase, so searching for 'colour vision' will yield papers on colour vision, but only the English language ones. Entering 'color vision' will find American articles. Searching for 'colo?r vision' will ensure that you tap both sets. Entering 'sleep*' yields 34,421 hits – far too many. Boolean operators will speed up and refine your search by cutting out irrelevant sites (see Figure 4.1). Entering 'sleep* + depriv*' yielded 1826 hits – a considerable reduction, but still rather too many for essay-writing purposes! If you refine your area of interest again, as in 'sleep*+depriv*+perform*-children', you hit 15 sites. A manageable research list.

Using root words, like Psychol*, will find all the words that have psychol as the first seven letters, like psychology, psychological and psychologist. Beware of using root* too liberally. Psych* will get psychiatric, psychiatrist, psychological,

Figure 4:1 Refining searches with Boolean operators

psychologist, which you might want, and psychic, psychopath, psychometrics and psychoanalysis, which you might not. The bracket convention can help refine a search: fat AND (consumption OR intake) will find fat and consumption, and fat and intake.

American and English spellings can be a nightmare; use both in keyword searches. Here is a starter list but add to these as you find them. Beware of the use of –ise (UK) and –ize (US) endings too.

English	American	English	American	English	American
ageing	aging	counsellor	counselor	focused	focussed
artefact	artifact	defence	defense	foetus	fetus
behaviour	behavior	dialogue	dialog	generalise	generalize
catalogue	catalog	draught	draft	labour	labor
centre	center	enclose	inclose	metre	meter
cheque	check	enquire	inquire	modelling	modeling
colour	color	extroversion	extraversion	oestrus	estrous

4.2 ELECTRONIC RESOURCES

Bibliographic databases

These contain information about journal publications, and some include book details. There are usually author, title and source details and, in most cases, an abstract or short summary. Databases may be networked, held in a library CD-ROM collection, or accessed via the Internet. Searching databases can help locate paper titles and abstracts, but it's no substitute for reading the whole paper.

For UK students, Web of Science is a goldmine and user-friendly. It holds details of academic papers in many journals. Check whether your library is networked to Web of Science, obtain a login name and password, and get on-line. You can search by authors and keywords. Explore the different options and menus to become familiar with what Web of Science has to offer. Mark items of interest as you search; you can download these via e-mail to your own filespace.

Here is a selected list of databases that are of interest to psychologists. What sources can your library access?

ASSIAnet is the Web version of Applied Social Sciences Index and Abstracts.

Best Evidence contains reviews of research papers designed to help solve clinical problems.

Cochrane Library contains several databases on evidence-based healthcare.

EMBASE is a major bibliographic database for information on the biomedical sciences, including neurology and pharmacology.

MEDBASE – another important bibliographic database for biomedical science.

POPLINE has information on demography, family planning services, maternal and child health and related health issues.

PsycLIT – a huge American database with information from all the major psychology journals (from 1887) and books (from 1987).

SOCIOFILE has citations and abstracts from journals in sociology.

Web of Science – an important collection of bibliographic databases for science, social sciences, education and the humanities.

World Wide Web (www)

The Web promises to be the most time-wasting of electronic resources in your degree, but it is fun, and gives the feeling of being busy on the computer all day. Use a keyword list (stress bereavement coping) and Boolean logic (stress+bereavement+coping) to exclude unwanted sites. Moving the cursor over highlighted text (known as *hypertext links*, usually blue) and double clicking the mouse will link to other documents. Book-marking 'favourite' pages will save you having to search from scratch for pages you use regularly. You should be able to e-mail documents to your own filespace, or save to floppy disc. On some computers you can open www and word-processing packages simultaneously, and cut and paste between the two (but be aware of plagiarism issues, see p. 60).

Major problems can arise if you print files with pictures or graphics. Make sure the printer will handle graphics, or you will clog printer queues and run up an enormous printing bill. The www response rate will be slow at some times of day. Be patient. Try before lunch or better still before breakfast, when users in different parts of the world are still asleep. Look around campus for the faster, newer machines. Check out some sites using **Try This 4.1.**

TRY THIS 4.1 – WWW resources for psychologists

Explore some of these sites. If a site address is defunct, use a search engine and the site title to locate the updated address, e.g. Association+Psychol*+Information.

The American Psychological Association at http://www.apa.org. Accessed 14 April 2000.

The American Psychological Society at http://www.hanover.edu/psych/APS.html. Accessed 14 April 2000.

The Australian Psychological Society at http://www.psychsociety.com.au. Accessed 14 April 2000.

The British Psychological Society at http://www.bps.org.uk. Accessed 14 April 2000.

CTI Centre for Psychology provides a gateway to a wide-ranging collection of academic sites of interest to students and teachers of psychology at http://www.york.ac.uk/inst/ctipsych. Accessed 14 April 2000.

Dana BrainWeb is a site provided by a philanthropic foundation dedicated to research on brain diseases and disorders at http://www.dana.org/brainweb. Accessed 14 April 2000.

Index of Psychology and psychology-related Journals at http://www.wiso.uni-augsburg.de/sozio/hartmann/psycho/journal.html. Accessed 14 April 2000.

Guardian newspaper at http://www.guardian.co.uk. Accessed 14 April 2000.

McConnell Brain Imaging Centre provides access to research on 3-D investigations of brain structure and functioning at http://www.bic.mni.mcgill.ca. Accessed 25 February 2000.

New Scientist at http://newscientist.com. Accessed 14 April 2000.

Psychology websites hosts an extensive list of psychology links at http://www.ums/edu/~mgriffin/genpsych/PsychWebsites.html. Accessed 14 April 2000.

Psyphile at http://memners.xoom.com/psyphile/home.html. Accessed 14 April 2000.

Social Psychology Network, 'the largest social psychology database on the network', with links to the Societies for Personality and Social Psychology and Experimental Social Psychology, respectively, at http://www.socialpsychology.org. Accessed 14 April 2000.

SOSIG (Social Science Information Gateway) provides links and mailing lists at http://sosig.ac.uk/welcome.html. Accessed 14 April 2000.

⚠ **Warning: Try This 4.2** could be totally useful or utterly frustrating. It is included because it will be useful to some people, but it may be obsolete by October 2001; everything changes fast in this area. Ask your librarian what is available to you. Do not get frustrated. Libraries and departments cannot possibly afford to pay for access to all these sites. Not being able to access a specific item will not cause you to fail your degree.

⚠ **Warning:** The fact that a database exists is no guarantee that it holds the information you need.

TRY THIS 4.2 – www addresses

To develop familiarity with the www and your library resources see how many of these databases you can access. Make a note of the www addresses. They will probably be worth bookmarking for future use. What other databases can you add to this list? The www addresses are given on p. 254 but can you find these using the search engines?

Cognitive and Psychological Sciences on the Internet	An index to Internet resources relevant to research in cognitive science and psychology, in particular, access to journals and magazines published by the Canadian Psychology Association.
CNN Interactive	The website for CNN (Cable News Network).
Animal Bytes Database	A website containing scientific classification, facts and biological values of most of the animal kingdom.
CHID Online	Combined Health Information Database. A US site providing titles, abstracts and citations for health information.
Mental Health Net	A comprehensive site of mental health information with a good search engine.
CyberPsychLink	Resource Directory of Sites Related to Psychology and Medicine.
Online Dictionary of Mental Health	A global information resource and research tool covering all of the disciplines contributing to our understanding of mental health.
Links2Go: Psychology	A directory of links to psychology-related topics and sites.
PsycLIT	The subset of the American Psychological Association's PsycINFO® database containing journals, books and book chapters, PsycLIT®, consists of over 1.3 million records from 1887 to the present.
Acoustical Society of America	Disseminates information about the physiological responses of man and animals to acoustic stimuli.
AGELINE	Provides bibliographic coverage of social gerontology, the study of ageing in psychological, health-related, social and economic contexts.
Wilson Social Science Abstracts	Abstracts and indexes 415+ English language social science journals. 1988–present.

⚠ **Warning:** www documents may be of limited quality, full of sloppy thinking and short of valid evidence. Some are fine, but be critical. Anyone can set up a www site. Look for reputable sites, especially if you intend to quote statistics and rely heavily on site information. Government and academic sites should be OK.

⚠ **Warning:** Think about data decay: which time period does the information relate to? If you have information on drug trials carried out in the 1980s, it will be fine for a review of the development of ideas and practice, but of more limited value in a report or an essay on recent research and current practice.

⚠ **Warning:** Do not plagiarise. You can cut and paste from the Internet to notes, but if you cut and paste to an essay the source must properly acknowledged. See pp. 100, 113.

E-journals

Increasing numbers of psychological journals are available on-line; witness the 1600+ listed at http://www.wiso.uni-augsburg.de/sozio/hartmann/psycho/journal.html. Accessed 14 April 2000. Some e-journals are only accessible if your university library has a subscription, but some have abstracts that can be viewed at no expense.

Check out the psychological journals available electronically through your library, and remember that journals from other subject areas may also be relevant, such as Sociological Research On-line at http://www.socresonline.org.uk or the British Medical Journal at http://bmj.com (both accessed 25 February 2000).

4.3 RESEARCH STRATEGIES

There are oodles of background research documents for just about every psychological topic, usually far too many. The trick in the library is to be efficient in sorting and evaluating what is available, relevant, timely and interesting.

A library search strategy is outlined in Figure 4.2. Look at it carefully, especially the recommendations on balancing time spent searching and reading. Library work is iterative. Remember that on-line searches can be done when the library is closed but computer laboratories are open. Become familiar with your local system, use **Try This 4.3** and **Try This 4.4** as a starting point. Good library research skills include:

✔ Using exploration and retrieval tools efficiently.

✔ Reading and making notes.

✔ Evaluating the literature as you progress.

✔ Recording references and search citations systematically, so that referencing or continuing the search at another time is straightforward.

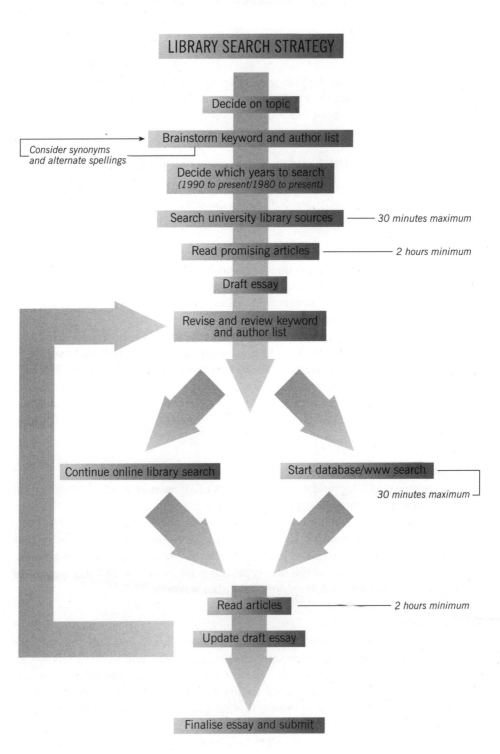

Figure 4:2 Library search strategy

TRY THIS 4.3 – Library search

Choose any topic from one of your modules. Make a list of three authors and six keywords. Do a search to explore the papers and texts available in your library. Compare the results with the reading list. Is there a paper that should be followed up which is not on the reading list?

TRY THIS 4.4 – Journal search

Use Web of Science databases to check the authors and keywords used in **Try This 4.3**, but only note the journals in your library, those that you can read later.

Set a maximum of 30 minutes for on-line searching, then read for at least 2 hours.

Beware the enticements of on-line searches. It is possible to spend all day searching electronic sources. You will acquire searching skills, know there is a paper with the ideal title in a library 5000 miles away or in a foreign language and have nothing for your essay.

Ignore enticing www gateways during initial research. For most undergraduate essays and projects the resources in the library are adequate; search and read these articles first. Look at wider resources later, after the first draft is written, and only if there is bags of time. Web searches are more appropriate for dissertation and extended project work. You cannot access and read everything: essays have short deadlines, and reading time is limited. The trick is to find documents available locally and at no cost.

Reading lists

Some lecturers give long reading lists with lots of alternative reading. This is vital where members of large classes will want to access documents simultaneously. Other lecturers give quite short reading lists, especially at Levels 2 and 3. They may include essential reading items, and a list of authors and keywords. This approach allows each student to explore the available literature independently. Where the reading lists are of the first type, it is wise to view it as a big version of the second! Use **Try This 4.5** to explore an author's work.

Review articles

These, especially those in *Psychological Review* and *Psychological Bulletin*, can give an illuminating synthesis of the recent literature and point you to other references. Some journals have themed issues. For example, in 1997 the *Journal of Infant and Reproductive Psychology* had a themed issue on early child maltreatment, and the November issue of the *British Journal of Psychology* had a special issue on the study of conscious experience in psychological science. You may start out with one reference but in a themed volume there will be papers on interrelated topics that are, at least, worth browsing.

Linked reading

If you happen to read Shotter and Katz (1998) you will quickly realise you need to read Anderson (1996). It may seem obvious, but having read article A you may need to read article B to understand A. Cross-referencing is a normal process. Take accurate notes of the references to follow up.

Be particularly critical of sources which may have a bias or spin. As Vujakovic (1998) points out, mass media materials are particularly vulnerable to personal or biased reporting. Use **Try This 4.6** to keep track of your reading and a balance between electronic searching (30 minutes) and real reading (2 hours).

TRY THIS 4.5 – Author search

Take one psychology author whose name appears on a reading list and design a library search to explore what that author has written. (Hint: include Science and Social Science Citation Indexes, Web of Science and PsycLit.)

TRY THIS 4.6 – Self-assessment of a library search

Use this grid to keep a tally of sources and authorities when doing a library search or preparing a report or essay. Check for an advantageous balance of recent citations and ensure that all the appropriate sources are used, in addition to those on the reading list.

Sources used in search for					
Books	Journal Articles			www sites	Other

Number of papers NOT on the reading list:					
None	1	2–4	5–7	7–10	11+

Number of papers from each time period:					
Pre-1980s	1980–4	1985–9	1990–4	1995–9	2000–date

4.4 WHY AM I SEARCHING?

Library searches are never done in isolation. Before starting, review your reasons for searching, and focus your keyword search. Put a limit on your searching time and on the types of document to include. Suggestions on this front include:

✔ Module essays: start with the reading list, and only explore further when you have an initial draft. Look critically at the gaps in your support material and use **Try This 4.6**.

✔ 'State of the art studies' exploring the current state of knowledge on a topic; limit searches to the last 2–5 years.

✔ An historical investigation of the development of an idea considering how knowledge has changed over 10, 20 or more years; aim for a balance between the older and newer references.

✔ A literature review should give the reader an outline of the 'state' of the topic. It may have a brief historical element, mapping the development of the subject knowledge, leading into a more detailed resumé of research from the past 5–10 years.

Do not forget international dimensions; the topic might be theoretical (language acquisition, adolescence, emotional expressiveness) but there may be cross-cultural examples that are worth considering, so check out the journals of other countries. The *Scandinavian Journal of Psychology*, the *Australian and New Zealand Journal of Psychiatry* and the *European Journal of Social Psychology* are international journals, but also contain articles reflecting national and regional concerns.

WRITE UP AS YOU GO, keep noting and drafting, and keep a record of references in full. Remember to add the reference, dates and pages on photocopies.

PSYCHOLOGIST'S BOOKSHELF

4.5 REFERENCES AND FURTHER READING

Anderson, T. (1996). Language is not innocent. In F. Kaslow (Ed.), *The Handbook of Relational Diagnosis*. New York: John Wiley and Sons.

Shotter, J. & Katz, A. (1998). 'Living moments' in dialogical exchanges. *Human Systems: The Journal of Systemic Consultation and Management*, **9**(2), 81–93.

Vujakovic, P. (1998). Reading between the lines: Using news media materials for geography. *Journal of Geography in Higher Education, Directions*, **22**(1), 147–55.

Winslop, I. & McNab, A. (1996). *The Student's Guide to the Internet*. London: Library Association Publishing.

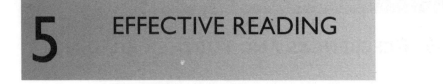

5 EFFECTIVE READING

Reading goes faster if you don't worry about comprehension.

You are 'reading' for a psychology degree, so it is not surprising that most time at university should (!) be spent with a book. Everyone reads – the knack is to read and learn at the same time. Pressure on library resources often limits the time books are available to you, so it is vital to maximise your learning. This chapter discusses some reading techniques, asks you to reflect on and evaluate what you do now, and to consider what you might do in future. As with playing the trombone, practice is required. There is a vast amount of information to grapple with in a psychology degree. Reading, thinking and note-making are totally interlinked activities, but this chapter concentrates on the reading element.

5.1 READING LISTS

Inconveniently, most psychology lecturers sort reading lists alphabetically by module, but you need them sorted by library and library floor location. Either use highlighter pen to indicate what is in which library, and take advantage of the nearest library shelf when time is limited, or make a list of the articles/chapters/papers you want to read each week. Now code it by *library* and by *floor* rather than by module (see Figure 5.1). This list needs to be twice as long as you can reasonably do in a week, so if a book is missing there are alternatives.

Author	Journal/Title	Class mark	Reading list	Library/Floor
Sternberg, R.J. & Grigorenko, E. 1997	*Intelligence, Heredity and Environment*	136.31	Individual Differences	Floor 10 Science Lib.

Figure 5:1 Library list sorter

- Carry reading lists at all times.

Reading lists are often dauntingly long, but you are not, usually, expected to read everything. Long lists give you choice in research topics and lots of options, especially where class sizes are large and copies of texts restricted. Serendipity cheers the brain. If a book is on loan, don't give up. There are probably three equally good texts on the same topic with the same library class number. Reading something is more helpful than reading nothing, and use the library's recall system to get hold of essential texts.

Students tend to request a module text and feel uncomfortable when a tutor says 'there is no set text'. Even where there is one, it is rarely followed in detail. Reading a recommended book is a good idea, but watch out for those points where a lecturer disagrees with the text. Perhaps the author got it wrong, or our understanding of a topic has moved forward, ideas have changed. Or perhaps your lecturer simply wanted you to be aware of the extent of the ongoing debate in the area. You do not have to buy all the set texts; buy as a group and share. Watch the noticeboards for second-hand sales.

Reading in support of lecture modules is the obvious thing to do, but 'Do you read for computing, statistics and practical classes?' Certainly the volume of reading expected for practical modules is less than for lecture modules, but zero reading is not right either. Class activities tend to stress the hands-on elements, BUT you should still allocate time for reading, to understand where practical activities fit with the art and science of psychology. If you don't actively make the connection between practicals and statistics and their psychological applications in Years 1 and 2, you are unlikely to use these techniques to best effect in projects and dissertations.

Top Tip

- READ FOR ALL MODULES!

5.2 READING TECHNIQUES

For most people there is a mega temptation to sit down in a comfy chair with a coffee and to start reading a book at page 1. THIS IS A VERY BAD IDEA. With many academic texts, by page 4, you will have done the ironing, cleaned the windows, fixed a motorbike, fallen asleep or all four and more. This is great for the state of the house but a learning disaster.

Everyone uses a range of reading techniques – speed reading of novels, skip-reading headlines, etc. – the style depending on purpose. As you look through this section reflect on where you use each technique already. For effective study adopt the 'deep study' approach.

Deep study reading

Deep study reading is vital when you want to make connections, understand meanings, consider implications and evaluate arguments. Reading deeply needs a strategic approach and time to cogitate.

Rowntree (1988) describes an active reading method known as SQ3R, which promotes deeper, more thoughtful reading. It is summarised in **Try This 5.1**. SQ3R is an acronym for Survey – Question – Read – Recall – Review. Give **Try This 5.1** a go; it may seem long-winded at first, but is worth pursuing because it links thinking with reading in a flexible manner. It stops you rushing into unproductive note-making. You can use SQ3R with books and articles, and for summarising notes during revision. You are likely to recall more by using this questioning and 'mental discussion' approach to reading. Having thought about SQ3R with books use **Try This 5.2**.

Browsing

Browsing is an important research activity used to search for information which is related and tangential, to widen your knowledge. In essence, it involves giving a broader context or view of the subject, which in turn provides you with a stronger base to add to with directed or specific reading. Browsing might involve checking out popular social science, history, science and introductory texts. Good sources of general and topical psychological information include *The Psychologist*, *New Scientist*, *Science*, and for UK students the Society supplements in the *Guardian* newspaper. Browsing enables you to build up a sense of how psychology as a whole, or particular parts of the subject, fit together. Becoming immersed in the language and experience of the topic encourages you to think psychologically.

Scanning

Scan when you want a specific item of information. Scan the contents page or index, letting your eyes rove around to spot key words and phrases. Chase up the references and then, carefully, (deep) read the points that are relevant for you.

Skimming

Skim read to get a quick impression or general overview of a book or article. Look for 'signposts': chapter headings, subheadings, lists, figures. Read first and last paragraphs/first and last sentences of a paragraph. Make a note of key words, phrases and points to summarise the main themes. Note that this is still not the same as detailed, deep reading.

Photoreading

Scheele (1993) describes a 'photoreading' method, one of many scanning techniques, which again requires you to identify your aims before scan reading and mentally and physically filing the contents.

TRY THIS 5.1 – SQ3R

SQ3R is a template for reading and thinking. Try it on the next book you pick up.

Survey: Look at the whole text before you get into parts in detail. Start with the cover; is this a respected author? When was it written? Is it dated?

Use the Contents and chapter headings and subheadings to get an idea of the whole book and to locate the sections that are of interest to you. First and last paragraphs should highlight arguments and key points.

Question: You will recall more if you know why you are reading, so ask yourself some questions. Review your present knowledge, and then ask what else you want/need to know. For example: What is new in this reading? What can I add from this book? Where does this fit in this course or other modules? Is this a supporting/refuting/contradictory piece of information?

Having previewed the book and developed your reasons for reading, you can also decide whether deep reading and note-making are required, or whether scanning and some additions to previous notes will do.

Read: This is the stage to start reading, but not necessarily from page 1; read the sections that are relevant for you and your present assignment. Read attentively but also critically. The first time you read you cannot get hold of all points and ideas.

On first reading – Locate the main ideas. Get the general structure and subject content in your head. *Do not make notes during this first reading*, the detail gets in the way.

On second reading – Chase up the detailed bits that you need for essays. Highlight or make notes of all essential points.

Recall: Do you understand what you have read? Give yourself a break, and then have a think about what you remember, and what you understand. This process makes you an active, learning reader. Ask yourself questions like: Can I explain this idea in my own words? Can I recall the key points without rereading the original text?

Review: Now go back to the text and check the accuracy of your recall. Reviewing should tell you how much you have really absorbed. Review your steps and check main points.

Are the headings and summaries first noted the right ones? Do they need revising?

Do new questions about the material arise now that you have gone through in detail?

Have you missed anything important? Do you need more detail or examples?

Fill in gaps and correct errors in your notes. Ask where your views fit with those of the authors. Do you agree/disagree?

The last question is 'Am I happy to give this book back to the library?'

TRY THIS 5.2 – SQ3R for papers

How do you adapt SQ3R to read a journal article? Work out a five-point plan and try it on the next article you read.

When reading ask yourself:

- 'Is this making me think?'

- 'Am I getting a better grasp of the subject material?'

If the answer is no then maybe you need to read something else or use a different technique. Reading is about being selective, and it is an iterative activity. Cross-checking between articles, notes and more articles, looking back to be sure you understand the point and chasing up other points of view are all parts of the process. Breaking for coffee is OK and necessary! Talking to friends will help to put reading in perspective. Have a go at **Try This 5.3**.

TRY THIS 5.3 – Where do you read?

Where do you do different types of reading? *'I need pen and paper in hand to read and learn effectively.'* How true is this for you? Three student responses to the first question are on p. 255. Have a quick look if you find reflecting on this difficult.

Academic journal articles and books are not racy thrillers. There should be a rational, logical argument, but there is rarely an exciting narrative. Usually, authors state their case and then explain the position, or argument, using careful reasoning. The writer should persuade the reader (you) of the merit of the case in an unemotional and independent manner. Academic writing is rarely overtly friendly or jolly in tone. You may well feel that the writer is completely wrong. You may disagree with the case presented. If so, do not 'bin the book'. Instead, make a list of your disagreements and build up your case for the opposition. If you agree, list supporting evidence and case examples.

Get used to spotting cues or signposts to guide you to important points and the structure; phrases like 'The background indicates . . .', 'The results show . . .', 'To summarise . . .' or see **Try This 5.4** to find further examples.

TRY THIS 5.4 – Spotting reading cues

Look through the book or article you are reading for psychology at present, and pick out the cue words and phrases which identify key points and structure. There are some examples on p. 255.

5.3 HOW DO YOU KNOW WHAT TO READ?

What do I know already?

Reading and note-making will be more focused if you first consider what you already know, and use this information to decide where reading can effectively fill the gaps. Use a flow or spider diagram (see Figures 4.2 and 8.1) to sort ideas. Put boxes around information you have already, circle areas which will benefit from more detail, check the reference list for documents to fill the gaps, and add them to the diagram. Then prioritise the circles and references, 1 to n, making sure that you have an even spread of support material for the different issues. Coding and questioning encourage critical assessments and assist in 'what to do next' decisions.

Be critical of the literature

Before starting, make a list of main ideas or theories. While searching mark the ideas that are new to you, tick those that reinforce lecture material and highlight ideas to follow up in more detail. Questions to ask include:

? Is this idea up to date?

? Are there more recent ideas?

? How does this paper or idea connect to the main thrust of the essay or argument?

? Do the graphs make sense?

? Are the statistics right and appropriate?

? Did the writer have a particular perspective that led to a bias in their interpretation/writing?

? Why did the authors research this area? Does their methodology influence the results in a manner that might affect the interpretation?

Library, author and journal searches start the process, and practice allows you to judge the relative value of different documents. After reading, look at your author and keyword list again. Do you need to change it? Exploring diverse sources will develop your research skills. Reading and quoting sources in addition to those on the reading list may seriously impress an examiner.

Narrow reading ➜ predictable essays and reports ➜ middling marks.

Wide reading ➜ more creative, less predictable responses ➜ higher marks (usually).

It does not usually matter what you read, or in what order. Read something.

How long to read for?

For most people two hours is long enough to concentrate on one topic. A short article from *The Psychologist* or *New Scientist* should take much less, but some reading takes longer. With longer documents you need a reading strategy, and you need to take breaks. Use breaks to look back at the SQ elements of SQ3R and decide whether your reading plan needs amending. If you cannot get involved with a text then it is possibly because you cannot get to grips with the point of the article, or do not know why you should be interested. So STOP READING and skim the chapter headings, skim your notes, refresh your brain on WHY you are reading and what you want to get out of it.

5.4 STYLES OF WRITING

There are differences in writing styles across the psychological literature, and some people have difficulty with reading and learning from certain kinds of writing. Styles range from the very direct through to the very discursive. This variety needs to be acknowledged from the start, and reading, note-making and discussion styles need to be matched to the different styles of writing. Much psychology literature is technical in tone, characterised by short sentences and an information-rich content. Most of the experimental psychology literature is in this style. In the qualitative psychology literature, you may find writing that is less direct and more discursive. Look for the broad themes rather than the detail. Writing styles reflect the conversational language and approach adopted in particular areas of the discipline, and becoming familiar with the different languages of psychology is part of your psychological training. The trick is to adapt your reading and note-making style to maximise your learning from different types of material.

For scientific, factual style writing see:

Andreassi, J.L. (1996). *Psychophysiology*, 3rd edn. Hillsdale, NJ: Lawrence Erlbaum Associates.

For an example of a more discursive style see:

Gergen, K. (1994). *Towards Transformation in Social Knowledge*, 2nd edn. London: Sage.

Top Tips

✔ If you find certain articles difficult to read, it may be due to unfamiliarity with the topic, its setting and related information, rather than the written style. If an article seems difficult, try looking at some related, scene-setting materials and then reread the paper.

✔ Ask yourself: Do I understand this? Ask it at the end of a page, chapter, paper, tutorial, lecture … and not just at the end!

5.5 References and further reading

Using on-line searching to locate reading skills texts in your library may produce a long list. Refine the search by excluding TEFL (Teaching English as a Foreign Language) and school-level texts.

Buzan, T. (1971). *Speed Reading*. Devon: David and Charles.
Girden, E.R. (1996). *Evaluating Research Articles from Start to Finish*. London: Sage.
Heffernan, T.M. (1997). *A Student's Guide to Studying Psychology*. Hove: Psychology

Rowntree, D. (1988). *Learn How to Study*.
    London: Warner Books.
Scheele, P.R. (1993). *The PhotoReading Whole Mind System*. Minnesota: Learning
    Strategies Corporation.

Psycho-Quick Crossword 1   Answers p. 255.

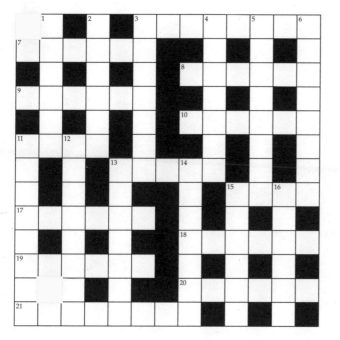

Across

3　Masculine pride (8)
7　Gut hi... (4)
8　Young blight (3, 4)
9　Environment; setting or situation (6)
10　Lazy person (slang) (6)
11　Weight (of evidence) (4)
13　The price of everything and the _____ of nothing (5)
15　Pendant, a long way to fall (4)
17　A throat swelling (6)
18　Mentally natural (6)
19　Academic case (6)
20　Hypnotic stupor (6)
21　Drowsiness (8)

Down

1　Sexual impulse (6)
2　One's people (6)
3　Inner tissue of pith, adds elm (anag.) (7)
4　A shimmering secretion (7)
5　A difficult situation, applies a strain (8)
6　Where an individual does not belong (8)
11　To cheer up (8)
12　Rule over arbitrarily (8)
13　Dizziness (7)
14　R... this way elevators (7)
15　It's not me; rejection (6)
16　Pub measures (6)

6 MAKING EFFECTIVE NOTES

Mental notes get lost.

There is a range of psychological information whizzing around in radio, video and ~~television~~, tutorials, discussion groups and in ~~BUT just~~

the idea that note-taking, when done ~~...~~ have a significant positive impact on learning – check out Harley (1998?).

Note-making which lets you learn requires your brain to be fully involved in asking questions and commenting on the ideas. Noting is not just about getting the facts down, it is also about identifying links between different pieces of information, contradictions and examples. Notes should record information in your own words, evaluate different points of view and encourage the development of your own ideas and opinions. Note-taking is a multipurpose activity; like snowboarding, it gets easier with practice. Good questions to ask when making notes include: 'Is this making me think?' or 'Am I getting a clearer understanding of the topic?'

Many people start reading and making notes without any sort of preview. A BAD IDEA. They make pages of notes from the opening section and few, if any, from later in the document. This is topsy-turvy since the first pages of a book usually set the scene, and notes may only be needed from conclusion and discussion sections. Sometimes detailed notes are required, but other times just noting keywords, definitions and brief summaries

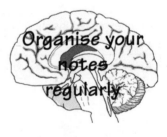

does the job. Use **Try This 6.1** to evaluate how the style and length of your note-making should change given different types of information, and consider how the SQ3R method (p. 49) fits in your note-making process. Then look at **Try This 6.2**, and reflect on what you do already. What could you do in future?

TRY THIS 6.1 – Styles of note-making

What styles of notes are needed for these different types of information? There are a couple of answers to kick start ideas.

Academic content	Style of notes
Significant article but it repeats the content of the lecture.	None, it is in the lecture notes, BUT check your notes and diagrams are up to date. Did you note relevant sources, authors?
Fundamental background theory, partly covered in the lecture.	
An argument in favour of point x.	
An argument that contradicts the main point	
An example from an odd situation where the general theory breaks down.	
A critically important case study.	
Just another case study.	
Interesting but off-the-point article.	A sentence at most! HOWEVER, add a cross-reference in case it might be useful elsewhere.
An unexpected insight from a different angle.	
An example/argument you agree with	
An argument you think is unsound.	1) Brief notes of the alternative line of argument, refs. and illustrative example. 2) Comment on why it does not work so the argument makes sense to you at revision.
A superficial consideration of a big topic.	
A very detailed insight into a problem.	

TRY THIS 6.2 – How do you make notes?

Look at this unordered jumble of note-making activities and ✔ those likely to assist learning, and put a ✗ against those likely to slow up learning.

What do you do already? Are there some ideas here that are worth adopting in the future?

Leave wide margins.	Ignore handouts.
Identify what is not said.	Code references to follow up.

Doodle lots.	Make short notes of main points and headings.
Turn complex ideas into flow charts.	Use cards for notes.
Ask lecturers about points that make no sense.	Order and file notes weekly.
Ask questions.	Jot down personal ideas.
Highlight main points.	Share notes with friends.
Natter in lectures.	Write illegibly.
Copy all OHTs.	Use coloured pens for different points.
Scribble extra questions in margins.	Write shopping lists in lectures.
Write down everything said in lectures.	Annotate handouts.
Take notes from TV documentaries.	Revise notes within three days of lectures.

People adapt their note-taking styles to suit different sorts of situations. A study by Van Meter, Yokoi and Pressley (1994) explored how some students vary their techniques according to their goals and background knowledge and experience, as well as the lecturer's style and the apparent relevance of the material. Taking a look at this paper might give you some food for thought. In the meantime:

6.1 MAKING NOTES FROM PRESENTATIONS

Psychology lectures and seminars are awash with information so memory meltdown syndrome will loom. Make notes of important points – you cannot hope to note everything. Listen to case studies and identify complementary examples. Highlight references mentioned by the lecturer, and keep a tally of new words. Your primary goal in presentations should be to participate actively, thinking around the subject material and to record a perfect transcript of the proceedings. Get the gist and essentials down in your own words.

Lecture notes made at speed, in the darkness of a lecture theatre, are often scrappy or illegible and usually have something missing. If you put notes away at once, you will not make sense of them a week later, let alone 21 hours before an exam. Try to summarise and clarify notes within a day of the lecture. This reinforces ideas in your memory, stimulates further thoughts and suggests reading priorities.

6.2 MAKING NOTES FROM DOCUMENTS

Noting from documents is easier than from lectures, because there is time to think about the issues, identify links to other material and write legibly. You can read awkward passages again, but risk writing too much. Copying whole passages postpones the hard work of thinking through the material but wastes time and paper. Summarising is a skill that develops given practice. Give **Try This 6.3** a go next time you read a journal article; it won't work for all articles but is a start to structuring note-making.

TRY THIS 6.3 – Tackling journal articles

Use this as a guide when reading a journal article or chapter.

1. **First read the article**.
2. Write down the reference in full and the library location so you can find it again.
3. Summarise the contents in two sentences.
4. Summarise in one sentence the main conclusion.
5. What are the strong points of the article?
6. Is this an argument/case I can agree with?
7. How does this information fit with my current knowledge?
8. What else do I read to develop my understanding of this topic?

Think about where you will use your information. Scanning can save time if it avoids you making notes on an irrelevant article or one that repeats information you have already. In the latter case, a two-line note may be enough, e.g.:

Withyoualltheway (2010) supports Originality's (2005) hypothesis with his results from a comparable study of The Prisoner's Dilemma.

or

> Dissenting arguments are presented by Dontlikeit (2010) and Notonyournellie (2010) who made independent, detailed analyses of risk-taking in the under 20s. Dontlikeit's main points are . . .

or

> Wellcushioned (2010), studying contraceptive choice in Brighton and New York, showed condom use to be most popular. His results contrast with those ~~of~~ (2010) report on condom use in Phuket, because . . .

Top Tips

✔ **New words.** Almost every psychology module has its specialist vocabulary. Keep a record of new words and check the spelling! The trick is to practise using the 'jargon of the subject' or 'psycho-babble'. Get familiar with the use of words like attribution, neuroleptic and epistemological. If you are happy with psycho-terminology, you will use it effectively.

✔ **How long?** 'How long should my notes be?' is a regular student query, and the answer relates to lengths of string. The length of notes depends on your purpose. Generally, if notes occupy more than one side of A4, or 1–5 per cent of the text length, the topic must be of crucial importance. Some tutors will have apoplexy over the last statement; of course there are cases where notes will be longer, but aiming for brevity is a good notion. **Try This 6.1** gave some guidelines.

✔ **Sources.** Keep an accurate record of all research sources and see Chapter 10 for advice on citing references. Don't just note Parker, when what you really need is Parker, Gellatly & Waterman (1999).

✔ **Quotations.** 'Eysenck, H., a man of note, wrote so many things to quote.' A direct quotation can add substance and impact in writing, but must be timely, relevant, fully integrated and fully referenced. A quote should be the only time when your notes exactly copy the text. Reproducing diagrams or pictures is a form of quotation and again the source must be acknowledged. If you rework secondary or tertiary data in a figure, table or graph, acknowledge the source, as in 'See Figure xxx from Drewit et al. (2010)', 'The data in Table xxx (taken from Wrotil, 1991) show that ...', 'Re-plotting the data (Graffit with) highlights ... (Figure xxx)'.

✔ **Plagiarism.** If you do not fully acknowledge your sources then the university may impose penalties which can range from loss of marks to dismissal from a course. The regulations and penalties for plagiarism will be somewhere in your University Handbook; something like: 'Any work submitted as part of any university assessment must be the student's own work. Any material quoted from other authors, must be placed in quotation marks and full reference made to the original authors. If you copy directly during note making, you run the risk of memorising and repeating the material in an essay. It is therefore vital to adopt good note making habits to avoid plagiarism. Read and think about ideas and main points, then make notes from your head, using your own language. Find new ways to express ideas. This is not as difficult as it seems, but practice helps. The original author wrote for a specific reason, but your reason and context for making notes is different. Keep asking questions and look for links to other references and modules. Notes should grab your attention, and make sense to you 10 weeks later. They may be longer or shorter than the original but paraphrased in your language. Just swapping a couple of words is not enough.

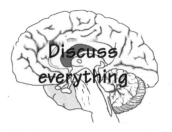

✔ **Diagrams.** Using flow or spider diagrams as a first step in note-making reduces the possibility of plagiarism. The style and language of the original author disappears behind a web of keywords and connecting arrows.

✔ **Check and share notes with friends.** Everyone has different ideas about what is important, so comparing summary notes with a mate will expand your understanding. (See O'Donnell and Dansereau, 1994.)

6.3 TECHNIQUES

Note-making is an activity where everyone has his or her own style. Aim to keep things simple, or you will take more time remembering your system than learning psychology.

Which medium?

Cards encourage you to condense material, or use small writing. Shuffle and re-sort them for essays, presentations and revision.

Loose-leaf paper lets you file pages at the relevant point and move pages around, which is especially useful when you find inter-module connections.

> Hang on while I staple this note to my floppy disk.

~~Notebooks keep everything together,~~ but you will need to leave spaces to add new

Multicoloured highlighting

Saunders (1994) suggests a colour code to highlight different types of information on *your own* notes, books and photocopies. He suggests: 'yellow for key information and definitions; green for facts and figures worth learning; pink for principal ideas and links between things; blue for things you want to find out more about . . .'. This approach requires lots of highlighter pens and consistency in their use, but it can be particularly useful when scanning your own documents. If this looks too complicated, use one highlighter pen – sparingly. On a PC changing the font colour or shading does the same task.

Coding

Coding notes assists in dissecting structure and picking out essential points. During revision, the act of classifying your notes stimulates thoughts about the types and relative importance of information. At its simplest use a ** system in the margin:

**** Vital	** Useful
?* Possible	↓ A good idea but not for this; cross-reference to . . .

A more complex margin system distinguishes different types of information:

I I	Main argument	B	Background or introduction
I	Secondary argument	S	Summary
E.G.	Case study	I	Irrelevant
[	Methodology, techniques	!!	Brilliant, must remember
R	Reservations – the 'Yes but' thoughts		
?	Not sure about this, need to look at . . . to check it out		

Opinions

Note your own thoughts and opinions as you work. These are vital, BUT make sure you know which are notes from sources, and which your own opinions and comments. You could use two pens, one for text notes and the other for personal comments. Ask yourself questions like: 'What does this mean?' 'Is this conclusion fully justified?' 'Do I agree with the inferences drawn?' 'What has the researcher proved?' 'What is s/he guessing?' 'How do these results fit with what we knew before?' 'What are the implications for where to go next?'

Space

Have spaces in notes, a wide margin or gaps, so there is room to add comments and opinions at another time. There is no time in lectures to pursue personal questions to a logical conclusion, but there is time when reviewing to re-focus thoughts.

Use abbreviations in notes but not essays: intro. for introduction; abst^n for abstention; reg^n for regression; emol for emotional and use symbols. ψ is a useful symbol for psychology, ψist for psychologist . . . and so on. You probably have a system already. Here are some sample abbreviations for speedier writing.

+	And	=	is the same as
→	Leads to	xxx^n	xxxion as in confabulation
↑	Increase	xxx^g	xxxing as in processing
↓	Decrease	//	Between
>	Greater than	Xpt	Except
<	Less than	←	Before
∴	Therefore	w/	With
?	Question	w/o	Without

Millions of unordered notes will take hours to create but will not necessarily promote learning. Aim for notes which:

- Are clear, lively, and limited in length.
- Add knowledge and make connections to other material.
- Include your own opinions and comments.
- Are searching and questioning.
- Guide or remind you what to do next.

Finally, feeling guilty because you haven't made some, or any, notes is a waste of time and energy.

6.4 REFERENCES AND FURTHER READING

Hartley, J. (1998). *Learning and Studying: A Research Perspective*. London: Routledge.

O'Donnell, A. & Dansereau, D.F. (1994). Learning from lectures: Effects of cooperative review. *Journal of Experimental Education*, **61**(2), 116–25.

Parker, A., Gellatly, A. & Waterman, M. (1999). The effect of environmental context .... .n memory: Dissociation between perceptual and conceptual .... *Cognitive Psychology*, **11**(4), 555–70.

.... *...dents of all Ages*, 3rd edn.

Van Merw.. ...
taking derived from thou ....
Psychology, **86**(3), 323–38.

What's my problem? Wordsearch 1 Answers p. 255.

You are looking for 25 problems.

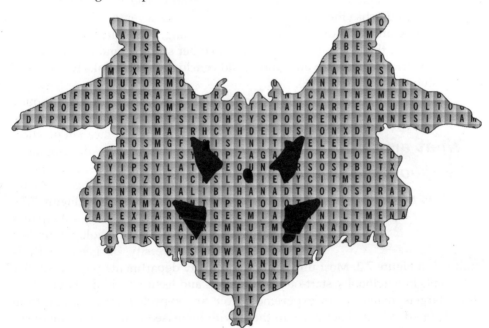

If I sound confused, it's because I'm thinking.

Few people set aside time to 'think'. Indeed refusing to go out on the grounds that 'I have to stay in and think about the implications of attachment style as a factor in the perpetuation of child abuse in three generations of a family' will not typically boost your street cred. Stick with 'washing my hair' or 'I want a quiet night in with EastEnders'. For most people the effective stimuli to thinking are conversation and discussion. Being asked: 'What is your position on the measurement of IQ?' or 'Are creativity and psychopathology related?' can stimulate thoughts you didn't know you had.

Psychology students are expected to apply their already well-developed thinking skills to a series of academic tasks and activities, to make reasoned judgements and arrive at conclusions about psychological issues. It is possible to pursue a psychology degree at a rather superficial level, learning and re-presenting information. This is called surface learning. The aim of a university education is to practise the skills that move beyond this level to deeper learning, to demonstrate understanding, be active in questioning, relate ideas and opinions to other parts of the psychology degree and to other subjects, and develop one's ability to interrelate evidence and draw valid conclusions. This links to the ideas of deep study reading (see p. 48).

A student's intellectual sophistication should mature during a degree course, but it is sometimes difficult to know what this might mean in practice. To convey some aspects of this development UTMU (1976) takes Bloom's (1956) list of cognitive skills for university students, and unpacks them by assigning a series of associated verbs (Figure 7.1). A qualitative description of the anticipated development process for psychology under-graduates at the University of Leeds, UK, is outlined in Figure 7.2. Most universities and many departments publish similar statements in handbooks, start-of-year briefings and lectures. Think about where these targets match your experience. You are expected to progress from knowledge-dominated activities to those with increased emphasis on analysis, synthesis, evaluation and creativity.

This chapter is a minimalist excursion into 'thinking'-related activities. It is very brief and partial, ignoring whole areas of philosophy, cognition and cognitive science that you may already be familiar with. It concentrates on three elements: 1) unpacking what it means to be critical; 2) reasoning; and 3) tackling questions

Knowledge	write; state; recall; recognise; select; reproduce; measure.
Comprehension	identify; illustrate; represent; formulate; explain; contrast.
Application	predict; select; assess; find; show; use; construct; compute.
Analysis	select; compare; separate; differentiate; contrast; break down.
Synthesis	summarise; argue; relate; précis; organise; generalise; conclude.
Evaluation	judge; evaluate; support; attack; avoid; select; recognise;

designed to encourage clear, focussed thinking. If your
could take a little more polishing then think through the ideas here. Like salsa
dancing, thinking gets better with time, not overnight. Thinking is tough.

7.1 THE PROCESS OF THINKING

Thinking is used to acquire understanding and answers. Adjectives used to
describe quality thinking include reasonable, clear, cogent, logical, precise,
relevant, broad, rational, sound, sensible and creative. You cannot think in the
abstract; there is purpose to your thinking, even if it is not immediately obvious.
Steps in quality thinking will involve:

- deciding on the objective (problem-solving; inferring general principles from
  particular facts)

- defining the background assumptions

- acquiring data and information in a rigorous way so as to be able to support a
  reasoned argument

- drawing conclusions from the available information

- considering the implications of the results.

Your thinking is a matter for personal development and self-assessment. When
tackling complex psychological problems make notes while thinking, plot your
ideas on spider diagrams, and record links and connections as they come to you.
Ideas float away all too easily, especially the really good ones.

	Knowledge	Analysis	Synthesis
Level at Year	Broad knowledge and understanding of areas of subject (s). Fluency in subject vocabulary.	Problem solving ability. Evidence of understanding. Ability to apply concepts to actual situations.	Ability to bring together different material, and to draw appropriate conclusions.
1	Demonstrate a basic understanding of core subject areas, happy with psychological terminology. Demonstrate a knowledge of appropriate supporting analysis techniques (stats, I.C., lab).	Apply psychological techniques to real problems through class and field examples. Understand that there may be unique or multiple solutions to any issue. Appreciate the relative validity of results.	Be able to handle material that presents contrasting views on a topic and develop personal conclusions.
2	Demonstrate a comprehensive knowledge of specific subject areas. Be able to question the accuracy and completeness of information. Appreciate how different parts of the subject interrelate.	Apply psychological theories to individual situations and critically examine the results. Understand that it may be appropriate to draw on multidisciplinary approaches to analyse and solve psychological problems.	To locate and comment on diverse material, add personal research observations and integrate literature-based information with personal results.
3	Demonstrate a deep understanding of a number of specialist subject areas and methods. Appreciate the provisional state of knowledge in particular subject areas.	Understand how to solve problems with incomplete information, how to make appropriate assumptions. To develop appropriate research hypotheses. Question and verify results.	Appreciate the breadth of information available. To identify and tap into key elements of the material. Produce coherent reports.
MSc MA	Demonstrate a broad, deep understanding of specialised subject areas and methods. Understand where this dovetails with the subject in general. Understand the current limits of knowledge.	Demonstrate an ability to propose solutions to psychological problems involving appreciation of different approaches, gaps and contradictions in knowledge or data. Differentiation of unique and non-unique answers. Appreciation of the reliability of a proposal and results given the constraints and assumptions involved.	Be able to collate materials from a wide range of psychology and non-psychology sources. Integrate personal research materials in a coherent, thoughtful and professional manner. Be able to work to a specified brief.

Figure 7:2 Skills matrix for psychologists

Evaluation	Creativity	Professionalism
Ability to review, assess and criticise one's own work and that of others in a fair and professional manner.	*Ability to make an original, independent, personal contribution to the understanding of the subject.*	*Ability to act as a practising psychologist, to present arguments in a skilled and convincing manner and to work alone or in teams.*
Draw conclusions from results and identify the relative significance of a series of results. Evaluate	Offer original comment on psychological material. Display or present information in different ways.	Be effective in planning and using time and psychological resources, including
Review existing literature and identify gaps, appraise the significance of results and conclusions.	Develop original independent research skills, interpret data and offer comment. Be able to display information in a variety of ways.	Confident use of computer packages for analysis and presentation. Confident group worker and collaborator in research activities. Produce written work to a high professional standard.
Critically appraise information, evidence and conclusions from personal and that of others' work.	Gather new information through personal research, draw personal conclusions and show where these insights link to the main subject areas.	Be able to set objectives, focus on priorities, plan and execute project work to deadlines. Produce well-structured and well-argued reports. Demonstrate fluency in oral and electronic communications.
Perform independent critical evaluation of information, evidence and conclusions, including reliability, validity and significance. Be able to form and defend judgements in the light of contradictory information.	Offer insights into the materials under discussion that are independent of data immediately available. Propose investigative approaches to psychology problems using psychological and non-psychological approaches as appropriate.	Make confident, effective and professional presentations, answer detailed questions thoughtfully and clearly. Produce substantive reports that are well structured, well reasoned, well presented and clear. Work effectively as a team member and team leader.

7.2 CRITICAL THINKING

Critical thinking involves working through for yourself, afresh, a problem. This means starting by thinking about the nature of the problem, thinking through the issues and aiming for a reasoned, logical outcome. During the process you also need to be aware of other factors that impinge – where bias may be entering an argument, the evidence for and against the issues involved – and by searching for links in other parts of psychology. Essentially, you need to be critically evaluating this material throughout the process.

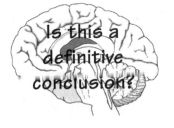

Being critical entails making judgements on the information you have at the time. It is important to remember that being critical does not require you to be negative and derogatory. It also means being positive, constructive and supportive. It involves commenting in a thoughtful way. A balanced critique looks at both the positives and negatives. Some students feel they cannot make such judgements because they are unqualified to do so. Recognise that neither you, nor your teachers, will ever know everything. In a year's time, with more and different information and experience, your views and values may alter. But for the moment you are making a judgement based on what you know now.

Discussion is a major thinking aid, so talk about psychology. It can be provocative and stimulating!

Where does *intellectual curiosity* fit into this picture? Psychological research is about being curious about psychological concepts and ideas. You can be curious in a general way, essentially pursuing ideas at random as they grab your imagination. We all do this. More disciplined thinking aims to give a framework for pursuing ideas in a logical manner, and to back up ideas and statements with solid evidence in every case.

Uncritical surface learning involves listening and taking notes from lectures and documents, committing this information to memory and regurgitating it in essays and examinations. The 'understanding' step is missing here. Aim for deeper learning.

7.3 REASONING

Strong essays and examination answers look at the psychological arguments, draw inferences and come to conclusions. Judgements need to be reasoned,

balanced and supported. First think about the
difference between *reasoned* and *subjective*
reactions, and reflect on how you go about
thinking. Subjective reaction is the process of
asserting opinions as facts, of making
unsupported statements. By contrast, reasoning
involves working out, on the basis of evidence, a
logical argument to support or refute your case
(Figure 7.3).

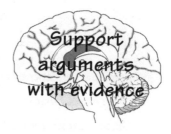

... rather than subjective statements with **Try This**

inferences on the basis of ... argument with caveats.

Subjective statement	Reasoned statement
Dementia affects lots of old people and is caused by disintegration of the brain tissue.	It has been estimated that between 5 and 10 per cent of individuals aged over 65 will develop dementia (e.g., Ritchie, 1997). The commonest form is dementia of the Alzeimer's type and is caused by neurofibrillary tangles and abnormal proteins that are found in various parts of the brain (cf. Foster *et al.*, 1997). The second commonest type results from a stroke.
A child will be happier if it has a sensitive mother.	Ainsworth's Strange Situation test (Ainsworth *et al.*, 1978) has allowed researchers to explore the nature of attachments between infants and their caregivers. One of the factors that appears to influence attachment is maternal sensitivity: secure attachment is best predicted by the mother's ability to respond positively to her baby's signals (e.g., Isabella & Belsky, 1991).

Figure 7:3 Examples of subjective and reasoned statements

TRY THIS 7.1 – Reasoned statements

Either write a fuller reasoned version of the four subjective statements below, OR pick a few sentences from a recent essay and rewrite them with more evidence, examples and references. For example responses see p. 255.

1 I have proved that girls are better at maths.

2 Questionnaires are the best way of measuring personality.

3 People who see life events as threatening are less healthy.

4 Working memory is vital to our everyday functioning.

7.4 QUESTIONS WORTH ASKING!

Being a critical thinker involves asking questions at all stages of every research activity. These questions could run in your head as you consider psychological issues. Questions such as:

? What are the main ideas here?

? Are the questions being asked the right ones; are there more meaningful or more valid questions?

? What are the supporting ideas?

? What counter-evidence is available?

? Is the evidence strong enough for you to reach a conclusion?

? How do these ideas fit with those from elsewhere?

? What is assumed?

? Are the assumptions justified?

? What are the strengths and weaknesses of the arguments?

? Is a particular social or cultural perspective biasing the interpretation?

? Are the data of an appropriate quality?

? Do the results really support the conclusions?

? Are causes and effects clearly distinguished?

? Is this a personal opinion or an example of intuition?

? Have I really understood the evidence?

? Am I making woolly, over-general statements? 'The cerebellum is involved with movement.' OK, but 'The cerebellum co-ordinates sensory information about the position of body parts with information from the frontal lobes about what movements are intended', or 'Without the cerebellum, the frontal lobes would produce jerky, uncoordinated, inaccurate movements' is better.

? Are points made/results accurate? 'The ear is sensitive to frequencies ranging from 30 to 20,000Hz.' This statement sounds clear, but is it right? Where/what is the evidence?

? Are the results/points precise? 'Variations in frequency cause vibrations at different points along the basilar membrane.' This statement is clear and correct, but we do not know how precise it is. Which parts of the basilar

distract and confuse the reader,

? Is the argument superficial? Have all the complexities of an issue been addressed? 'Is deliberate reinforcement necessary for language learning?' A clear 'No, because . . .' will answer the question, but this is a very complex issue requiring consideration of the importance of child-directed behaviours and the interplay between biology, cognition and the social environment.

? Is there a broad range of evidence? Does the answer take into account the range of possible perspectives? The question 'Discuss the arguments for and against the definition of dyslexia as a disorder' could be argued from an educational psychology perspective, but a broad essay might also consider clinical, developmental and cognitive psychological research. You will not have time to cover all points in equal depth, but aim to make the reader aware that you appreciate that there are other views or approaches.

? Are the arguments presented in a logical sequence? Try to check that thoughts and ideas are ordered into a sequence that tells the story in a logical and supported way.

? How does this idea or hypothesis fit with the wider field of enquiry? You might be looking at a paper on drug treatments for depression, but where does it fit with individual differences, biological psychology *or* psychotherapy?

? What examples will reinforce the idea?

? Can this idea be expressed in another way?

? What has been left out? Looking for 'gaps' is an important skill.

? Is this a definitive conclusion or a probable conclusion?

? What are the exceptions?

Take a little time to think before jumping into a task with both feet. Having completed a task or activity, spend a few minutes reflecting on the results or [illegible] Try This 7.2 and Try This 7.3 are two exercises that develop critical skills. Both provide frameworks for thinking about, evaluating and synthesising psychological material.

TRY THIS 7.2 – Gutting a paper

Select one paper from a reading list, any paper, any list! Make notes on the following:

Content:	What are the main points?
Evidence:	What is the supporting material? Is it valid?
Counter-case:	What are the counter-arguments? Has the author considered the alternatives fully?
Summary:	Anything else that might flesh out an exam answer tables/ diagrams, etc.
What else?:	Is there relevant material from other sources that the author might have included, but has omitted or has only alluded to?

How well did the author meet his or her stated objectives?

TRY THIS 7.3 – Comparing papers

Take three papers that are on the same or related topics, from any module reading list.

Write a 1000-word review that compares and contrasts the contributions of the three authors. (Use the guidelines from the previous exercise.) Write 250 words on where these three papers fit with material from the module.

This seems like a major effort, but it really will improve your comprehension of a topic, so treat it as a learning exercise rather than an isolated skills exercise. Pick three papers you are going to read anyway. It is another approach to reading and noting.

In practice, few lecturers would argue that a logical perspective is the only way to deal with questions. Express your emotional responses within an essay, ONLY if they are relevant and appropriate. An essay on 'storm and stress in adolescence' requires consideration of gender, physical development, friendship networks and parenting with references and examples. A polemic answer describing the horrors of your experience of puberty and early romantic relationship disasters will not do.

Can you improve the quality of your thinking alone?

Yes, but it takes practice. You will probably become more disciplined in your thinking by discussing issues regularly. This is because the act of talking over an idea sparks off other ideas in your own mind. When someone else voices their point of view, you get an insight into other aspects of the problem. Thinking of arguments that run against your own position is difficult. A discussion group might do the following:

✔ start by summarising the problem

[text obscured] to follow through

✔ summarise the outcomes.

A good reasoner is like a good basketball shooter, becoming more adept through practising.

Where to think?

Thoughts and ideas arrive unexpectedly and drift off just as fast unless you make notes. Take a minute to recall where you do *your* thinking. There are almost as many varied answers as people, but a non-random sample of individuals in a lecture (N = 67) showed that favoured locations include in bed at 4 a.m., while walking to work, jogging, swimming, working out in the gym, cleaning the house or cutting grass! There is certainly a common element of useful thinking happening while one is otherwise engaged in an activity that allows the mind to wander in all sorts of directions, without distractions like phones and conversations. The majority of students who offered 'walking' and 'the gym' as their best thinking opportunities are evidence of this. Writing down ideas is vitally important, but is incompatible with aerobics. Recognise this problem by taking 10 minutes over a drink after exercise, or a couple of minutes at a bus stop, to jot down thoughts and plans. This makes aerobic exercise or travelling by bus an effective multi-tasking activity.

Avoiding plagiarism

Good thinking habits can minimise your chance of inadvertently plagiarising the work of others. Get into the habit of engaging with and applying concepts and ideas, not just describing or reporting them. That means thinking over the ideas to find your own contexts and alternative examples. Make sure you include your own thoughts, opinions and reflections in your writing. Be prepared to draft and redraft so that the thoughts are in your own language, and acknowledge your ᴜᴏᴜʀᴄᴇꜱ. Leave time to link ideas coherently. Finally, put the full reference for your citations at the end of each piece of written work. Thinking and understanding involve a commentary in your head. Writing a summary in your own words is a good way to check you understand complex ideas. Ask:

'Do I understand this?' Ask at the end of a page, chapter, paper, tutorial, lecture . . . and not just at the end.

7.5 REFERENCES AND FURTHER READING

Ainsworth, M.D.S., Blehar, M.C., Waters, E. & Wall, S. (1978). *Patterns of Attachment.* Hillsdale, NJ: Lawrence Erlbaum Associates.

Bloom, B.S. (Ed.) (1956). *Taxonomy of Educational Objectives: 1 Cognitive Domain.* London: Longman.

Foster, J.K., Black, S.E., Buck, B.H. & Bronskill, M.J. (1997). Age and executive functions: A neuroimaging perspective. In P. Rabbitt (Ed.), *Methodology of Frontal and Executive Function.* Hove: Psychology Press.

Halpern, D.E. (1996). *Thought and Knowledge: An Introduction to Critical Thinking,* 3rd edn. Mahwah, NJ: Erlbaum.

Isabella, R.A. & Belsky, J. (1991). Interactional synchrony and the origins of infant–mother attachment: A replication study. *Child Development,* **62**, 373–84.

Logie, R.H. (1999). Working memory. *The Psychologist,* **12**(4), 174–8.

Ritchie, K. (1997). Establishing the limits of normal cerebral ageing and senile dementia. *British Journal of Psychiatry,* **173**, 97–107.

UTMU (1976). *Improving Teaching in Higher Education.* London: University Teaching Methods Unit.

Van den Brink-Budgen, R. (1996). *Critical Thinking for Students: How to Use Your Recommended Texts on a University or College Course.* Plymouth: How To Books.

Psychojumble
Four items appear in the top picture but not in the bottom one and vice versa. Which are the eight items appearing once only? Answers on p. 256.

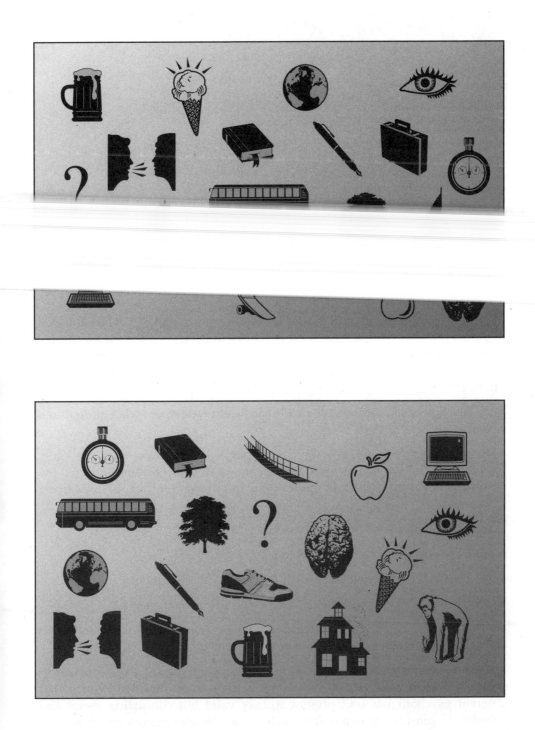

8 CONSTRUCTING AN ARGUMENT

Look, this isn't an argument, it's just a contradiction!

At the centre of every quality psychological essay, report or presentation is a well-structured argument. This is an argument in the genre of a fully supported and referenced explanation of an issue. In producing an argument you are not looking to provide a mathematical proof, or evidence that is strong enough to support a legal case. You are trying to establish a series of facts and connections that link them, so that your deductions and conclusions appear probable. If you establish enough links and supply the case evidence through real psychological examples, your argument cannot be rejected as improbable.

At the start think about your motive for putting pen to paper. Not just 'I want a 2.1'; what are you trying to say? Most psychological issues can be viewed from a number of perspectives and exemplified with a wide range of material. This means unpacking the elements of an argument and structuring it logically. Your aim might be:

- to develop a point of view, as in a broadsheet newspaper-style editorial or a debate

- to persuade the reader, possibly your psychology examiner, that you know about 'the role of heuristics in the elicitation of complex emotions' or 'the advantages and disadvantages of the test–retest method of measuring reliability'.

You may be more specific, perhaps wanting to define:

- how one concept differs from previous concepts

- the implications of using one idea or concept rather than another one

- whether a decision is possible or 'Are we still sitting on the fence?'

- what would need to be adapted or amended, what would work and what would not, if an idea or concept were transferred to a new environment.

Some arguments are linear, others rely on an accumulation of diverse threads of evidence which, collectively, support a particular position. Recognise that different psychologists will present equally valid but conflicting views and opinions. In considering issues around the prescription of neuroleptic drugs you could seek information from a psychiatrist, biochemist, psychopharmacologist, psychotherapist, community mental health nurse, pharmaceuticals company representatives, mental health campaigning groups, people taking the drugs in question, and their friends and families. In developing a statement about the use of neuroleptics you would need to present the different views and consider:

? What are the limitations of each view?

? What elements are entrenched?

? How might a consensus be formed?

A psychology research project can leave you overwhelmed with evidence. 'Thinking' is involved in designing an approach to maximise your understanding ~~of ... and interactions between~~ different facets and elements of the data

8.1 STRUCTURING ARGUMENTS

Any argument needs to be structured (Figure 8.1) with reasoned evidence supporting the statements. A stronger, more balanced argument is made when examples against the general tenet are quoted. Russell (1993) describes three classic structures that can be adopted in arguing a case (Figure 8.2). We contend that at university level the third model should be used every time, and that in every discussion, oral presentation, essay, report and dissertation you should be able to point to each of the six sections and to the links between them.

8.2 UNPACKING ARGUMENTS

It is all too easy when speaking and writing to put too much information into a sentence, or to make very general statements. One might say 'Newborn babies are faster at imitation than 2- to 3-month-old babies'. This is true but hides much information. A fuller statement would be something like: 'Infants only 36 hours old have been observed discriminating between the facial expressions happy, sad and surprised, and imitating these expressions. While 2- to 3-month-old babies are perfectly capable of imitating, they are slower to do so than newborns because

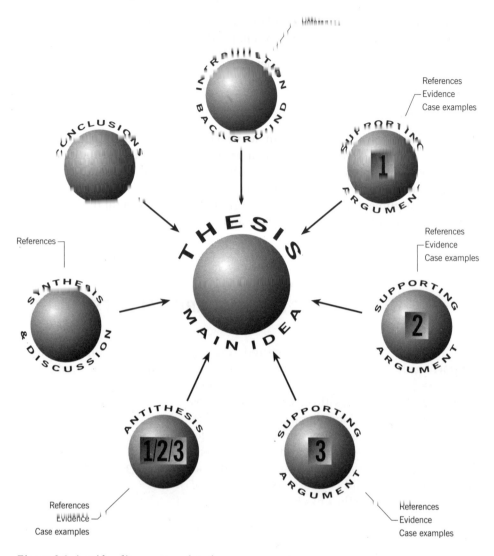

Figure 8:1 A spider diagram template for an argument

they attempt to play social games with adults who make interesting faces and gestures.' To further strengthen this example add references: '. . . interesting faces and gestures (Watchett & Sea, 2005)'.

Another statement meriting some unpacking is 'Anorexics have distorted body images of themselves'. A more detailed statement might say, 'People with anorexia have been demonstrated as seeing themselves as heavier than they actually are. When presented with a photograph of herself an anorexic is significantly more likely than a matched control to adjust that image so that it is

the development of monocular depth perception' is a ~~ g
and might be an essay title (just add Discuss). Another version, gaining more
marks by adding detail, might read,

> The visual cliff consists of a board placed across a sheet of glass, with a
> surface of patterned material directly under the glass. The appearance of
> depth – the visual cliff – is created by a dramatic change in the texture
> gradient in the patterned material. If an infant aged 6–7 months is placed on
> the board, with one of her eyes covered to eliminate binocular cues, she will
> crawl across the 'shallow side' of the board to her mother, but will not cross
> the 'cliff'. Thus when an infant is old enough to crawl her monocular depth
> perception is also relatively well developed.

When reviewing your own writing, try to identify general sentences that could
benefit from fuller explanation.

8.3 RATIONAL AND NON-RATIONAL ARGUMENTS

Arguments are categorised as being rational and non-rational. The non-rational
are to be avoided wherever possible. Here are five examples:

1 'Punishment is the best form of reinforcement for achieving better behaviour.'
  Aside from being arguable, this is hyperbole. It might sell newspapers but it is
  not an argument unless supported by data.

2 'People become obese primarily because they overeat. Students overeat when
  they are stressed, therefore they are more at risk of becoming obese around
  exam time.' This is a very poor argument and untrue in the majority of cases.

Some students are obese, some are thin, some overeat at stressful times, some forget to eat altogether. Everyone's weight fluctuates over time.

3 'Politicians have been documented using styles of language that enable them to avoid giving direct answers to questions' is a more considered and academic statement than 'All politicians employ the most roundabout linguistic constructions that convey absolutely zero, because they are inherently incapable of giving straight answers to important questions'. Going OTT with language or throwing in jargon to impress the reader is a typical journalistic device, involving an emotional rather than a factual appeal to the reader.

4 'It is unquestionably clear that a central executive controls all cognitive function. Words which sound very strong – *clearly, manifestly, undoubtedly, unquestionably, all, naturally, obviously* – will influence the reader into thinking the rest of the statement must be true. Overuse of strong words is unhelpful, the written equivalent of browbeating or shouting. Used sparingly they have greater effect.

5 'An extrovert would always choose to go to a party rather than stay at home and read a book' or 'All adolescents have problems at some stage communicating with their parents' involve over-generalisation. The scope of psychology means that an exception can be found to almost every generalisation.

Inductive or deductive? Which approach?

In presenting an argument, orally or on paper, give some thought to the ordering of ideas. If you write deductively you begin with the general idea and then follow on with examples. Inductive writing starts with specific evidence and uses it to draw general conclusions and explanations. You must decide what suits your material. In general, use the inductive approach when you want to draw a conclusion. The deductive approach is useful when you want to understand cause and effect, test a hypothesis or solve a problem. The examples given here of an inductive (A) and a deductive (B) approach are in paragraph form, but the same principles apply to essays and dissertations. There is an enormous leap here from a single study to broad general statements about healthy social development in children; the whole could do with further unpacking of the argument and more examples.

(A) In a study of children aged 3–6, Stein and Levine (1989) reported that children as young as three years were able to predict positive or negative emotional responses in others as a function of whether or not the others' goals had been fulfilled. The development of children's language abilities and their understanding of their own and others' emotions in terms of internal mental states is a major stepping stone in the development of the young child's social life. It is especially important in the development of co-operative relations between peers and family members. The socialisation of emotion is a fundamental aspect of child development.

(B) When children reach the age of about 2–3 years their language ability has developed to the point where it becomes possible for researchers to explore children's emotional lives more closely. Research suggests that as children grow older their understanding of the causes of emotion is increasingly related to their own beliefs, desires and goals as well as those of people around them. For example, Stein and Levine (1989) read stories of various types to children aged 3–6. In some stories the child wanted something but didn't get it, and in others the child didn't want something but got it anyway. The results of the study showed that children as young as three were able to predict positive or negative emotional responses in a story as a function of whether or not the characters' goals were fulfilled. Fabes *et al.* (1991) have provided additional support for this through a naturalistic study of 3-year-olds in a nursery-school setting.

8.4 POTENTIAL MINEFIELDS

Watch out for bad arguments creeping into your work. The following examples are rather obvious. Be critical in reviewing your own work: are there more subtle logic problems? It is easy to spot logical errors when sentences are adjacent, but they may be less easy to see if there are a thousand words in between.

✗ **Circular reasoning:** Check that conclusions are not just a restatement of your original premise.

Aversive events can be used in the learning of new responses. We know this because we see new responses happening when unpleasant events occur.

✗ **Cause and effect:** Be certain that the cause really is driving the effect.

Students are forced to live in crime-ridden areas, so crime becomes part of student life.

✗ **Leaping to conclusions:** The conclusion may be right in some cases, but steps in the argument are missed (see unpacking arguments, p. 77). Some arguments are simply wrong.

Many people look back on their lives and achievements as they approach the end of life. The final years of life may be spent in despair.

Sons of alcoholic fathers are more likely than sons of non-alcoholic fathers to develop alcoholism. This tells us that alcoholism is hereditary.

Be clear about the difference between arguments where the supporting material provides clear, strong evidence, and those where there is statistical or experimental evidence supporting the case but uncertainty remains. In student projects and dissertations, time often limits experimental or field work. If there should have been 60 participants, but unfortunately there was only time to get 12, be clear about the limitations. Statements like 'On the basis of the six participants tested we can suggest that . . .' or 'The statistical evidence suggests . . . However, the inferences that may be drawn are limited because sampling occurred just before the Christmas break and all participants were psychology students' are very acceptable. Qualifying statements of this type have the additional merit of implying that you have thought about the limits and drawbacks inherent in the research results.

Is this a good argument?

Watch out for arguments where the author gives a true premise, but the conclusion is dodgy. Just because you agree with the first part of a sentence does not mean that the second part is also right. Keep thinking right through to the end of the sentence. Having articulated an argument, do you buy it? Why? Why not? What is your view? Look at **Try This 8.1** as a starter.

TRY THIS 8.1 – Logical arguments?

Consider the following statements. What questions do they raise? Are they true and logical? What arguments could be amassed to support or refute them? See pp. 256–7 for some responses.

1. It is evident from the observation of children at play that boys are more aggressive than girls.
2. Motion sickness comes about when the vestibular organs receive information about movement that do not fit with the information about the relative motion between the person and the external visual field (e.g., Reason and Brand, 1975). Forward-facing seats lead to a lower incidence of motion sickness.
3. Burt's (1955) work with twins showed that the heritability of intelligence was 80 per cent, and this finding has been highly influential in the development of work in this area.
4. Categorisation is a cognitive mechanism that helps us categorise the world we live in. This helps us understand the world and simplify our perception of it. There are infinite numbers of social categories like Liberal Democrats and mothers.

Language that persuades

If you use strong statements like 'Clearly it has been demonstrated . . .', 'This essay has proved . . .' or 'The evidence has unquestionably shown . . .', be sure that what you have written really justifies the hype. It is worth thinking about your stock of linking phrases. Use **Try This 8.2** to review what you currently use, and then look at the answers to see if there are others to add.

TRY THIS 8.2 – Logical linking phrases

Identify words and phrases that authors use to link arguments by scanning through a couple of papers or chapters you are going to read next anyway. Some examples are given on p. 257.

- When reviewing your work read the introduction and then the concluding paragraph. Are they logically linked?
- Keep all parts of your brain engaged.

8.5 OPINIONS AND FACTS

It is important in both reading and writing to make a clear distinction between facts supported by evidence, and opinions, which may or may not be supported. Telling them apart is a matter of practice in looking to see what evidence is offered and what else might have been said. Has the author omitted counter-arguments? In **Try This 8.3** there are some short extracts to practise your discrimination skills. Which are facts, which opinions and which have evidence offered in support?

TRY THIS 8.3 – Fact or opinion?

Are these statements factual or based on opinion? Briefly describe the argument advanced by the writer. (All statements are taken verbatim from articles and reviews in *The Psychologist*, 12(1), 1999, authors and page numbers as shown.) Suggested answers are on pp. 257–8.

Organisations provide the individual with an interpersonal arena in which, among other emotions, the experiences of love, companionship, betrayal and envy may influence performance and service delivery. Yet these experiences are barely represented in mainstream academic organisational literature. This omission is interesting. (Walsh, p. 20.)

There is a growing interest in affect and organisation and management theory generally, yet it remains under-researched in the arena of strategic management processes. (Daniels, p. 24.)

Each stage also involves social activity (Daniels, p. 24.)

Even generating worry in others is sometimes necessary to promote behavioural change, as when a doctor issues a health warning to a patient (Ostell, Baverstick & Wright, p. 30.)

It is important not to treat all emotional reactions in the same way, as different emotions tend to be provoked and sustained by different patterns of thinking. (Ostell, Baverstick & Wright, p. 32.)

There are now internet sites covering virtually every aspect of psychological research. (Johnson, p. 41.)

A major problem with **Try This 8.3** is that only part of a paragraph is reproduced, and inevitably some opinions are based on limited information. As in life, if you start looking for arguments you will find them. **Try This 8.4** is a way of getting into analysing arguments. Use it as a framework next time you read something psychological.

TRY THIS 8.4 – Spot the argument

As you read any psychological article: (a) highlight the arguments; (b) highlight the statements that support the argument; and (c) highlight the statements that counteract the main arguments. Is the information presented balanced?

8.6 UNFASHIONABLE ARGUMENTS

Examining all sides of a question can be particularly difficult if unfashionably moral or ethical elements are involved. Consider how you would discuss the causes of rioting. You might say that people riot because it is a group reaction, an example of hysterical contagion, a way of livening up a dull, hot evening, a predictable response to misunderstood political action. You could talk about the 'fact' that some people 'are evil', not 'made evil by circumstance' and state that behaviour is not solely determined by upbringing, social background and employment prospects. A less biased response might focus on the effects of inequality in social support, health, education, etc., on unemployment, drug misuse and racial tension. The rioters could be portrayed as victims of circumstance (it's not their fault) or as inciters, throwers of bricks and bottles and people responsible for their own actions.

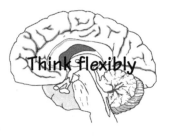

These issues are, of course, difficult and complex, interlocked, interlinked and coloured by personal understanding of background and culture. Is it possible for you to be an unbiased reporter? The challenge is to try to see all perspectives, including the 'moral' and the unfashionable. If the issue is 'drug addiction', is it because the pharmaceutical companies hold too much sway? If juvenile delinquency is related to parenting style, should parents be held to account?

Another way into thinking about these issues is to think of headlines that will never make the papers:

NO DRUGS IN SWANSEA/TORONTO/NEW DEHLI CLUBS ON 36,518 DAYS LAST CENTURY

Why have there been no drugs in these cities' clubs on most nights of the twentieth century?

8.7 EXAMPLES OF ARGUMENTS

It is impractical in this text to reproduce an essay and discuss the quality of the arguments. Rather, some students' answers, together with some examiners' comments, are used to make points about the adequacy of the arguments. This section could also be useful when revising for short-answer examination questions.

As an exercise in exemplified brevity, expressing ideas or concepts in two or three sentences or a maximum of 50 words is a good game. Consider these three answers to the question:

1   Define feedback. (2 sentences maximum)

(A) *Feedback occurs where part or all of the output from one process is also the input for another process. This can be positive, negative or both.* (26 words)

(B) *This is where the system effectively alters itself. Positive feedback is where the signal is reinforced, the converse is called negative feedback.* (22 words)

(C) *Feedback is the action by which an output signal from a process is coupled with an input signal (Figure 8.3). Feedback may be positive, reinforcing any changes, e.g. escalation of argument, or negative which ameliorates any changes, e.g. homeostatic control of body temperature.* (49 words including the diagram and its caption)

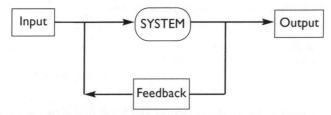

Figure 8:3 A simple feedback loop

These are not perfect answers, but the third statement has a little more psychology and the diagram reinforces the argument. This, and the next question, asks for a supported factual response rather than an argument.

2   What is habituation?

(A) *Habituation is the most primitive form of association learning and is considered to be a more primitive form of learning than classical conditioning. Habituation can be defined as a progressive decrease in response amplitude or the frequency of occurrence of a response to discrete and repetitive stimuli.* (47 words)

(B) *Habituation refers to the reduction in the strength of a response to a repeated stimulus. In general almost any stimulus will produce habituation; for example, when working at a computer a student may habituate to the levels of ambient noise from whirring disc drives and fellow students' muttering, and so be able to focus on her work.* (57 words)

We think both these definitions would get full marks since both define habituation. If there is negative marking for padding or making unsupported (or unsupportable) statements, then the first answer would lose out. What is meant by 'primitive', and where is the evidence for the second half of that sentence? If there are bonus marks going, or within an essay, the second answer has some added value. Using an example relevant to everyday experience makes this answer clearer than the first, and shows signs of understanding the concept rather than learning by rote.

The next examples build up arguments with evidence.

3   Explain the steps involved in deduction in experimental psychology.

(A) *Deduction is where a relationship is deduced from psychological phenomena, whereas induction looks for relationships within data or information. In deduction a general idea, such as 'more older adults live by the coast', is formulated as a hypothesis that may be tested, as in: 'population demographics change as you move from inland areas to the coasts'. Having defined the hypothesis it can then be tested in a scientific manner in order to verify or disprove it. Tests might involve primary data collection through questionnaires, observation, or analysis of census and ward data or local authority data. Following analysis the hypothesis will be accepted, rejected or accepted with exceptions. Appropriate deductions might involve a statement like 'The hypothesis was shown to be generally true for the Sunshine, Crown-Green and Wrinkly coasts, but there was no evidence of this demographic pattern applying to the Wildwoollynorth coast. Here the coastal towns are awash with bright young drilling engineers (Figure xxx) and very low proportions of older adults.'*

The first sentence is a little bald but indicates that the writer is aware of an alternative, inductive approach. The remaining sentences have integrated examples, following a case example through the reasoning. We hope you will agree that this answer gets more marks than the following bullet-style answer:

(B) *The steps in deductive reasoning are: Have an idea; develop a working hypothesis; test the hypothesis experimentally through data collection and analysis; decide whether to accept or reject the hypothesis and further explain how the world works in this case, and then reassess or redefine the problem if the research is to continue.*

This short statement answers the question at a level that will get a pass mark, but it has no psychology content. The first answer will score additional marks if the lecture or main text example is not to do with migration of older adults to the so-called 'sunshine states'.

4   Evaluate the practical relevance of the trait approach to measuring personality.

Tests such as the Eysenck Personality Inventory (EPI) and 16PF have been used extensively in personnel selection. If the test has good validity then we would expect it successfully to predict aspects of job performance. Blinkhorn and Johnson reviewed several studies in which these tests had been used to predict job performance, but found that fewer than 10 per cent of the correlations between test score and job performance were statistically significant. This suggests that the tests actually have poor validity. If personality scores are poor predictors of real-world behaviour then this suggests that the usefulness of the trait/factor approach to measuring personality is limited. However, a further study has shown that when candidates for jobs are warned that the test contains lie scales that can detect distorted responses, the correlation between personality and job performance is much stronger.

This question looks for the respondent to take a position, which in turn requires an argument – 'evaluate' is a keyword. The author demonstrates immediately that she can think of examples of tests that are based on the trait approach to measuring personality by naming them and summarising one of their most popular uses. Then she displays deductive reasoning in her second sentence. The third sentence is good but would be that bit more impressive with the date of the study included. So far, the material presented supports the idea that the tests have very limited relevance, but the author cites some counter-evidence. Unfortunately, the study details are missing. Although somewhat abrupt, the final sentence shows that the author is aware that there may be techniques for improving the validity and relevance of these tests.

5   Discuss the value of a structured interview compared with a questionnaire approach.

A structured interview has the benefits of being more personal, the interviewer gets a 'hands-on' feel for the data, and problems can be detected and dealt with as the interviews progress, for example by extending, adding or dropping some questions. The interviewee should feel involved, which is likely to encourage full answers and s/he may volunteer additional information. There is a problem with the honesty of answers in all survey research, but a one-to-one interview is more likely to elicit honest responses. The number of interview refusals is likely to be small. Conversely, interviews are very time-consuming in both administration and analysis, especially if there are audiotapes to transcribe.

A questionnaire can feel very impersonal; there is little motivation to complete. Since the number of returns from a postal questionnaire may be as low as 15 per cent, it must be sent to a large population to allow for non-returns. The respondents may misunderstand some questions, so instructions must be clear and questions unambiguous.

Both approaches require careful preparation, with questions structured in user-friendly order. A pilot survey should be carried out in each case and the schedule adjusted in response to the results.

If we are looking at argument in isolation then this is good. BUT, this answer would be as useful in a sociology or geography essay and gain the same marks. It has argument, structure and lots of good points but no links to psychology. There are no psychological examples and no references to the many authors who have written about social survey techniques in psychology. In a psychology examination it would score 45–50 per cent, a pass; it needs the psychological angle to do better.

Top Tips

- Avoid cop-out statements like 'Others disagree that . . .' – who are these others? There are more marks for 'Knowitall (2010) and Jumptoit (2010) disagree, making the point that . . .'.
- No examiner will give marks for the use of '. . . etc.'.

Yes but . . .

In addition to logical linking phrases keep a list of caveat or 'yes but' statements handy. There are alternatives to 'however' like *consequently; as a result; by contrast; thus; albeit; therefore; so; hence; nonetheless; despite the fact that; although it has been shown that.* More extended versions include: 'A rigorous qualitative psychologist might argue that the results of this research are ethereal, confused and disorganized, and that some structure would have helped the project'; 'The author gives an interesting but superficial account of . . .'; 'The figures show that . . . but were not able to support or refute the main hypothesis because . . .'; 'The succeeding tests support this criticism because . . .'; 'The outcome may be influenced by . . .'; 'Only a few of the conclusions are substantiated by the experimental analyses'; 'The argument is stated but the supporting evidence is not given'; . . . 'Although this is an entirely reasonable exploratory approach it neglects . . . and . . . thereby weakening the inferences that may be drawn'; 'Therefore the criticism should be directed at . . . rather than at . . .'; 'The outcomes, therefore, relate to a different set of conditions to those initially outlined'. Build on this list as you read. As you research use these 'yes but . . .' phrases to help focus thinking and to draw valid and reasoned inferences.

Be critical (within reason) of your writing and thinking. This means allocating time to read critically, remove inappropriate clichés and jargon, and add caveats and additional evidence.

✔ Write in clear sentences, with psychological cases and references to support the statements.

✔ Give due weight to arguments that support and refute your main argument.

✔ Talk through your arguments with friends. Explaining and persuading someone of your case usually clarifies arguments.

✔ Ask 'Does this persuade me?'

✔ Use Figure 8.1 as a template to check that you have a balanced argument.

8.8 REFERENCES AND FURTHER READING

Some genuine references were embedded in the extracts, the full citations can be found at http//www.geog.leeds.ac.uk/staff/p.kneale/skillbook.html or a Web of Science search will find them.

Fairbairn, G.J. & Winch, C. (1996). *Reading, Writing and Reasoning: A Guide for Students,* 2nd edn. Buckingham: Open University Press.

Russell, S. (1993). *Grammar, Structure and Style*. Oxford: Oxford University Press.

Toulmin, S., Rieke, R. & Janik, A. (1979). *An Introduction to Reasoning*. New York: Macmillan.

> Strong words often connote weak arguments.

Psych-ladders

Change one letter at a time to make new words each time you move down the ladder. Answers on p. 259.

T	E	S	T
P	O	N	S
W	A	V	E
B	O	D	Y
L	U	N	G
M	A	Z	E

M	O	D	E
H	A	L	O
F	O	O	T
C	E	L	L
M	I	N	D
L	O	B	E

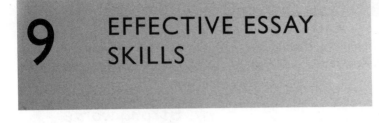

9 EFFECTIVE ESSAY SKILLS

When I write I discover what I think

Many of the chapters in this book start with some reasons as to why practising a particular skill might be a moderately good idea. Now demonstrate your advanced creative skills by designing your own opening. Create two well-argued sentences using the following words or phrases: reports, communication, language, persuasion, cheerful examiners, lifelong, clarity. Reorganise the following jumble to make a coherent sentence: with needs solos . practise, bagpipe As writing

The paragraph above may give you an insight into how annoying examiners find disjointed, half-written paragraphs, with odd words and phrases rather than a structured argument. Such paragraphs have no place in essays. If this is the first chapter you have turned to, keep reading!!

This chapter picks up some important points for psychology essays, but many texts discuss writing skills in more detail. Mature students who 'haven't written an essay in years' or students who did science A-levels and 'haven't written an essay since . . .' should find Fairbairn & Winch (1996), Heffernan (1997) or Russell (1993) valuable. Many universities run essay-skills classes, and the fact that so much psychology assessment is still essay-based should encourage *everyone* to go along. For tips on using English, grammar and spelling, Kirkman (1993) is particularly good and delightfully short.

Tutors are often asked what a good answer looks like. The most helpful response involves comparing and evaluating different pieces of writing. This chapter includes some examples of student writing at different standards. You are asked to compare the extracts to get a feel for the type of writing you are expected to produce. Space restricts the selection, but you could continue by comparing essays with friends and other members of your tutor group.

All essays need good starts and ends, lots of support material and a balance of personal research and lecture-based evidence. This usually requires an initial plan, some rethinking, writing, further research, and rewriting. Typically this is followed by a heavy editing session where the initially long sentences are cut down to shorter ones and paragraphs are broken up, so that each paragraph makes a separate point. The first version of anything you write is a draft, a rough-and-ready first attempt, requiring development and polish before it is a quality product. Many marks disappear because the first draft is submitted as the final product. Check out Mahalaksi's (1992) or Norton's (1990) research showing the relationship between features of essay writing and getting good marks.

9.1 WHAT KINDS OF ESSAYS ARE THERE?

The 'what do you know about . . .' style essay should be disappearing from your life. University questions usually require you to *think* about information that you have researched and to *weave* it into an argument. You are asked to analyse, criticise, examine and debate ideas in a structured way, using apt examples to illustrate your arguments. Essays that get high marks interweave lecture material with personal research findings and ideas. Facts from lectures, by themselves, are not enough. Painful but true. Reproducing the facts and arguments as presented in a lecture may get you a mark of 30–50 per cent. To get 50 per cent plus you need to show an examiner that you have thought about the issues. This involves adding other information gleaned through reading, sorting out what it all means for you, and restating the argument in your own words (Figure 9.1). OK, that is our opinion. Ask your psychology tutors what they think about this; get your own department's view.

You will increasingly be asked for *discussion* rather the *descriptive* essays, where counterbalanced arguments are required. Compare these sets of questions:

Descriptive: Describe the place of modern technology in the modern organisation.
Discussion: To what extent might the use of new technology in modern organisations be considered dangerous?
Descriptive: Outline the sensory, physiological, cognitive and social abilities of the newborn infant.
Discussion: To what extent does the infant arrive in the world ready for human interaction?

The descriptive essay title tends to have pointers to the structure and the type of answer required. The discussion essay clearly needs more thought and planning. You must establish your own structure and write an introduction that signposts the structure to the reader. This should be followed by linked arguments supported by evidence, leading to a conclusion that follows from the points you have made. Including material that veers off at a tangent, or is irrelevant, or presenting evidence in ways that do not really support your case, loses marks.

Many psychology essays involve a question with no right answer. You consider the various dilemmas and decisions that are the essence of real situations, provide evidence and reach a balanced conclusion. Questions like this might be, 'Discuss the contention that personality tests are only as valid as the theories of personality they reflect'; 'The mere division of people into categories is sufficient to evoke intergroup discrimination. Discuss'; 'Are theories of learning either necessary or useful?' and 'Discuss the relative contributions of studies of normal and abnormal readers to our understanding of the processes involved in reading'.

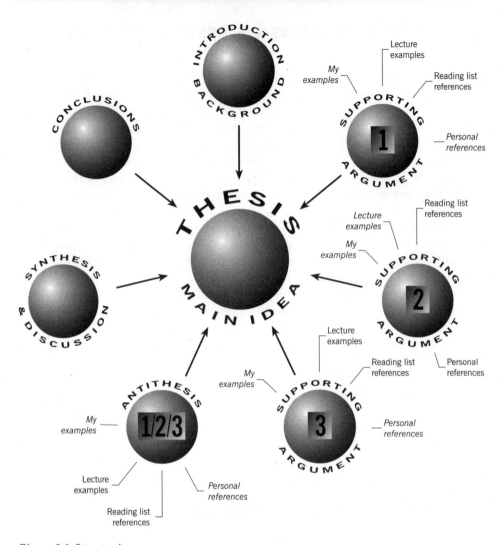

Figure 9:1 Structuring an essay

9.2 CAREFULLY ANALYSE ESSAY TITLES

The wording of a question can give you guidelines for your answer. Take time to analyse the question. For example:

Discuss how the study of visual illusions may give clues to more general mechanisms of visual perception.

What are the keywords? Anyone who thinks that this is an essay centred on visual illusions is in trouble. It is an essay about brightness and shape constancies, figure and ground and the Gestalt organisational laws, monocular and binocular perceptions of depth, movement perception and the impact of culture – a perceptual mechanisms essay. Specific illusions are used to organise discussion of the different mechanisms; for example the Poggendorf illusion to introduce the idea of perspective, or virtual contours to illustrate Gestalt organisational law of continuation. Equal weight needs to be given to the different sections of the essay – 'the study of visual illusions' and 'more general mechanisms of visual perception'. Notice that second element – the question is not about explaining the occurrence of the illusions, it's about what we can learn from these phenomena about visual perception in general.

> Describe and critically evaluate the factors that are considered to impact on employee well-being.

What are the keywords? The problem with this essay is that there is too much information that can be used: the influence of organisational size and structure, communication systems, the introduction of new technologies and consequent impact on job definition and security, down-sizing, management styles, personal style, job satisfaction, person–environment fit, social support and family situation. There is an excess of knowledge material. Most students attempt to include all the knowledge and thereby throw away the 50 per cent of the marks for the 'critically evaluate' section. Treat the titles in **Try This 9.1** in a similar manner, or use essay titles from your own modules.

Top Tip

✔ Assume all essay questions include the phrase 'with reference to specific psychological examples'.

TRY THIS 9.1 – Keywords in essay questions

What are the keywords and potential pitfalls with the following titles? Answers on p. 259.

1 'Many psychologists working today in an applied field are keenly aware of the need for close co-operation between theoretical and applied psychology' (Lewin, 1955). With specific reference to research in the area of job design evaluate the extent to which you believe this to be true.

2 Can simple conditioning theories explain complex behaviours?

3 Describe the relationship between reliability and validity in relation to any one psychological measure.

4 Discuss the difficulties in defining intelligence.

5 ECT is not only barbaric and damaging to the brain, it is also therapeutically ineffective. Discuss.

Getting started – 'red and blue pen modes'

Having analysed the essay title start with a spider diagram or plan to get started. Think about using a particular colour (blue) to write down all the things that come to mind. Let your ideas flow; don't get self-critical just yet, don't look for the exact technical term, phrase or reference. When you have done the free and creative bit, take a different coloured (red) pen and annotate your work for structure, style, references, grammar and spelling. This approach can help take the 'fear' out of writing, and you don't waste time searching for references and digging out the thesaurus in mid-flow.

9.3 EFFECTIVE INTRODUCTIONS

A good introduction serves two purposes. It outlines the general background or position and signposts the structure and arguments that follow. It gives the reader confidence that you are in command of the topic. There is no reason for the introduction to be long, 100–200 words or half a side is usually plenty. If the introduction is longer, consider editing it and putting the material later in the essay.

Introductions require some thought. *Planning time is vital*. A provocative, headline opening, grasping the imagination of the reader is a good wheeze, BUT it must be integral to the essay. Lengthy case material and examples are not usually good opening material. If there is an example in the first paragraph, limit it to one sentence; further details belong in the body of the essay. Here is a reasonably good introduction (it could be improved):

What functions are served by non-verbal behaviour? Illustrate your response with specific examples.

People often wonder why they can't lie effectively. Why is it that when they do their best to conceal something or try to persuade people of something which is not true, something always gives them away? After all, everyone uses language to communicate, and language can be manipulated to suit the speaker's purpose. Therefore anyone should be able to tell a lie effectively, but this is not usually the case. The world might be a different place if language was the only means of communication. But it's not. What actually gives us away are the huge number and variety of non-speech signals that we send while speaking – our non-verbal behaviour. (110 words.)

This grabs the reader's attention by kicking off with an example of a function of non-verbal behaviour implied in the very first sentence, deception, and then signposting a problem with the system, lack of complete control over our signalling. It moves quickly on to define the concept by making a contrast with verbal behaviour, and indicates that the subject area is broad and the behaviour potentially impactful. A lot of clues to the content in just over 100 words.

The next example contains a series of true statements, but the style of the essay is not to be imitated.

Non-verbal behaviour is a very broad category, and the different functions it can serve play an important role in human social interaction. The functions of non-verbal behaviour are many and vary immensely, from the communication of motive or intent, communication of emotion, or as an aid to verbal communication. In animals, the function of non-verbal behaviour is usually to express the animal's motive or intent as to what it will do next. Most animals exhibit species-specific behaviours, that is, they have displays specific to their species. These act as communication signals. These displays are also known as expressive displays because they 'express' the mind state of the animal. There are several examples of these expressive displays that can be given. (120 words)

The content of the first two sentences is fine, if a little long-winded. It could read, 'Non-verbal behaviour encompasses many different behaviours that can play an important part in social interaction. Its functions are many and varied, including the communication of emotion and intent'; 28 words instead of 49. Most tutors would expect this essay to focus on humans; the use of the term 'non-verbal' is the clue here. It's a bit of a surprise, then, to find that the whole of the rest of this opening is about animals. The fourth sentence is a rather unfortunate circular definition. Sentence 6 is also circular; it suggests the author believes it possible to understand the thoughts of animals. The final sentence cues the reader to expect examples that aren't there.

Pretend to be an assessor and take a critical look at **Try This 9.2**. Then try the same technique with your recent essays.

TRY THIS 9.2 – EVALUATE AN INTRODUCTION

Pretend to be an examiner looking at these four introductory paragraphs to the same essay. You need no knowledge of personality, nature or nurture, in fact a small gap in your knowledge will help here because you can concentrate on the main issues for good opening paragraphs. Questions to ask include:

Is the general case outlined and explained? Does the introduction indicate how the author will tackle the essay? Is the language suitably technical (or 'grown up' as a tutee once described it)?

Some comments are on pp. 260–1.

Is personality a matter of nature or nurture?

Version 1

All of the things which make up the human body and mind can be assumed to have come from either our genetic makeup, which we have inherited from our parents, or from external factors in the environment which have affected us since we were conceived. The fascination for this debate was largely prompted by Galton's ideas about eugenics and his attempt to show that genius was hereditary by tracing back the family line of high-achieving families. Although his results showed a strong positive effect of a good 'pedigree' he completely failed to take into account the environmental effects such breeding also entails.

Version 2
For many, especially those not well acquainted with the subject, psychology is seen as a way of predicting an individual's personality by simply observing a few token gestures and key bodily positions. In reality, this particular ability is not among the talents of psychologists, nor among their aims; instead, the study of personality is a much more in-depth affair. Put simply, our personality is the defining part of us that makes us who we are. It comprises our emotional set, our memories, the way in which we behave and react in certain situations, and the way in which we interact with others. It also includes our likes and dislikes, our talents and abilities and, although we may possess some traits in common with others, each individual has an entirely unique personality. Put shortly, our personality is what allows other people to distinguish us from everybody else.

Version 3
Personality has dozens of meanings: popular, legal, grammatical, ethical, religious, economic and psychological (Allport, 1937). At the core of all these different meanings, however, is a common feeling. A person is both unique and important. The very origin of the word personality suggests a relationship between the dramatic rendering of character and psychologists' attempts to understand it. The word itself comes from 'persona', the mask that the Greek and Roman actors wore to indicate the character that they played; and Allport defined it simply as 'the dynamic organisation of traits within the self that determine the individual's unique way of playing his social roles'.

Version 4
Genes determine our eye colour and blood type. This much is easy to accept. Genes regulate hormones, contribute to the shape of our fingers and the length of our lives. As living beings we share the biological roots that genes co-ordinate, but these roots aren't the ones we usually value. Although each life begins with a combination of genes different from any other – making us, quite literally, a new experiment of nature – when we think about what makes any one person unique it is learning and environment that interests us most, much more it seems than heredity. Our environment after birth is considered the only potent moulder of our lives.

9.4 THE MIDDLE BIT!

This is where to put the knowledge and commentary, developed in a logical order, like a story. *You need a plan.* Subheadings will make the plan clear to you and the reader, but whether you use subheadings mentally or mentally and physically is a matter of personal taste. It may be worth asking your tutors if they mind. Most tutors will not, but some are vitriolically against sub-headings in essays. Find out first.

Examples are the vital evidence that support the argument. Where you have a general question like 'Describe the impact of TV on children's violence', aim to include a range of examples. BUT if the question is specific – 'Comment on the impact of Tellytubby TV' – then the essay needs to mostly be about Tellytubby TV. In the 'impact of TV' essay, remember to make the examples relevant to children's violence. There is a 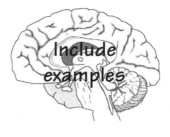 tendency for some students to answer questions like this with evidence pertinent to children's development generally. Our advice is to use as many relevant examples as possible with appropriate citations. As a rule, many examples described briefly get more marks than one example retold in great depth. Examples mentioned in the lecture will be used by 80 per cent of your colleagues. Exhilarate an examiner with a new example.

Graphs, figures, and pictures should illustrate and support the arguments, and do so with fewer words than a description of the same material. Put them in. Label them fully and accurately, and refer to them in the text. If there is no instruction to a reader to look at Figure X they will get to the end of your document without looking at it, and the inclusion is wasted. One advantage of labelling figures is that they can be cross-referenced from elsewhere, especially the discussion and conclusion sections, in the essay.

Reference appropriately. All sources and quotations must be fully referenced (see Chapter 10 for details), including the sources of diagrams and data. Try to avoid the over-obvious: 'Drugs can have a significant effect on brain function (Dye, 2010)'. OK, they can, and Dye may have said it as part of a Level 1 Bio lecture but this is not really an appropriate example of referencing, whereas, 'TCH, the active ingredient in marijuana, interferes with concentration and memory and distorts perceptions of the passage of time (Howlett, 1990)' is a proper and highly desirable example of referencing.

9.5 SYNTHESIS AND CONCLUSION

Synthesis

The discussion or synthesis section allows you to demonstrate your skill in drawing together the threads of the essay. In style terms it can help to express the main points in single sentences with supporting references, but this is just one suggestion. Here is an example of a synthesis paragraph. In answer to the essay question, 'Discuss recent research on sibling relationships in early childhood', paragraphs 1–6 introduced, described and commented on some developmental studies (the knowledge section of the answer). The essay went on:

> On the whole sibling relationships appear rather less important than peer relationships (Burhmester, 1982), and children aged between five and eleven are far more likely to turn to parents and friends than to siblings for comfort. On the other hand researchers have identified a series of different relationship patterns on the basis of retrospective work with young adults (e.g., Murphy, 1973). There is evidence from this work that some siblings act as either carers or buddies with each other, but many are either quite conflictual or completely uninvolved (e.g., Stewart et al., 1985). Sibling rivalry is most strongly associated with families where the children are within four years of age of each other, and in which the parents are not very happy with their own relationship (Kinsman, 1988). Overall, rivalry tends to be highest among boy-boy pairs, and friendliness highest among sisters. The importance of these relationships is superseded by relationships with peers, which become hugely influential in the later transition of adolescence from dependence to independence.

So what do you think? Looks like a useful summary, with some references – should get good marks. HOWEVER, the authors are all developmental researchers, and some of them did do the work referred to, though not in the years cited. One of the references is a complete spoof – examiners and tutors notice these things. Another problematic feature is that none of the references is later than 1988. This would be bad enough in any essay, but the title specifically asked for discussion of recent research.

Conclusion

The conclusion should sum up the argument but without repeating statements from the introduction. Introducing new material can cause examiners to comment 'The conclusions had little to do with the text'. It is hard to judge the standard of conclusions in isolation, because the nature and style of a conclusion depends on the content of the essay, but it helps to look at other examples. Despite this caveat criticise the examples in **Try This 9.3**.

TRY THIS 9.3 – Good concluding paragraphs

Read the following concluding paragraphs and consider their relative merits. Comments on each can be found on p. 261.

Version 1

It is becoming increasingly clear from the aforementioned research that an either/or requirement of the nature–nurture debate falls short in explaining the richness and complexity of people's lives. This polarised debate should be dismantled to allow consideration of the complementary series of influences that lie on a continuum bounded at one end by heredity, and the environment at the other. In between, where we find most individual charms and characteristics, lie the complex interactions of the two. The continuum of influences is shaped differently for each individual, which is one reason why trying to reduce a person's characteristics to numbers and ratios is too simple. It reduces an ever-changing and developing being into a static thing – not a useful goal for a psychologist to achieve.

Version 2
In conclusion, while there is evidence to support both personality as nature and personality as nurture, an interactionist approach is a more logical path to take. Statistics suggest that personality is 40 per cent inherited, with 5 per cent attributable to shared environment and 35 per cent to non-shared environment. Therefore, it seems sensible to conclude that personality is due to neither independently, but to a combination of the two.

Version 3
There are, however, a number of cases where the environment has not accounted for much. The only really valid studies of genes versus environment have been studies of identical twins separated at birth and reunited as adults. Rosen (1987) describes twins who didn't meet until adulthood – when they finally did meet, they discovered that they were both volunteer fire-fighters, both held their beer bottles (same brand) in the same unusual way, and both tended to make similar remarks when joking. In another example, twins discovered that they smoked the same brand of cigarettes, drove the same make of car and had the same hobby. Each of these twins grew up in very different environments. However, there are not enough examples of twins separated at birth. It is a statistical nightmare to deduce anything from such studies: how much is due to chance, and how many other traits do they share?

Version 4
While much of the evidence seems to point towards personality being genetically determined, this clearly is not the full picture as the 0.5 correlation for identical twins shows. There are clearly other contributing factors, but to attribute these to the environment would be to ignore the same correlation occurring for identical twins who are raised apart, the low similarity between adopted children and their adoptive siblings. An alternative hypothesis is that we are all born with a range of personality attributes, say eight. Assuming that people could only express the extremes of those eight traits (not at all X or extremely X), then we would have 256 possible different personalities. If we now assume that each person can express tiny variations all the way along the eight continua, then we have a potentially infinite number of different personalities. The most important issue then is identifying which traits our children have and the most effective means by which to foster or discourage them.

9.6 ASSESSMENT AND PLAGIARISM

Assessment

Use either your department's assessment criteria or Table 9.1 and Figure 9.2 to critically review your writing. In Figure 9.2 the percentage equivalents are given for guidance, but these values vary. Self-assessing a first draft can indicate where to focus your next research and writing effort.

Another way of developing your evaluation skills is to use **Try This 9.4**, which builds on an idea from note-making by using codes to locate the different sections of the essay and to compare their relative weights. **Try This 9.5** presents another way of creating essay structures, by posing some questions about the mark distribution. If the balance of the reward changes then so does the content.

TRY THIS 9.4 – Analysing essay structures

Look at any essay you have written. With five coloured pens, or a code system, mark in the margin the sections which show Knowledge, Analysis, Synthesis, Evaluation, and Creative abilities. Now think about the relative content.

?   How would you rewrite this essay to increase the analysis section?

?   How would you redesign to increase the evaluation content?

?   Is there a good opening paragraph?

?   Does the argument flow logically?

?   Are the examples relevant?

?   Are the arguments summarised effectively?

?   Are the conclusions justified?

?   Where could the balance of the essay be altered to improve it?

TRY THIS 9.5 – Marks for what?

Take any essay title (the last or next) and work out a plan for researching and answering the question when the mark distribution is:

1 Knowledge 20 per cent; Analysis 20 per cent; Synthesis 20 per cent; Evaluation 20 per cent; Professionalism 20 per cent.

AND

2 Knowledge 10 per cent; Analysis 50 per cent; Synthesis 20 per cent; Evaluation 10 per cent; Creativity 10 per cent.

AND

3 Knowledge 30 per cent; Evaluation 70 per cent.

Consider how the plans change as the mark distributions alter.

Criterion	First 70–100%	2(i) 60–69%	2(ii) 50–59%	Third 40–49%	Ordinary 37–39%	Fail 0–36%
Structure: organisation, logical order of material, aims, conclusion	Well organised throughout. Logical flow between sections. Aims and conclusion appropriate and specified clearly.	Mostly well organised, appropriate structure. Aims and conclusion specified.	Structure attempted. Evidence of organisation. Sound aims and conclusion.	Some attempt at structure or organisation but inappropriate.	Little attempt at organisation.	Disorganised. No structure, aims or conclusions.
Accuracy and understanding of material, focusing on the question	Accurate and thorough understanding focused on the question throughout.	Good understanding of the subject, mostly focused on the question.	Sound understanding of the subject but not effectively focused on the question. Some inaccuracies or misunderstandings.	Inaccuracies evident. Some limited understanding of the subject, not applied to the question.	Some glimpses of understanding but much work inaccurate or unfocused.	Totally fails to address the question posed. Fails to demonstrate understanding of the subject.
Coverage: comprehensiveness, relevance, evidence of reading/research, use of examples	Developed own ideas based on thorough understanding of the relevant literature. Comprehensive coverage of material. Excellent use of illustrative examples.	Demonstrates evidence of reading well beyond lecture material. References are relevant. Good use of illustrative examples.	Covers lecture material reasonably well. Mostly accurate and comprehensive. Some evidence of further reading. Some relevant examples provided.	Lecture material only, but not comprehensive. Little evidence of further reading. Some examples given but not all relevant.	Much irrelevant or missing material. Too brief but some knowledge of the general topic. Little attempt to exemplify.	Lack of relevant material. No use of examples.
Clarity of argument: coherence, fluency, criticality, innovation	Excellent coherence and clarity of expression. Demonstrates application of critical thought. Shows innovation in handling arguments.	Mostly coherent. Some attempt at critical analysis and innovative argument.	Generally coherent but some lack of clarity of thought or expression.	Some clarity but too simplistic.	Somewhat disjointed and lacking in development.	Incoherent. Disjointed.
Presentation: grammar, spelling, legibility, referencing system	No errors. Clear, relevant and consistently accurate referencing.	Few errors. Referencing relevant and mostly accurate.	Occasional errors. Minor inaccuracies or inconsistencies in referencing.	Frequent errors. Referencing with some inaccuracies or inconsistencies.	Very frequent errors. Referencing inaccurate or inconsistent.	Riddled with errors. Referencing absent.

Table 9:1 Essay assessment criteria

Essay title..						
	I	2.1	2.2	3	Fail	
Knowledge 30%						
Topics covered in depth						Superficial responses
Appropriate psychological content						Limited/no psychological content
Structure and argument 40%						
Logical presentation						Disorganised
Good synthesis and evaluation						No synthesis and evaluation
Clear, succinct writing style						Rambling and/or repetitious
Creativity 20%						
Includes new ideas						No new ideas
Innovative presentation						Incoherent presentation
Presentation 10%						
Fully and correctly referenced						No references
Correct spelling and grammar						Poor spelling and grammar
Good use of illustrative materials						Poor/no use of illustrative materials

Figure 9:2 Essay self-assessment form

Avoiding plagiarism

Academic staff are good at noticing material that is copied from texts and papers without acknowledgement. They spot changes in the style of writing, use of tenses, changes in format and page sizes, the sudden appearance of very technical words or sentences that the writer doesn't seem happy with, and quotations without citations. The advice is 'never cut and paste any document', whether from the www or from friends. Think through the point you want to make, express it in your own way and cite sources as you write. Put all quotations in quotation marks and cite the source.

Getting advice

Showing a draft essay, or any document, to someone else for comment is not cheating. It is normal practice in business and academic publishing, as shown by the acknowledgements at the end of many published papers. For example, in *Clinical Psychology: Science and Practice*, **7**(1), 2000, there are thanks for reviewers' comments and suggestions on pages 11, 62, 83, 91 and 103. You do not have to take note of all the comments but having an independent check on grammar and spelling and someone asking awkward questions about content does no harm.

9.7 GETTING THE ENGLISH ~~RIGHT~~ BETTER

Try ~~NEVER~~ to cross anything out!! Keep sentences short wherever possible. See **Try This 9.6** for starters!

TRY THIS 9.6 – Shorten these sentences
Answers on p. 262.

Wordy	Better
In addition to all the previous arguments there is the point that X.	
One of several important factors in reading is phonological awareness.	
The illusion of outgroup homogeneity refers to the fact that often people tend to assume that other people from different groups are much more similar than other people in the same group.	
Being as how the brain is in charge of the release of glucocorticoids . . .	
Moving to another point in the debate . . .	
The reaction times were measured before and after eating, respectively.	
Chi-square is a kind of statistical test.	
One of the models that offers the best kind of explanations says that . . .	
People who have suffered damage or trauma to the right side of the brain tend to have difficulty with spatial perception, and in particular with spatial tasks such as reading a map.	
The nature of the problem . . .	
There are all sorts of problems with the way the experiment was run that mean these results may not be very reliable.	

Wordy	Better
One prominent feature of the ear is the pinna, which serves the function of . . .	
It is sort of understood that . . .	
There is such a huge amount of information covered by this title that it will be impossible to cover it all, so I have decided to only look at . . .	
The body of evidence is in favour of . . .	

Technical terms

Good professional writing in any subject uses technical language, defining technical terms when necessary. There is no need to define technical terms that are in everyday use and where you are using the word in its usual sense; assume the reader is intelligent and well educated. In an essay on the effect of drugs on brain and behaviour, paragraph 2 started with: 'The brain is situated in the head, and consists of many billions of cells; it is sometimes referred to as our grey matter.' In our view this student wasted time with this sentence; we know where the brain is, and it was not appropriate to define it this way in the context of this essay.

Use technical language to make your communication efficient, but do make sure you know what the terms mean. Marks will be deducted for assuming that free-floating anxiety refers to fear of swimming without armbands. Use the correct technical terms when appropriate, but keep your language simple and direct overall. Avoid the temptation to compete for the prize for long-windedness, as in 'the production of speech is in great measure the consequence of a multifarious collection of synchronised muscular activation in the regions of the visage, oral cavity and the anterior passage of the neck'.

Startling imagery

'It is a truth, universally acknowledged, that a man in possession of a large-screen satellite TV on Cup Final Day, must be in want of a six pack.' The impact is greater for being the antithesis of Jane Austen. However, this comment, while arresting, is also stereotypical and far from politically correct. Creative use of language is great, but avoid the temptation to tabloidise in an inappropriate manner.

One idea per paragraph

In a lengthy essay, restricting paragraphs to one idea plus its supporting argument should make your message clearer. Use **Try This 9.7** to analyse one of your own essays.

TRY THIS 9.7 – One idea per paragraph

Look back through your last essay and underline the ideas and supporting statements. If each paragraph has a separate idea and evidence, award yourself a chocolate bar and cheer. If not, redesign a couple of paragraphs to disentangle the arguments and evidence. The challenge is to make the evidence clear to the reader by separating out the different strands of the argument.

N.B. This is a good exercise to do at the end of the first draft of every essay.

Synonyms (equivalents/alternatives/correspondences/ transposables . . .)

Part of the richness of English comes from the huge vocabulary that adds variety, depth and readability to writing. Take care to write what you mean to write! There are very few words in English that mean exactly the same, that are true synonyms, and there are lots of similar words and meanings that get confused. A common error is to confuse infer and imply; they are not synonyms. Infer is used when drawing a conclusion from data or other information; imply means to suggest or indicate. We might infer from the records of a group's beliefs that they fear that the world is ending, or a lecturer might imply during a discussion that group x believe the world is ending. Have a practice with **Try This 9.8** and **Try This 9.9**. Look at any sentence you have written, and play around with a thesaurus (book or electronic) to find synonyms you might use. If you tend to overuse certain words, make a list of synonyms and substitute some of them WHERE APPROPRIATE.

TRY THIS 9.8 – Synonyms for psychos?

Which of the alternatives makes most sense? Answers on p. 263.

1 The study <u>relates/reports</u> statistically significant differences between the groups.

2 I am working on a research project that uses in-depth interviews as its <u>main/ paramount</u> data source.

3 A new set of guidelines has been <u>deployed/developed</u> as a result of the study.

4 In the absence of any <u>experiential/empirical</u> evidence of a causal link . . .

5 The findings are <u>conforming/consistent</u> with those of older adults.

6 The main factor <u>underlying/undermining</u> people's risky health behaviours is . . .

7 The <u>effectualness/effectiveness</u> of the system can only be demonstrated by . . .

8 This phenomenon is best <u>illustrated/illuminated</u> by the example of X.

9 The <u>inconsistency/discrepancy</u> between the two methods is likely to be an important factor.

10 The notion of greater autonomy <u>reverberates/resonates</u> well with psychological theory.

TRY THIS 9.9 – More synonyms

These two grids show a perfectly acceptable sentence and some of the synonyms that might be substituted. Some synonyms are acceptable, others make no sense at all. Which are useful substitutes?

			society						
	exploration	covering	family		sharers			honest	proportion
Full	enquiry	containing	persons	due to	partners	bears		good	extent
Complete	examination	subsuming	bodies	during	players	owns	the	upright	measure
All	*research*	*involving*	*people*	*as*	*participants*	*has*	*an*	*ethical*	*dimension*
Every	delving	numbering	public	while	associates	shares	a	virtuous	capacity
Wide	scrutiny	embracing	folk	since	contestants	holds		moral	limit
		concerning	populations		colleagues				gauge

	total				whole			pieces
	round		larger than		aggregate			characters
	ensemble	exists	better than		total			bits
The	*whole*	*is*	*greater than*	*the*	*sum*	*of*	*its*	*parts*
	entirety	lives	superior to		tally			compartments
	solid		beyond		amount			branches
	sum				score			slices

Use of analogy

Argument by analogy can be very useful, but the following example shows it can also get out of hand: 'Overcrowding has been linked to aggression. Thousands of chickens can be really happy in a field but will peck each other to death in a hen house.' The first sentence would be better standing alone, especially if it read, 'Overcrowding has been linked to aggression (Calhoun, 1962)'.

Rereading and correcting

I know what I meant! Trying to get students to reread and correct written work is an uphill battle for most tutors. Reread to spot illogical statements or those where a crucial word was missed. Here for your amusement are some psychology essay statements that do not exactly convey the writer's original intention: 'Males can mate loads of times without making any difference to the gene pool'; 'Illusions can be misinterpreted by the brian'; 'Dawkins called his approach regrettable'; 'Ethics help psychologists to debrief participants without paying them'; 'The unconcious mind doesn't really know what it is doing'; 'In old age people carry on getting older until they die'; 'Factor analysis is difficult to measure because it measures everything that is under the data'; 'Many people argue that electrolysis is a poor alternative to one of the so-called talking therapies'.

Abbreviations and acronyms in text

Replacing long words or phrases with initials or abbreviations is regarded as lazy by some tutors. However, with well-known and established acronyms (see p. 249) and phrases like NIMBY (Not in my back yard) it is reasonable to adopt this approach. Consider your response to abbreviations in **Try This 9.10**. When using abbreviations, the full definition must be given the first time the phrase is used with the abbreviation immediately afterwards in brackets.

TRY THIS 9.10 – Abbreviations

Look at Chapter 16. How do you feel about the use of ES as an abbreviation throughout this chapter? Is it a procedure you would wish to adopt?

Colloquial usage

Regional or colloquial terms may not be universally understood so are best omitted. Writing as you speak can also be a trap, as in these examples from students' essays: 'We could of tried a slightly different methodological approach that . . .' should read 'We could have tried a slightly different approach that . . .', and 'She therefore put to greater emphasis on . . .' should be 'She therefore put too great an emphasis on . . .'.

Punctuation and spelling

The excessive use of exclamation marks!!!!!!!!!! is also less than good practice! *And never* start a sentence with And, But or BUT unless you are making a strong additional or contrasting point. There are plenty of examples of its usage in this book, where BUT and capitalisation are used to emphasise points.

For some, spelling is a minefield. Use the spell checker but remember that it will not pick up the errors in the following examples: 'The soul participant', 'simplify the task by braking it down into', 'Children acquire there understanding of', 'Gibbon's theory of direct perception' (should be Gibson's), 'rewards were bight sized cubes of cheese', 'a negative sine (sign)', 'the weal of life', 'Participants were asked to shout until they were horse'.

Less or fewer?

Less is used with quantities, as in 'less weight was attached to the significance of the result, due to inadequate sampling', whereas fewer is used with numbers, so 'there are fewer than seven participants per group'. You may prefer to think of less being used with uncountable items: it will

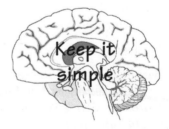

take less time if you do it this way. By contrast, fewer is used with reduced numbers of countable items: 'There were fewer of us at the tutorial today.'

When editing, check that you have not overused certain words. Find synonyms or restructure the paragraph if repetition is a problem. Keep sentences short and TO THE POINT. Ensure paragraphs address one point only. Be consistent in your use of fonts and font sizes, symbols, heading titles and position, bullet points and referencing. Decide on your style and stick to it. If you feel you have trouble with your style of writing, or you are unsure about the use of colons, semi-colons and apostrophes see Kahn (1991), Kirkman (1993) or Russell (1993).

Top Tips

✔ Read and revise everything you write. It is worth taking time at the end of an essay to reread and redraft, correct spelling, insert missing words, check grammar, tidy up diagrams and insert references.

✔ Check that your arguments are logical.

✔ Read what is written, not what you meant to write.

✔ Work with a friend.

9.8 REFERENCES AND FURTHER READING

Genuine references were embedded in some of the essay extracts, and the full citations would normally appear at the end of the essay. They are not included here. A Web of Science search will find them or see http//www.geog.leeds.ac.uk/staff/p.kneale/skillbook.html.

For grammar queries see:

Dummett, M. (1993). *Grammar and Style for Examination Candidates and Others.* London: Duckworth.

Kahn, J.E. (Ed.) (1991). *How to Write and Speak Better.* London: Reader's Digest.

Kirkman, J. (1993). *Full Marks: Advice on Punctuation for Scientific and Technical Writing,* 2nd edn. Malborough: Ramsbury Books.

Most study-skills books discuss essay writing, but see also:

Barrass, R. (1982). *Students Must Write – A Guide to Better Writing in Course Work and Examinations.* London: Routledge.

Fairbairn, G.J. & Winch, C. (1996). *Reading, Writing and Reasoning: A Guide for Students,* 2nd edn. Buckingham: Open University Press.

Heffernan, T.M. (1997). *A Student's Guide to Studying Psychology.* Hove: Psychology Press.

Mahalaski, P.A. (1992). Essay-writing: Do study manuals give relevant advice? *Higher Education,* **24**, 113–32.

Norton, L.S. (1990). Essay writing: What really counts? *Higher Education,* **20**, 411–42.

Russell, S. (1993). *Grammar, Structure and Style.* Oxford: Oxford University Press.

Psycho-Cryptic Crossword 1 Answers p. 263.

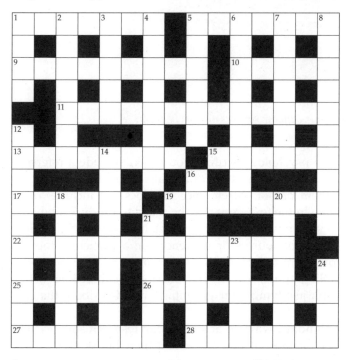

Across

1 Eggs prepared to join endless test (7)
5 A flutter on someone throwing knives? (7)
9 'Far out man!' (9)
10 Chips away at the leather covering stool (5)
11 Gestures may pass them (6, 7)
13 Verifiable check on the inebriate's tab length (8)
15 Implode, and lose mass leaves spongy skull tissue (6)
17 Sorts out the third period (6)
19 Take a friend to the theatre (8)
22 The rational couldn't be, could they? (13)
25 Tiles came unstuck from the little refuge (5)
26 Get into the writers alien pay scale (9)
27 Stopped the sea hitting the trunk (7)
28 Enquires about the dead? (7)

Down

1 Reg took the lead from William in raising vegetables (4)
2 Four tomes needed to explain reasons for action (7)
3 Re-site the junction away from the street, gives shade (5)
4 Appropriate formal dress for the competent person (8)
5 A charm makes a shift east (6)
6 A spotless characteristic (9)
7 With a sense of personal omnipotence (4-3)
8 A searcher for hazards? (4-6)
12 Descriptors of data (10)
14 Goes through the motions step by step (9)
16 Caption takes a left but still is lacking sensual desire (8)
18 On the spur of the moment the mule took a sip (7)
20 Refuse to take the sailor's Mark (7)
21 Senseless Greek, symbol found in stables (6)
23 Bowler misses, the bullseye (5)
24 Apprehension of loud impacts on the audio system (4)

10 CITATIONS, REFERENCES AND SOURCES

May your caffeine sources always be fresh.

At the end of every piece of psychology writing you MUST include a reference list. This is an alphabetical list of all the sources actually quoted in your document, whether you read them or not. A reference list does not include 'other things I read but didn't quote in the text'. You may be asked to produce a bibliography, either in addition to your reference list or as a task in its own right. A bibliography is an alphabetical list of sources or references on a particular topic; a complete bibliography would aim to include every document relating to a topic. To create an 'annotated bibliography', sort the references into subsections with a brief statement or paragraph justifying your groupings and describing the contents.

There are a number of standard ways to acknowledge research sources. The references in any good text or journal will show you their house style. Some psychology departments have their own preferred style for essays and dissertations, so check the student handbook, or follow the advice here. These recommendations follow a standard pattern and adopt conventions of the BPS (British Psychological Society) and the APA (American Psychological Association). The skill with referencing is consistency. Decide on a style and stick to it.

10.1 CITING PAPER SOURCES IN TEXT

Within text, a book or article is cited by the author's family name and the year of publication. When there are two authors both are quoted. Conventionally, when there are three or more authors all authors are named in the first citation, and the *et al.* convention is adopted thereafter, but if there are many authors this can look very odd and the *et al.* system is used even at first mention. For example, 'Discussing the patterns of chocolate consumption by adolescents, Thornton

(2010) showed that the preferences for different percentages of cocoa solid described by Bitter and Sweet (2007) were inaccurate, whereas the effect of celebrity advertising analysed by Rich, Famous and Beautiful (2008) bore a much stronger relationship to rates of consumption. Specifically, Rich *et al.*'s (2008) study demonstrated . . .'.

Where information in one text refers to another, quote both: 'As reported by Figure (2010), Ground (2009) found that . . .'. Both the Figure (2010) and Ground (2009) references should appear in the reference list. Similarly: 'In an extensive review of bullying, Tuffy (2010) shows the field approach taken by Gore (2005) is unreliable, and therefore the methodology adopted by Gore is not followed.' Again quote both sources, even though you have probably only read Tuffy. Quoting both tells the reader how to locate the original. If you want to make clear that you have acquired your information from a secondary source use a sentence like 'High frequencies are mediated nearest the oval window, and low frequencies at the farther end of the basilar membrane (Cochlear 2005, cited Implant *et al.* 2010)'. In this type of case it is important to give the two dates which indicate the age of the original data, 2005, rather than 2010 date of the reference you read. You should quote both Cochlear and Implant *et al.* in the references. The Cochlear reference should be cited in the Implant *et al.* paper, so not including it would be lazy. If Implant *et al.* does not cite Cochlear, use a Web of Science search (see p. 37) to find the source.

Take care with oriental names where given names are second, the family name first. It is all too easy to reference by the given name.

Referring to government publications, where the author is awkward to trace, is also problematical. There are no absolute rules; use common sense or follow past practice. This example is a classic referencing nightmare:

CSICSC (1992). *China Statistical Yearbook 1992*. Fan, Z., Fang, J., Liu, H., Wang, Y. & Zhang, J. (Eds) Beijing: China Statistical Information and Consultancy Service Centre.

There is no single right way to cite this source; even librarians have different views on how to handle this one. Some would reference it by the editors as 'Fan *et al.* (1992)', others by the full title 'China Statistical Yearbook (1992)'. In a library search you might have to try a number of search options. Searching by title is likely to be the fastest successful route to locating this volume.

Referencing by initials can be convenient and time-saving. You might refer in your document to DoH (1999) or GHS (2004), but you must give the full title in the reference list:

DoH (Department of Health) (1999). *Effective Care Co-ordination in Mental Health Services: Modernising the Care Programme Approach – A Policy Booklet*. London: Department of Health.

or

GHS (General Household Survey) (2004). *General Household Survey 2002*. London: HMSO.

Finally, if there doesn't seem to be a rule, invent one and use it consistently.

10.2 CITING PAPER SOURCES IN REFERENCE LISTS

The key is consistency in format, including standard use of commas, stops, italics and initial capital letters.

Citing a book
Template:
Author(s) (Year). *Title*, edition (if not the first). Place of publication: Publisher.

Example:
Walker, A.E. (1997). *The Menstrual Cycle*, 2nd edn. London: Routledge.
Bee, H. (2000). *The Developing Child*, 9th edn. Boston: Allyn and Bacon.

Citing a chapter in an edited volume
The authors of the chapter or paper in an edited text are cited first, followed by the book editors' details. Note that it is the title of the book that is placed in italics, not the chapter title.

Template:
Author (Year). Chapter title. In Editor's Name (Ed.)/Editors' Names (Eds), *Book Title*. Place of publication: Publisher.

Example:
North, M.M., North, S.M & Coble, J.R. (1997). Virtual reality therapy: An effective treatment for psychological disorders. In G. Riva (Ed.), *Virtual Reality in Neuro-Psycho-Physiology*. Oxford: Oxford University Press.

Citing an edited book
Template:
Editor/s (Ed.)/(Eds) (Year). *Title* (Edition, if necessary). Place of publication: Publisher.

Example:
Tavecchio, L.W.C & van Izendoorn, M.H. (Eds) (1987). *Attachment in Social Networks: Contributions to the Bowlby–Ainsworth Attachment Theory*. Amsterdam: North Holland.

Citing a journal article
Template:
Author (Year). Article title. *Journal Title*, **volume number** (issue number), page numbers.

Examples:
Silvester, J., Anderson, N.R. and Patterson, F. (1999). Organisational culture change: An inter-group attributional analysis. *Journal of Occupational and Organizational Psychology*, **72**(1), 1–23.

Smith, L. (1999). A good night's work. *Management of Health Safety and Environment Journal*, **3**(4), 26–30.

Citing a conference paper

Template:
Author (Year). Article title. *Conference Title*. Location of conference. Date (month and year).

Example:
Collins, A., Smith, L.R. & Gardner, P.H. (1998). Bright Light Technology: Implications as an intervention for shiftworkers. *II European Symposium of Ergonomics – Working Time: Change in Work and New Challenges.* Troia, Portugal. April 1998.

Citing a newspaper article

Most newspaper articles have an author attribution and should be referenced alphabetically by the author, for example Meikle (1995). Where there is no author, use the first couple of words of the title or a couple of main words as the cross-reference and the full title in the reference list, as in Children's English (1995).

Template when an author is cited:
Author. Full Date. Title. *Newspaper*, Volume number if applicable, page number(s).

Example:
Meikle, J. 19 April 1995. Children using geatt words instead of standard English 'is dead wrong'. *Guardian*, National News, p. 7.

Template for an unattributed item:
Title, Full date. *Newspaper*, Volume number if applicable, page number(s).

Example:
French face Welsh racism inquiry, 16 March 1699. *Daily Groat*, 3.

Citing unpublished theses

Thesis citations follow the general guidelines for a book; then add 'unpublished', and enough information for another researcher to locate the volume.

Careless, I.M. (1999). *Attitudinal Ambivalence amongst Clubbers.* University of Life: Unpublished BSc thesis, School of Psychology.
Fletcher, W.F. (1994). *Sources and Effects of Stress among Teleworkers.* University of Leeds: Unpublished PhD thesis, School of Psychology.

10.3 CITING ELECTRONIC SOURCES

A standard template for citing electronic sources of information is not yet agreed. These notes follow recommendations from various library sources. If you are writing for a publication, check whether an alternative method is used. The crucial new element is adding the date when you accessed the information, because the contents of electronic sites change. The next person to access the site may not see the same information.

Referencing within text

Internet and other electronic sources should be treated in the same way as a book or journal reference. For example, 'from studies of residence for older adults (Age Concern, 1998) we estimate . . .'.

Citing individual Internet sites

To cite Internet sources use the document's URL (Internet) address. Addresses tend to be long, so typing needs careful checking. If the citation is longer than one line the URL should only be split after a forward slash / in the address. ThecaSe/ofchaRacters/inTheAddress/sHouldnOt/bealterEd.EVER.

Template:
Author/editor (Year). *Title* [on-line] (Edition). Place of publication: Publisher (if ascertainable). URL. Accessed Date.

Example:
Age Concern (1999). *Local authority charging procedures for residential and nursing home care* [on-line]. http://www.ace.org.uk/fs10/further.htm. Accessed 12 April 2000.
National Institute for Occupational Safety and Health (1999). *Stress at work* [on-line]. US Department of Health and Human Services: NIOSH. http://www.cdc.gov/niosh/stresswk.html. Accessed 14 April 2000.

When the electronic publication date is not stated write 'no date'. The term [on-line] indicates the type of publication medium. Use it for all Internet and e-journal sources. The 'Accessed' date is the date on which *you viewed or downloaded* the document.

'Publisher' covers both the traditional idea of a publisher of printed sources, and organisations responsible for maintaining sites on the Internet. Many Internet sites show the organisation maintaining the information, but not the text author. If in doubt, ascribe authorship to the smallest identifiable organisational unit.

Example:
Center for Advancement of Learning. (1998). *Assessment – Learning and Study Strategies Inventory (LASSI), Learning Strategies Database* [on-line]. Center for Advancement of Learning Muskingham College. http://muskingham.edu/~cal/DATABASE/lassi.html. Accessed 12 April 2000.

Citing e-journals (electronic journals)
Template
Author (Year). Title. *Journal Title*, volume (issue), [on-line] page numbers or location within host. URL. Accessed date.

Example:
Claudio-da-Silva, T.S and Rocha do Amara, J. (1999). Drug abuse. *Brain and Mind*, 3(8), [on-line]. http://www.epub.org.br/cm/n08/doencas/drugs/abuse_i.htm. Accessed 12 April 2000.

In some electronic journals the 'page' location is replaced by screen, paragraph or line numbers.

Citing personal electronic communications (e-mail)

For reference to personal e-mail messages use the 'subject line' of the message as a title and include the full date. Remember to keep copies of e-mails you reference.

Template:
Sender (sender's e-mail address), Day Month Year. *Subject of Message*. E-mail to Recipient (recipient's e-mail address).

Example:
Carston, D. (1234psyc@Leeds.ac.uk), 21 October 2000. *Essay for Second Tutorial*. E-mail to P. Booth (8901psyc@Leeds.ac.uk).

✔ **Authors**. Generally an author's name can be found at the foot of an electronic document. Authors of journal articles are usually cited at the beginning of the article as in hard copy. Where the identity of the author is unclear, the URL should indicate the name of the institution responsible for the document. However, this organisation may only be maintaining the document, not producing it, so take care to assign the right authorship.

✔ **Date of publication**. This is often at the foot of the page with the author's name, and sometimes with 'last updated' information. In newer versions of Netscape and other browsers, select *Document Info.* on the *View* menu. This shows the 'last modified date' of the document.

✔ Keep accurate records of the material you access. Using an on-line database bibliographic package can help to keep track of research resources.

Producing correct reference lists is an important skill, demonstrating your attention to detail and professionalism. Correct **Try This 10.1** to develop this skill. The ultimate test of a reference list is that someone else can use it to locate the documents. Check your citation lists meet this standard.

TRY THIS 10.1 – The nightmare reference list

There are many deliberate errors here. If a reference list like this appears at the end of an essay or dissertation the marks will drift away. How many errors can you spot in five minutes? (The corrected version is on pp. 263–4). PLEASE DO NOT USE THIS LIST AS AN EXAMPLE OF GOOD PRACTICE! Use the corrected version instead.

Hayes, N. (1998). Foundations of Psychology: An Introductory Text, 2nd edition. Surrey: Thomas Nelson. Chapter 4.

Rosch, E.H., Mervis, C.B., Grey, W.D., Johnson, D.M. & Boyes-Braem, P. (1976). *Basic objects in natural choice categories*. Cognitive Psych, **8**, 382–439.

Kline, P. (1993). *The Handbook of Psychological Testing*. Routledge

Miura, I.T., Okamoto, Y., Kim, C.C., Chang, C.-M., Steere, M. & Fayol, M. Comparisons of children's cognitive representation of number: China, France, Japan, Korea, Sweden and United States. *International Journal of Behavioural Development, 17*.

American Psychiatric Association (1994). *Diagnostic and Statistical Manual of Mental Disorders, 4*th *E*. Washington, DC: American Psychiatric Association.

Moscovici, S. & Hewstone, M. (1983). Social representations and social expectations: from the 'naïve' to the 'amateur' scientist. In Hewstone, *Attribution Theory: Social and Functional Extensions*. Oxford: Blackwell.

Prichard (1837). *Treatise on Insanity and Other Disorders Affecting the Mind*. Philadelphia, PA.: Haswell, Barrington and Haswell.

Vallbo, A.B. (1995). Single-afferent neurons and somatic sensation in humans. In M.S. Gazzaniga (Ed), *The Cognitive Neurosciences*. Cambridge: MIT Press.

Spearman, C.E. (1927). The *Abilities of Man: Their Nature and Measurement*. London: Macmillan.

Wagner, H.L., C.J. MacDonald & A.S.R. Manstead (1986). Communication of individual emotions by spontaneous facial expression. Journal of Personality and Social Psychology, 50, 737–743.

Rick, J et al., (1997). *Stress: Big issues but what are the problems?* [on-line] Institute for Employment Studies, Report 331. http://www.employment-studies.co.uk/summary/331sum.html. Accessed 31 October 1998.

10.4 SOURCES AND FURTHER READING

BUBL (Bulletin Board for Libraries) (1998). *Bibliography* [on-line]. BUBL Information Service, Strathclyde University. http://link.bubl.ac.uk/bibliography. Accessed 12 April 2000.

ISO (1998). *Bibliographic references to electronic documents* [on-line]. International Organization for Standardization, National Library of Canada. http://www.nlc-bnc.ca/iso/tc46sc9/standard/690-2e.htm. Accessed 10 April 2000.

TAFIS Reference Collections (2000). *Writing References and Bibliographies: Guides available on the Web, Guides to Citing Printed Sources* [on-line]. http://www.tay.ac.uk/tafis/references/other-citations.html. Accessed 12 April 2000.

University of Vermont (1997). *Electronic Sources: APA Style of Citation* [on-line]. http://www.uvm.edu/~ncrane/estyles/apa.html. Accessed 10 April 2000.

Xia, L. & Crane, N.B. (1996). *Electronic Styles: A Handbook for Citing Electronic Information*, 2nd edn. Medford, NJ: Information Today Inc.

Can you name a psychological rock group?

Pink Freud.

11 | LISTENING AND INTERVIEWING

He knew the precise psychological moment to say nothing.

Psychology lectures, seminars and discussion groups can involve 12 or more hours of listening each week, so listening skills are important. Listening is often considered an automatic activity, but is increasingly quoted by employers as a vital skill for effective business performance (Gushgari Francis and Saklou, 1997). In business, valuing the customer or client and taking the time to understand what the speaker is conveying is important. In professional psychological work with clients, such as clinical, educational, organisational, counselling, health and forensic, good listening skills are essential. Interviewing is a standard research methodology in many areas of psychology. Being good at listening has the potential to enhance the quality of your research understanding and inferences.

Listening is not the same as hearing; it is a more active and interactive process. Listening involves being ready to absorb information, paying attention to details and the capacity to catalogue and interpret the information. In addition to the actual material and support cues like slides and OHTs, there is information in the speaker's tone of voice and body language. As with reading, the greater your psychological background, the more you are likely to understand. This means listening is a skill involving some preparation, a bit like hosting an end-of-term celebration.

11.1 LISTENING IN LECTURES

Arriving at a lecture full of information about last night's activities or juicy scandal is normal, but the brain is not prepared for advanced information on specific language impairments or algorithms and heuristics. Some lecturers understand that the average student audience needs 5 minutes' background briefing to get the majority of brains engaged and on track. Others leap in with vital information in the first five minutes because 'everyone is fresh'! Whatever the lecture style, but especially with the latter, you will get more from the session having thought, 'I know this will be an interesting lecture about . . .' and scanned notes from the last session. Assuming from the start that a lecture will be dull ensures that it will seem dull.

Top Tips

- A lecturer's words, no matter how wise, enter your short-term memory, and unless you play around with them and process the information into ideas, making personal connections, the words will drop out of short-term memory into a black hole. Think about the content and implications as the lecture progresses.

- You may feel a lecturer is wildly off beam, making statements you disagree with, but do not decide automatically that he or she is wrong: check it out. There might be dissertation possibilities.

- Keep a record of a speaker's main points.

- Be prepared for the unpredictable. Some speakers indicate what they intend to cover in a lecture, others whizz off in different directions. This unpredictability can keep you alert!, but if you get thoroughly lost, then ask a clarifying question (mentally or physically) rather than 'dropping out' for the rest of the session.

- If you feel your brain drifting off ask questions like 'What is s/he trying to say?' and 'Where does this fit with what I know?'

- Have another look at p. 5, expectations of lectures.

- Treat listening as a challenging mental task.

11.2 LISTENING IN DISCUSSIONS

Discussion is the time to harvest the ideas of others. With most topics in psychology there is such a diversity of points of view that open discussion is vital. Try to be open-minded in looking for and evaluating statements that may express very different views and beliefs from your own. Because ideas fly around fast, make sure you note the main points and supporting evidence (arguments) where possible. Post-discussion note collation is crucial, mostly involving ordering thoughts and checking arguments that support or confute the points. Have a look at **Try This 11.1** and think about how you score on effective listening.

11.3 TELEPHONE LISTENING

Some research interviews are conducted over the telephone, and companies are increasingly conducting first job interviews on the telephone. Listening and

TRY THIS 11.1 – Assess your listening effectiveness in discussions

Think back over a tutorial or a recent conversation and rate and comment on each of these points. Alternatively score this for a friend or fellow tutee, and then think about your skills in listening, compared with theirs.

Score your effectiveness on a 1–4 scale, where 1 is No, and 4 is Yes		Comment
Did you feel relaxed and comfortable?	1 2 3 4	
Did you make eye contact with speaker?	1 2 3 4	
Did you make notes of main words and personal thoughts during the discussion?	1 2 3 4	
Did you discuss the issues?	1 2 3 4	
Did you think about what you were going to say next while the other person was still talking?	1 2 3 4	
Did you ask a question?	1 2 3 4	
Did you get a fair share of the speaking time?	1 2 3 4	
Did you try to empathise with the speaker?	1 2 3 4	
Did you accept what the others said without comment?	1 2 3 4	
Did you interrupt people before they had finished talking?	1 2 3 4	
Did you drift off into daydreams because you were sure you knew what the speaker was going to say?	1 2 3 4	
Were you distracted by the speaker's mannerisms?	1 2 3 4	
Were you distracted by what was going on around you?	1 2 3 4	

talking under these circumstances are difficult to do well. If video-conferencing facilities are available you can pick up on facial and body-language clues, but these are missing in a telephone interview. This skill improves with practice. Pilot interviews are vital – practise with a friend.

General

☎ Find a quiet room to call from, and get rid of all distractions.

☎ Lay your notes out around you and have two pens ready.

Research calls

☎ Plan the call in advance. Have your schedule of questions, prompts and probes ready so you can really concentrate on the responses and implications.

☎ Make notes of main points rather than every word, and leave time after the call to annotate and order the responses while they are fresh in your brain.

☎ Query anything you are unsure about. Be certain you understand the respondent's nuances.

☎ Show you are listening and interested without interrupting, using fillers like 'yes', 'mmm', 'OK' and 'great'.

☎ Be aware of the non-verbal cues, like a changed tone of voice, pauses, chuckles to help you 'hear between the lines'.

☎ Don't assume you know all the answers already. If you disengage, the interviewee will become less engaged and less enthused, and will be a less productive informant.

☎ Curb your desire to jump in and fill pauses; let the speaker do most of the talking. Silences are OK.

Job interviews

✔ Prepare in advance, as you would for a visit to an organisation, by researching the organisation's background and make-up.

✔ Make notes of points as you speak, and query anything you don't understand.

✔ Be enthusiastic! All psychologists have lots to offer.

✔ Be formal in your conversation: there is a job in prospect. It is easy to drop into a colloquial, conversational mode as if chatting to a friend, which you would not do in a face-to-face interview.

11.4 INTERVIEWING

As you know from experience and Research Methods classes, different styles of interview are useful for collecting different kinds of information. In survey research you administer interviews (or questionnaires) to random samples of the population, asking closed/fixed-choice questions. The responses to these lend themselves to quantitative analysis. More qualitative approaches are less structured, more free-flowing and use open-ended questions. These require a different kind of coding and exploration, but are associated with richer and more authentic understanding of people's experiences. The approach you choose will depend on your research questions. Some issues are common to the design, planning and running of interviews, whatever the type.

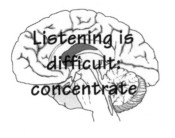

It is important when planning to make sure that the questions make sense to your interviewee, that they appear relevant and appropriate and do not cause offence. Have your mates, your supervisor, a representative of your sample population check your first, second, third ... drafts. When recruiting interviewees, make sure they are fully informed about what will be expected of them. What anonymity and confidentiality checks have you in place? (See Chapter 19 on Ethics.)

Have a run-through of the interview with a friend as a final check. Is everything you want in there? Does your friend understand all the questions? How long does it take? Answering your friend's queries about contents and procedure will be good practice for the real thing.

11.5 FACE-TO-FACE INTERVIEWS

Most of the tips for telephone interviews apply equally to personal interviews. One obvious difference is that in a face-to-face interview it is a good idea to look neat and clean and friendly – this helps give people the impression that you are a respectable, trustworthy person, worth taking seriously. Check whether your interviewee will be happy to have you tape the conversation. This will save you having to scribble down everything while allowing you to demonstrate your prowess in giving good non-verbal listening cues. Don't forget to consider issues of confidentiality and ownership of the tape post-transcription. Choose locations where you will not be interrupted. Take a coffee break in a long session to give both your own and your interviewee's brain a break. Remember people can speak at about 125 words a minute, but you can listen and process words at 375 to 500 words a minute so it is easy to find your brain ambling off in other directions. Don't wool-gather!

Jumping to conclusions in discussion is dangerous: it leads you to switch off. Check your understanding by reflecting back to the interviewee. Possibly the speaker is going in a new direction, diverting to give additional insights. Watch out for those 'yes but . . .' and 'except where . . .' statements.

Got a difficult customer? Let them talk; they will feel in charge and get the idea that you agree with their discourse, which you may or may not. They're not being as responsive as you'd hoped? Check your questioning style, throw in a few more open-ended queries – 'Can you tell me more about . . .?' 'Can you help me understand . . .?'.

Top Tips

☺ Really good listeners encourage the speaker by giving feedback, checking their understanding, nodding, making good eye contact, being respectful and interested. Verbal feedback is often better as a statement that confirms what you have heard, rather than a question that will probably be answered by the speaker's next statement anyway. Unhelpful feedback includes yawning, looking out of the window, checking your watch every few seconds, writing shopping lists and going to sleep. Relating similar personal experiences or offering solutions to problems does not help. The aim is to show your interest in your interviewee, not turn the conversation round to the more interesting subject of your own experience!

☺ When you are listening, interruptions need sensitive management. If you answer the phone or speak to the next person to arrive, your interviewee may feel they are less important than the person who interrupts. If you do this to someone in business, they are very likely to take their business elsewhere. So turn the phone off and shut the door.

☺ If you are emotionally involved you tend to hear what you want to hear, not what is actually said. Try to remain objective and open-minded.

☺ Keep focused on what is said. Your mind does have the capacity to listen, think, write and ponder at the same time. There is time to summarise ideas and prepare questions, but it does take practice.

☺ Make a real attempt to understand what the other person is saying.

☺ Think about what is not being said. What are the implications? Do these gaps need exploring?

11.6 REFERENCES AND FURTHER READING

Gushgari, S.K., Francis, P.A. & Saklou, J.H. (1997). Skills critical to long-term profitability of engineering firms. *Journal of Management in Engineering*, **13**(2), 46–56.

Hargie, O.E. (Ed.) (1997). *The Handbook of Communication Skills*. New York: Routledge.

Howarth, J. (1996). *Psychological Research: Innovative Methods and Statistics*. London: Routledge.

What did the sign
on Pavlov's Lab
door say?

Please knock.
DON'T ring the bell.

12 DISCUSSION

Great minds discuss ideas, small minds discuss people.

Psychologists develop their research abilities through discussion in workshops, tutorials and seminars. Talking through the details of a topic leads to a greater degree of understanding and learning. In most jobs and especially as a professional psychologist, being able to discuss topics calmly, fairly and professionally is essential, so discussions are valuable opportunities to practise.

To learn effectively from discussions there needs to be a relaxed atmosphere where people can think about the content and note what others are saying. Ineffective discussions occur when people worry about what to say next, and run through it mentally, rather than listening to the person speaking. Some of this is nerves, which will calm down with practice, but in the meantime, preparing fully is the best way to lower your stress levels. You have plenty of psychology background and specific information to share.

Be positive about seeking the views of others and value their contributions. Employ open-ended questions, those which encourage an elaborated, rather than a brief yes or no answer. 'What are the main features of aerobic exercise?', is an open-ended question and more useful than 'Do you like . . . aerobic exercise?' 'What do you think about pheromes / left-handedness / psychoticism?' are good questions, but the phrase 'What do you think . . .?' is a bit general. Be more specific: 'What are the advantages of . . . computerised tomography?' or 'In what ways do you consider . . . the Internet's global, unrestricted data will influence the actions and attitudes of individuals?' or 'What is undervalued about . . . the role of caregivers in the community?'

Keep up the quality of argument in discussion. For example, you might discuss the relationship between unemployment and ill health. You might make a general point like, 'There is evidence that the unemployed are more likely to perceive themselves as being in bad health, that the shaming element in unemployment has related health consequences'. This is a general argument that would be strengthened, getting more marks, by adding references and examples as you speak. You might say, 'Hanse and Engstrom in their 1999 study of the effect on workers of closing a Volvo plant in Sweden suggest that sense of coherence has a greater impact on the psychological symptoms among those workers who remain unemployed than amongst those who have been re-employed'. By adding an example and citing the authors, you make the argument stronger and more memorable. For top marks, take examples from more than one source.

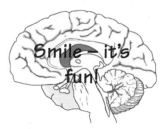

12.1 TYPES OF DISCUSSION

Brainstorming

Brainstorming is a great way of collecting a range of ideas and opinions and getting a group talking. The process involves everyone calling out points and ideas. Someone keeps a list, maybe on a flipchart so everyone can see. A typical list has no organisation; there is overlap, repetition and a mix of facts and opinions. The art of brainstorming is to assemble ideas, including the wild and wacky, so that many avenues are explored. The points are reordered and arguments developed through discussion, so that by the end of a session they have been pooled, ordered and critically discussed. Have a go at **Try This 12.1** as an example of working with a brainstormed list, and use **Try This 12.2** with your next assignment.

TRY THIS 12.1 – Working with a brainstormed list

Brainstorming produces a list of ideas with minimal detail and no evaluation. This list was compiled in five minutes with a group. Items overlap and repeat, facts and opinions are mixed, and there is no order. Take five minutes to categorise the items. A possible sort is given on p. 264.

Eating	Personal perception of	Bone decay as a result –
Anorexia nervosa	your body: is it a visual	increased osteo
Thinness is a desirable aim	or weight issue?	problems?
Eating disorder	Abuse of laxatives and	Is it a first-world problem
Athletics – reduced	diuretics	only?
performance	Appropriate nursing care	Middle class, parental
Bulimia	Is it a positive, pleasurable	locus of control
Hormone release	state for some / in some	Transgenderism
Do hormones control	situations?	A cause of distress in
eating?	High-calorie drink	individuals
Adolescent disorders	substitutes	Stunkard–Messick Eating
Young men are often	Who is observing?	Questionnaire
ignored	How do you know when	Twin studies might give
Cultural influences – fact	you have a problem?	insight into . . . ?
or fiction?	Body dissatisfaction	Cultural identity –
Social implications	Social implications	thinness has different
Eating Attitudes Test	Hunger	values in different
Low-calorie diet	Hypertension	cultures or
Gender differences in	Depression results from	communities?
eating attitudes and	an individual's	Altered sex drive – short-
behaviours	dissatisfaction with their	and long-term?
Eating Disorders	body	
Association	Families are disrupted	

TRY THIS 12.2 – Brainstorm an essay plan

Using your next essay title or a revision essay or assignment, brainstorm a list of ideas using the blue/red pen technique (p. 94), alone or with friends, including references and authors, and use this as the basis for essay planning. Brainstorming 'what I know already' at the start of essay planning can indicate where further research is required.

Role-play exercises

These may involve the simulation of a meeting, as for example where family conflicts are explored through a family group therapy meeting. You will prepare a role in advance, not necessarily a role you would agree with personally. Procedure depends on the type of topic. It may lead to a decision given by the chairman, or a 'jury' vote from the observers.

Debate

The normal format for a debate presupposes that there is a clear issue on which there are polarised opinions. A motion is put forward for discussion. It is traditionally put in the form 'This house believes that . . .'. One side proposes the motion, and the other side opposes it. The proposer gives a speech in favour, followed by the opposer speaking against the motion. These speeches are 'seconded' by two further speeches for and against, although for reasons of time these may be dispensed with in 1-hour debates. The motion is then thrown open so everyone can contribute. The proposer and the opposer make closing speeches in which they can answer points made during the debate, followed by a vote. Issues in psychology are rarely clear-cut and a vote may be inappropriate, but a formal debate is a useful way of exploring positions and opinions, and for eliciting reasoned responses.

Oppositional discussion

Oppositional discussion is a less formal version of debate, in which each side tries to persuade an audience that a particular case is right and the other is wrong. You may work in a small group, assembling information from one point of view, and then argue your case with another group that has tackled the same topic from another angle. Remember that all your arguments need supporting evidence, so keep case examples handy.

Consensual discussion

Consensual discussion involves a group of people with a common purpose pooling their resources to reach an agreement. Demonstrations of good, co-operative discussion skills are rare; most of the models of discussion on TV and radio and in the press are set up as oppositional rather than consensual. Generally you achieve more by discussing topics in a co-operative spirit and one of the abilities most sought after by employers of graduates is the ability to solve problems through teamwork.

Negotiation

Negotiation, coming to an agreement by mutual consent, is another useful business skill as well as being vital for therapists. One practises and improves negotiation skills in everyday activities like persuading a tutor to extend an essay deadline, getting a landlord to do repairs or persuading someone else to clean the kitchen. In formal negotiations:

- Prepare by considering the issues in their widest context, in advance.

- Enumerate the strengths and weaknesses of your position. This reduces the chances of being caught out!

- Get all the options and alternatives outlined at the start. There are different routes to any solution and everyone needs to understand the choices available.

- Check that everyone agrees that no major issue is being overlooked, and that all the information is available to everyone.

- Appreciate that there will be more than one point of view, and let everyone have their say.

- Stick to the issues that are raised and avoid personality-based discussion. Another member of the group may be an idiot BUT saying so will not promote agreement.

- Assuming decision deadlines are flexible, break for coffee, or agree to meet again later, if discussion gets over-heated.

- At the end, ensure that everyone understands what has been decided by circulating a summary note.

There are many books on discussion, assertiveness and negotiation skills. See Drew and Bingham (1997) or Fisher, Ury and Patton (1997), or do a keyword search to see what your library offers.

Top Tips

- Being asked to start a discussion is not like being asked to represent your country at football. You are simply 'kicking off'. Make your points clearly and 'pass the ball' promptly. Focus thoughts by putting the main points on a handout or OHT.

- Don't wait for a 'big moment' before contributing. Ask questions to get a topic going.

- Don't be anxious about the quality of your contributions. Get stuck in. Early in a discussion everyone is nervous and too concerned about his or her own contribution to be critical of others.

- Keep discussion points short and simple.

- Use examples to illustrate and strengthen your argument.

- Share the responsibility for keeping the group going.

- Have a short discussion before a tutorial to kick ideas about. Meet somewhere informal, perhaps in the bar, or over coffee or supper.

12.2 ELECTRONIC DISCUSSIONS

It is not always possible to get people together for a discussion. Electronic discussions can solve groupwork timetabling problems, and are especially useful for part-time students and those off-campus on years abroad or in work-placements. They are also good practice for business discussions. One advantage of electronic discussions is that you can build research activities into the process. Having started a discussion, you may realise that you need additional information. You can find it and feed it in as the discussion progresses. Electronic discussions are held via e-mail and bulletin boards, or you may get involved in computer conferencing. The methodology depends on the local technology (Aldred, 1996; Bonk and King, 1998; Rapaport, 1991).

Here are some suggested ground-rules to make electronic discussions successful, with possible times and numbers for an e-mail tutorial discussion in brackets.

- Agree a date to finish (2 weeks).

- Everyone must make a minimum number of contributions (three).

- Agree to read contributions every x days (two or three).

- Appoint someone to keep and collate all messages so there is a final record (Joe).

- Appoint a 'devil's advocate' or 'pot stirrer' to ask awkward questions and chivvy activity (Sandy).

- Ask someone to summarise and circulate an overview at the end (the basis of a group report for everyone to amend if the discussion is assessed).

- Be polite. In a conversation you can see and hear when someone is making a joke or ironic comment. The effect is not always the same on the screen.

- Where further research is required, attempt to share tasks evenly.

- Replying instantly is generally a good idea; that is what happens in face-to-face discussion, and first thoughts are often best.

In all discussions some people 'lurk' quietly, listening rather than commenting. The second item in the list above should overcome this issue to a certain extent. One of the more off-putting things that can happen in an electronic discussion is someone writing a 3000-word essay and mailing it to the group. This is the equivalent of one person talking continuously for an hour. It puts off the rest of the group; they feel there is little to add. Try to keep contributions short in the first stages. One good way to start is to ask everyone to brainstorm four to six points to one person by the end of Day 2. Someone collates, orders and mails a full list around the group as the starting point for discussion and research. (See **Try This 14.1 – E-mail in action**, p. 150.)

12.3 GROUP MANAGEMENT

The quality of discussion depends above all on the dynamics of each particular group. Some work spontaneously without any problems, others are very sticky. There are no hard-and-fast rules about behaviour in group discussions but here are some general points to consider. Meetings flow well when members:

- Steer the discussion to keep it to the point, sum up, shut up people who talk too much, and encourage and bring in people who talk too little.

- Keep track of the proceedings.

- Inject new ideas.

- Are critical of ideas.

- Play devil's advocate.

- Calm tempers.

- Add humour.

Formal meetings have designated individuals for the first two tasks (chair and secretary), but in informal meetings anyone can take these roles at any time. Everyone is better at one or two particular roles in a discussion; think about the sorts of roles you play and also about developing other roles using **Try This 12.3**.

TRY THIS 12.3 – Discussant's role

Here is a list of the actions or roles people take in discussions (adapted from Rabow *et al.*, 1994). Sort them into those which are positive and promote discussion, and those which are negative. (Suggested answers on p. 265.) How might you handle different approaches?

Asks for examples.	Seeks the sympathy vote.
Asks for opinions.	Keeps arguing for the same idea, although the discussion has moved on.
Encourages others to speak.	Asks for reactions.
Helps to summarise the discussion.	Is very defensive.
Ignores a member's contribution.	Gives examples.
Is very (aggressively) confrontational.	Offers opinions.
Is very competitive.	Summarises and moves discussion to next point.
Keeps quiet.	Diverts the discussion to other topics.
Mucks about.	Gives factual information.
Offers factual information.	Asks for examples.
Speaks aggressively.	

12.4 ASSESSING DISCUSSIONS

At the end of each term or as part of a learning log (see Chapter 2) you may be asked to reflect on your contribution to discussion sessions, and in some cases to negotiate a mark for it with your tutor. The attributes an assessor might check for are included in **Try This 12.4**. Assess friends, seminar and TV discussants on this basis, and consider what you can learn from those with high scores. Having analysed what makes a good discussant, have a look at **Try This 12.5**.

TRY THIS 12.4 – Assessment of discussion skills

Evaluate a discussant's performance on a 1–5 scale and note what they do well.

Assessment of discussion skills	1 (useless), 3 (average), 5 (brilliant) Comment on good points
Talks in full sentences.	
Asks clear, relevant questions.	
Describes an event clearly.	
Listens and responds to conversation.	
Discusses and debates constructively.	
Speaks clearly and with expression.	
Selects relevant information from listening.	
Responds to instructions.	
Contributes usefully to discussion.	
Reports events in sequence and detail.	
Is able to see both sides of the question.	
Finds alternative ways of saying the same thing.	
Listens to others, and appreciates their input efforts and needs.	

Reflect on the tips you can pick up from 4–5 point performers.

TRY THIS 12.5 – Self-assessment of discussion skills

Level 1 students at Leeds brainstormed the following list of 'skills needed to argue effectively'. Look down the list and select three items where you would like to be more effective. Do you have items to add to the list?

Having got your list, plot a strategy to work on each of these three issues at your next group discussion (e.g. I will not butt in; I will ask at least one question; I will say something and then shut up until at least three other people have spoken).

Being open-minded.	Staying cool.
Listening to both sides of the argument.	Being tolerant.
Using opponents' words against them.	Using good evidence.
Playing devil's advocate.	Being willing to let others speak.
Summing up every so often.	Only one person talking at a time.
Thinking before speaking.	Being firm.

Some final points

Getting better at discussion and argument needs practice, and hearing one's own voice improves one's self-confidence. You can practise in private. Listen to a question on a TV or radio discussion programme. Then turn the sound down, take a deep breath to calm down, and use it as thinking time. What is the first point? Now say it out loud. Subject matter is not important; get in there and have a go. Respond with two points and then a question or observation that throws the topic back to the group or audience. That is a good technique because you share the discussion with the rest of the audience, who can contribute their range of views. You might want to tape a programme and compare your answer with the panellists, remembering to look at the style of the answers rather than their technical content.

Where points of view or judgements are needed, you may want to seek the opinions of people with different academic, social and cultural backgrounds and experience. Their views may be radically different from your own. Seminars, workshops and tutorial discussions in psychology are explicitly designed to allow you to share these kinds of complementary views. To get the most out of a discussion or conversation:

- Be positive.

- Ask yourself questions, like 'How will this help me understand ... *driver behaviour in 18- to 25-year-olds?*'

- Make eye contact with the group.

- Give the speaker feedback and support.

- Aim to be accurate and to the point.

- Include psychological examples and references as you speak.

12.5 REFERENCES AND FURTHER READING

Aldred, B.K. (1996). *Desktop Conferencing: A Complete Guide to its Applications and Technology*. London: McGraw-Hill.

Bonk, C.J. & King, K.S. (Eds) (1998). *Electronic Collaborators: Learner-centered Technologies for Literacy, Apprenticeship, and Discourse*. Mahwah, NJ: Erlbaum Associates.

Drew, S. & Bingham, R. (1997). Negotiating and Assertiveness. In S. Drew & R. Bingham (Eds), *The Student Skills Guide*. Aldershot: Gower, 121–34 and 255–62.

Fisher, R., Ury, W. & Patton, B. (1997). *Getting to Yes: Negotiating an Agreement without Giving In*, 2nd edn. London: Arrow Business Books.

Hanse, J.J. & Engstrom, T.E. (1999). Sense of coherence and ill health among the unemployed and re-employed after closure of an assembly plant. *Work and Stress*, **13**(3), 204–22.

Rabow, J., Charness, M.A., Kipperman, J. & Radcliffe-Vasile, S. (1994). *William Fawcett Hill's Learning Through Discussion*, 3rd edn. Thousand Oaks, CA: Sage.

Rapaport, M. (1991). *Computer Mediated Communications: Bulletin Boards, Computer Conferencing, Electronic Mail, and Information Retrieval*. Chichester: John Wiley.

Psychograms 2

Try these psychological anagrams. Answers on p. 265.

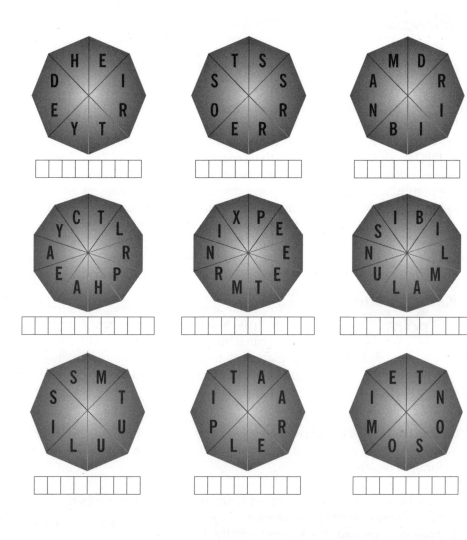

13 ORAL PRESENTATIONS

Always try to stop talking before people stop listening.

Most psychology degrees are littered with speaking opportunities. This is a really good thing! Somewhere on your CV you can add a line like, 'During my university career I have given 25 presentations to audiences ranging from 5 to 65, using OHTs, slides and inter-active computer displays'. This impresses employers, but many psychology graduates fail to explain that they have had these opportunities to hone this very saleable skill. Speaking lets you get used to managing nerves, become familiar with the question and answer session that

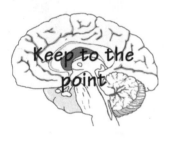

follows, and generally be a happy lapin. So grab all opportunities to practise your presentation skills. They all count as CV experience, from 5-minute presentations in tutorials to seminars and mini-lectures.

You need a well-argued message supported with psychological information, one that enraptures (maybe), the audience. Other chapters explain how to get the information together; this one is about practical presentation skills. The four most important tips are:

1   Suit the style and technical content of your talk to the skills and interests of the audience. Making the content accessible, so the audience wants to listen, will encourage a positive response.

2   Buzan & Buzan (1993) show that people are most likely to remember:
    ☺ Items from the start of a learning activity.
    ☺ Items from the end of a learning activity.
    ☺ Items associated with things or patterns already learned.
    ☺ Items that are emphasised or highlighted as unique or unusual.
    ☺ Items of personal interest to the learner.

    Tailor your presentation accordingly. Help the audience to think and understand.

3   Get the message straight in your head, organised and ready to flow. Lack of confidence in the content ➜ insecure speaker ➜ inattentive audience = bad presentation.

4   Remember the audience only gets one chance to hear you, so pare down a short presentation to the essential points. Make clear links between points and add brief, but strong, supporting evidence. You must have a plan, and stick to it on the day. Basically it is down to PBIGBEM (Put Brain In Gear Before Engaging Mouth).

13.1 STYLE

- **Can I read it?** Reading a script will bore both you and the audience. Really useful (frightening but useful) tutors will remove detailed notes and ask you to 'tell the story in your own words'. You are allowed bullet points on cards, to remind you of the main points, but that is all. Illustrate your talk with cartoons, equations and diagrams on OHTs (overhead transparencies), but remember that reading OHTs aloud is another cop-out.

- **Language.** A formal presentation requires a formal speaking style. Try to minimise colloquial language, acronyms and paraphrasing, and limit verbal mannerisms like the excessive use of *Hmm, Umm, err,* and *I mean.* Put new words or acronyms on a handout or OHT.

- **Look into their eyes!** Look at the audience and smile at them. If they feel you are enthusiastic and involved with the material, they will be more involved and interested. Psychologists study behaviour – so study your audience.

- **How fast?** Not too fast, slower than normal speech, because people taking notes need time to absorb your ideas, to get them into their brains and onto paper. The ideas are new to the audience. Watch the audience to check if you are going too fast, or they are kipping.

- **Stand or sit?** Position is often dictated by the room layout and normal practice. Given the choice, remember that sitting encourages the audience to feel it is a less formal situation, one where it is easier to chip in and comment.

- **How loud?** So that the audience can hear, but do not feel you are shouting. Ask someone you trust to sit at the back and wave if you are too loud or too quiet; getting it right takes practice. Tape record yourself sometime. When you have finished laughing at the result, have a think about whether you speak at the same pace and pitch all the time. Changing pace and pitch, getting excited about the material and showing enthusiasm are all good techniques for keeping your audience attentive and involved.

- **What about repeating material?** You can emphasise primary points by repetition, or by simultaneously putting them on an OHT or board, but only repeat the important points.

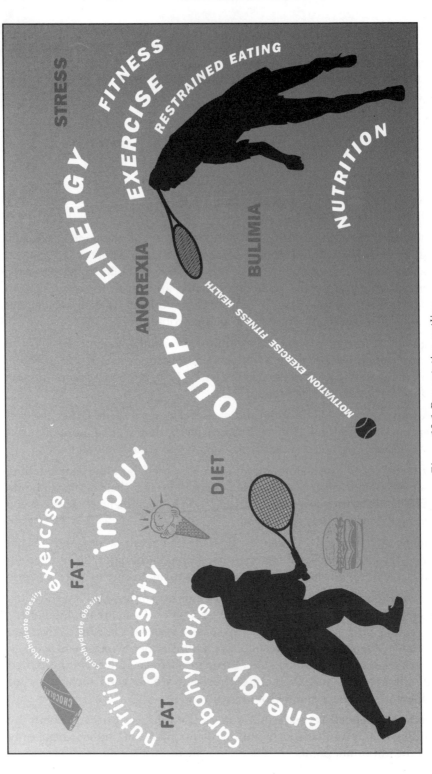

Figure 13:1 Presentation outline

13.2 CRUTCHES (OHTs, SLIDES, FLIPCHARTS)

Audiences need to understand your message. Visual assistance could include some or all of:

- A title slide that includes your name and (e-mail) address, so the audience knows who you are and where to find you!!

- A brief outline of the talk; bullet points are ideal, but adding pictures is fun, just make sure the message is clear. Is Figure 13.1 clear enough or OTT (over the top!)?

- Diagrams (colours on complex ones help to disentangle the story).

- Graphs and pictures.

- Finally, a summary sheet. This may be the outline slide shown again at the end, or a list of the key points you want the audience to remember.

OHTs

An OHT is shown on an OHP (overhead projector). Preparing good OHTs and managing OHPs takes practice.

What does not work: Small writing, too many colours, untidy handwriting, and writing from edge to edge (leave a 5cm margin at least). Misuse of, or inconsistent Use of capitals Doesn't help Either.

Good practice includes:
- OHTs prepared carefully in advance.

- SPELL CHECK EVERYTHING.

- Print in large font (18pt+) and then photocopy onto overhead film. (Putting overhead film through a computer printer will work with a few machines; usually you bust the printer.)

- A cartoon, clipart item or picture will make a message more memorable, and lighten the atmosphere if part of the material is seriously technical or a tad dull.

- Keep writing **very big** and messages short!

- It is fine to use diagrams from books and papers, but usually you need to **enlarge** them and always cite their source.

- Some audience members will be colour blind, so avoid green and red together, black with blue, and black on red. Yellow and orange do not show up well in large lecture theatres, orange and brown are not easy to distinguish from 30 rows back.

- Number your OHTs in case your 'friends' shuffle them or you drop them.

- If you have lots of information, and time is short, give the audience a handout with the detailed material, using the talk to summarise the main points.

Before giving a talk, investigate the projector, find the on/off switches, the plug and how to focus the transparency. 'Sod's law of talk giving' says that the previous speaker will breeze in, move the OHP, give a brilliant talk and leave you to reset the stage while the audience watches you!! KEEP COOL, and DON'T PANIC. Have a pen or pencil handy to act as a pointer. Pointing at the transparency on an OHP shows greater cool than demonstrating your javelin technique with a pointer at a screen beyond your reach.

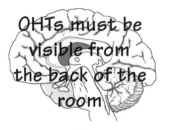

OHTs must be visible from the back of the room

Slides

Make sure the room has a projector and can be blacked out and that there is a carousel available. Run the slides through the projector in advance to ensure they are the right way round. Mixing overhead and slide projectors is a nightmare for novices and always wastes time in a talk. Try to use one medium or the other, so if you want to use slides get the title and talk outline slides onto film as well. Slides can be made from computer graphics package images. Just watch the cost and time for production. OHTs are fine for most purposes except very large audiences (over 300).

Flipcharts

Make sure your pens are full of ink and, again, **write big**. Left- and right-handed persons need the chart in slightly different positions. Check beforehand what the audience can see, and adjust your position accordingly. If spelling is a problem, flipcharts are a BAD IDEA. Irritatingly, the audience will remember your spelling error rather than your message.

13.3 WHAT TO AVOID

☹ **Getting uptight.** All speakers are nervous. THIS IS NORMAL. Take deep breaths and relax before the event. If you are well prepared there is the time to walk slowly to the venue and have a coffee beforehand. Get to the session early enough to find the loos, lights and seats. Ensure that the projectors, computer display system, flipchart, handouts, notes and a pen are in the right place for you and the audience. Then take a lot of deep breaths. YOU WILL BE FINE.

😕 **Showing the audience you are nervous.** Ask your mates to tell you what you do when speaking. Everyone gets uptight, but fiddling with hair, pockets, clothes, keys, pencil, ears and fingers distracts the audience. They watch your mannerisms and remember very little of the talk. Practise speaking.

😕 **Overrunning.** As a rule of thumb, reckon you can speak at about 100-120 words per minute. Practise in advance with a stopwatch (there is one on most cookers), reducing the time by 10 per cent.

13.4 HANDLING STICKY SITUATIONS

😊 **Late arrivals** should be ignored, unless they apologise to you, in which case smile your thanks. Going back interrupts your flow and irritates the people who arrived on time.

😊 **Time is up and you have 20 more things to say.** This is bad planning and usually only happens when you have not practised the material aloud. You can read your material much, MUCH faster than you can speak it. However, if you do run over time then either skip straight to your concluding phrases OR list the headings you have yet to cover and do a one-line conclusion.

😊 **Good question, no idea of the answer.** Say so. A phrase like 'That's a brilliant thought, not occurred to me at all, does anyone else know?' will cheer up the questioner and hopefully get others talking. If you need time to think, offer variations on 'I'm glad this has come up . . .', 'I wanted to follow up that idea but couldn't find anything in the library, can anyone help here?', 'Great question, no idea, how do we find out?'

😊 **The foot–mouth interface,** exemplified by such psychologists' classics as 'they took both a top-down and bottoms-up approach', 'changes for boys at puberty include the deepening of their vice', 'asexual activity occurs in lower-class orgasms', 'Let's go round the group and see what ideas we can all throw up' – sad when the topic is bulimia. They happen.

Top Tips

● **Assessment.** Self-assess your bathroom rehearsals against your department's criteria, or use the guidelines in Figure 13.2 to polish a performance.

Oral Presentation Criteria

Name ....   Title of talk ....

		Great	Middling	Oh dear!	
Rendition					
Speed	Spot on				Too fast/slow
Audibility	Clear and distinct				Indistinct
Holding attention	Engaged audience				Sent them to sleep
Enthusiasm	Ebullient delivery				Boring delivery
Substance					
Organisation	Organised, logical structure				Scrappy and disorganised
Pertinence	On the topic				Random and off the point
Academic accuracy	Factually spot on				Inaccurate
Support materials					
Suitability	Tailored to talk				None, or off the topic
Production quality	Clear				Unclear
Treatment	Professionally presented				Poorly integrated and presented
Question time					
Handling queries	Thoughtful answers				Limited ability to extend the discussion
Adaptability	Coped well				Limited, inflexible responses
Teamwork					
Co-ordination	Balanced, team response				Unequal, unbalanced response

Figure 13:2 Oral presentation assessment criteria

- **Use technical, psycho-language.** Try not to use colloquial speech or to substitute less than technical terms: 'The results seem a bit iffy', 'He ate loads and loads', or 'subliminal influences, mmm, yes . . . when you don't notice you're doing it'. Strive in presentations to use a formal, technically rich style.

- **Practise your talk** on your rabbit, the bathroom mirror, etc. Speaking the words aloud will make you feel happier when going for the Gold Run. It also gives you a chance to pronounce unfamiliar words like autotopagnosia, psychoneuroimmunology, tetrahydrocannabinol and get them wrong in the privacy of your own bus stop. If in doubt about pronunciation ask someone – the librarian, your mum, anyone.

- **Most marks are given for content**, so research the psychology thoroughly.

13.5 REFERENCES AND FURTHER READING

Anholt, R.R.H. (1994). *Dazzle 'Em with Style: The Art of Oral Scientific Presentation.* New York: Freedman.

Buzan, T. & Buzan, B. (1993). *The Mind Map Book.* London: BBC Books.

Sides, C.H. (1992). *How to Write and Present Technical Information*, 2nd edn. Cambridge: Cambridge University Press.

I'm crazy about big words.

That's called being psycholinguistic.

14 RESEARCHING AND WRITING IN TEAMS: IT'S FUN AND EFFICIENT

My team will beam down, get the data, create the report and then come back alive and unhurt.

Employers look for people who work happily in teams. A soloist may be very useful, but if s/he cannot get on with colleagues, explain and relax in management situations, that person may impede progress. More importantly, teamwork allows the exploration of more material than is possible for an individual. Team members can bounce ideas off each other. Where resources are limited, getting involved in co-operative activities and sharing has benefits for everyone. The skill benefits include teamwork, developing professional standards in presentation, problem-solving, negotiation and responsibility.

A bunch of psychologists having supper together may talk about Prof. Ism's lecture on prejudice. Everyone has different ideas. If some people decide to chase up further information and pool it, they are beginning to operate as a team. In some modules you will research and write as a team, but remember you can use team skills and approaches to tackle other parts of your course. Two to five people in the same flat, hall of residence or tutor group can team up to extend and optimise research activities, and talking psychology together will develop your discussion skills and broaden your views.

This chapter raises some of the issues associated with groupwork and suggests some ways of tackling group tasks. There are pitfalls. Not everyone likes teamwork and sharing. Some people feel they may be led down blind alleys by their team-mates. We think the advantages of team research outweigh the disadvantages, but if this is an issue that bothers you, brainstorm as to which group members are a disadvantage. Possibly:

☹ Those who do not pull their weight.

☹ The perennially absent.

☹ Those who do not deliver on time.

☹ The over-critical who put others down, suppressing the flow of ideas.

☺ Anyone who gets touchy and sulks if their ideas are ignored.

If you are aiming to benefit from team activities, these are some characteristics to suppress! You may not like working in teams, but when you do, it is in everybody's interests for the team to pull together and derive the benefits. Having identified unhelpful teamwork characteristics, consider what good team qualities might include:

☺ Making people laugh.

☺ Getting stuff finished.

☺ Communicating well.

☺ Being reliable.

☺ Making friends.

☺ Keeping calm in arguments.

☺ Speaking your mind.

☺ Resolving disputes.

Reducing tension in a group promotes cohesion and encourages learning.

There is a natural pattern in life that is also seen in the normal reaction of people to teamwork and life in general. Map these natural reactions to an event in your life, or to an assignment as in Figure 14.1. Each time you are given an assignment you are likely to experience all these reactions. The people who realise 'where' they are in the sequence, and push on to the Recovery and Getting on Track stages, give themselves more time to do the task well.

Natural reactions	Reactions mapped to an essay	Reactions mapped to a team project
Shock	I know nothing about . . .	We know nothing about . . .
Recrimination	I didn't want to do this module, who made it compulsory?	I don't want to work in groups/ with them.
Disagreement	No motivation, nothing done.	Everyone does their own thing, or nothing.
Reorganisation	2 weeks to go, do a plan.	There are 2 weeks to go, we have to get it together! Make a plan.
Recovery	Parts of this are quite interesting.	Everyone knows which bits to do. Some people start to enjoy it.
Getting on track	Got parts of two sections sorted, and found some more references.	It is coming together, disks are swapped and ideas evaluated.
Partial success	Drafted the essay, needs editing and references.	Mostly done, but no cover, diagrams missing and needs editing.
Frustration	Printer's not working, forgot to spell check.	We can't find Jim, who has it all on disk!
Success	Final version handed in.	Report completed.

Figure 14:1 Natural reactions to groupwork

14.1 RESEARCHING IN GROUPS

Groups can cover more material than an individual, but having decided to share research outcomes, recognise there will be difficulties and tensions at times. Group members are only human. Everyone has a different way of researching and note-making, so shared information will 'look' different on paper, BUT you can learn from the way other people note and present information. Figure 14.2 summarises thoughts from three groups after a shared research task. They give some insights into what can happen.

One meeting or three? How often does a group need to meet? Generally:

Two or more meetings ➜ more chat ➜ greater exchange of views ➜ more interactions ➜ more learning.

Have electronic meetings (see p. 149) when time is tight.

14.2 WRITING IN TEAMS

Team writing is a normal business activity. Typically it involves a group brainstorming an outline for the document, individuals researching and drafting sub-sections, circulation of drafts for comment, the incorporation of additional ideas and views, and someone editing a final version. The same approach can be adopted in university writing. Like ensemble recorder playing, writing as a team is difficult and discordant the first time you do it, but very useful experience.

One valuable approach involves team members volunteering to research and draft specific sub-sections and volunteering for a 'writing role' (Figure 14.3). Discussions are more lively and focused when individuals can use their role to offer alternatives and new approaches. The critic has the licence to criticise; the linker can say 'Yes, that's great, but how do we use Weber's Law and TPB to explain "storm and stress" in adolescents?' Adopting writing roles can depersonalise criticism, which is especially important when working with friends. Be critical and stay friends.

Style and layout

Decide on the general layout at the start, on the format, fonts and style of headings, and the format for references. Make decisions about word length, like 'each sub-section has a maximum of 200 words'. Early word-length decisions limit waffle. Nevertheless, length needs looking at later in the project: some parts of the argument will deserve expansion. Keep talking to each other about ideas and their relative importance and position in the narrative.

Finally, someone (or some two) has to take the whole document and edit it to give it a consistent voice and style, BUT everyone needs to provide graphs, diagrams and references in the agreed style.

Task	Reflection
Tutorial essay on memory Individual essays Two-week deadline	We had only met the week before so we didn't really know each other. We had a quick meeting to arrange another time to meet and we all said we would look up some of the references. Met on day 5 and no one had done anything. Ali offered to look at the Loftus and Darwin papers, Emily said she would do a Web of Science search for really recent articles and the rest of us split up the RL bits between us. Agreed to meet two days later. Emily had lots of stuff and Sandy had found a couple of recent BSc project reports. We ended up with lots of photocopies and web pages. Ali had made notes on the background papers which were added to the pile and we had a quick discussion about what we could write. We had to set our own titles, all different, which meant we talked a lot and probably wasted reading/writing time but no one got upset. We could have emailed some of the web refs and electronic journal articles to each other to save lots of printing. Getting lots of refs together meant I wrote a very different essay to normal. I wouldn't have looked at so many different resources on my own and because we talked about it all I knew more in the end.
Seminar preparation Aggression and video games 15-minute presentation followed by 10-minute discussion Class of 40	We started with a meeting over beers in the Union and talked about what we could do. Everyone had lots of ideas and views and we talked a lot about films we liked and cinema stories. Began to realise that we were going to need some more factual material and real references. Dave decided to see if the Cinema literature had anything to say. Alice and Clara said they would do a www and newspaper search. Tim offered to do the Web of Science search. Agreed to meet on Friday, watch a couple of videos and organise the next stage. We got lots of info from really odd places like *Cosmopolitan* and *The Times* as well as journals. Downloaded video covers from www to make cool OHTs and got posters from the video shop for displays. As the seminar was at 3.00 we met in the morning to sort it out. Bad idea. Should have met the day before, had too many ideas, not enough structure and everyone wanted to get their piece in. We got a running order but no real introduction and we hadn't got a good OHT to finish. Questions went OK cos everyone started offering their experience of cinema but it wasn't a very academic discussion so I don't think we will get that many marks. It was great getting to know the group and it was a really interesting subject but we were probably too general and not analytical enough.
Group research: pregnancy shrinks the brain? Six people Group report	We were pleased to get the class practical time to work on the project but soon realised we were way behind and worked late to try to put things right. For sub-sections to be compiled individually all of the group had to know what they were supposed to cover and to have similar ideas about the arguments we wanted to make. Once we had a first draft other people added further information and someone else did the draft introduction and conclusion. It was amazing to me to watch us arguing about individual sentences and words. I learned a lot about revising from this. Editing the final document meant five people sending me an assortment of materials and I felt that I was making a patchwork of a report – I learned a lot about the formatting features and generated the table of contents electronically. We had a big argument about whether the conclusion should be an optimistic paragraph on 'where do we go from here' or a summary of the content. Some members didn't like sentences starting with And or But, younger members were less constrained by punctuation. Eventually the editor made the final decision but I think this was with some reluctance as they wondered if I would make the right decision. Too much material, we needed to plan earlier and make decisions sooner. Six people writing gave us too much text. Next time we need to set word limits for each section.

Figure 14:2 Experiences of group research

Writing role	Responsibilities
Summariser	Introduction, conclusions, abstract
Visuals/graphics	Smart graphs, figures, indexes, contents page
Critic	Faultfinder, plays devil's advocate
Academic content	Subject reporters
Linker	Checks connections between arguments, sections and the introduction and conclusion
Discussant	Evaluates and discusses

Figure 14:3 Roles in writing

Duet writing

Two people sitting at a PC can be very effective in getting words on disk. The exchange of ideas is immediate, two brains keep the enthusiasm levels high and you can plan further research activities as you go. It is advantageous to have two people together doing the final edit, keeping track of formats and updates and being cheerful!

Timetabling issues

A team-writing activity cannot be done like the traditional psychology essay, on the night before submission after the pub. People get ill and things happen, so the timetable needs to be generous to allow for slippage AND team members have to agree to stick to it. It usually works: it's too embarrassing to be the only non-contributor. It may assist planning if you put some dates against the points in Figure 14.4.

1	Brainstorm initial ideas, assign research tasks and data collection. *(Day 1)*
2	Research topics. *(Days 2–5)*
3	Draft sub-sections and circulate. *(Days 6–9)*
4	Meet to discuss progress, decide on areas that are complete, assess where additional research is needed, assign further research and writing roles and tasks. *(Day 10)*
5	Redraft sections and circulate. *(Days 10–14)*
6	Are we all happy with this? *(Day 15)*
7	Editor's final revisions. *(Days 16–18)*
8	Finalisation of cover, contents and abstract. Check and add page numbers. Check submission requirements are met. *(Day 18)*
9	Submit. *(Day 18!)*

Figure 14:4 Timetabling team writing

Keeping a team on track? Need a chairperson?

One of the pitfalls of working with a group of friends is that more time is taken making sure everyone stays friends than getting on with the task. One vital issue that emerges is the initial division of labour (see Figures 14.2 and 14.5). It is vital that everyone feels happy, involved and equally valued. So the chairman, or the person that emerges as the chairman, must endeavour to ensure there is fair play, that no one hogs the action excluding others, and equally that no one is left out (even if that is what they want). The chairman is allowed to goad you into action, that's her/his job. It is unfair to dump the role of chairman on the same person each time: share it around. Chairing is a skill everyone should acquire.

If a group feels someone is a serious dosser they may want to invoke the 'football rules', or ask the module tutor to do so. The rules are one yellow card as a warning, two or three yellow cards equal a red card and exclusion from the group. The same system might be used to reduce marks (see p. 151). A red-carded person does not necessarily get a zero but in attempting to complete a group task alone they are unlikely to do better than a bare pass.

Top Tips

✔ The time required to tidy up, write an abstract, make a smart cover, do an index and acknowledgement page and cross-check the references is five times longer than you think: split the jobs between the team.

✔ It saves hours of work if everyone agrees at the start on a common format for references, and everyone takes responsibility for citing the items they quote.

The key to team writing is getting the STYLE and TIMETABLE right, although CONTENT also matters.

Plagiarism

Where groupwork leads to a common report then obviously collaborative writing is involved. BUT, if you are required to write independent reports from group research or group activities you must ensure your reports are independently written, not copies or cut-and-paste versions of each other's documents. In this situation share reading, float and discuss ideas, BUT write independently. This means planning to finish the research three days, or more, before the deadline so everyone has time to draft and correct their reports.

14.3 COMMUNICATION BY E-MAIL

It is vital that everyone has access to a group report, so a method of circulating the most recent version of a document is needed. Using e-mail with attachments is ideal, and saves printing costs. You can share thoughts, drafts and updates while working at the most convenient place and time for you. Have a go at **Try This 14.1**.

TRY THIS 14.1 – E-mail in action

Research a tutorial essay or practical report, sharing resources and ideas, without physically meeting. HINT: the first time, it helps to have everyone in the same computer laboratory: you can resolve any problems quickly.

Open a new word-processing document and:

1 Type in the title, the keywords you would use in a library search and write very briefly about two or three issues, say three sentences for each.

2 Then save the document. Open e-mail, attach and mail the document to your mates.

3 With a bit of luck other people will be doing the same thing at the same time, so there should be e-mails arriving from them. Save your colleagues' files in your own workspace, but check whether they have used the same file name as you; if so it will need changing to avoid over-writing.

4 Return to the word-processing package, open your original document and the new ones. Copy the material into a single file and reorganise it to make a coherent set of comments. While collating keep track of ideas, perhaps through subheadings. Reflect on your colleagues' comments. At the immediate supportive level there is the 'That's a new / good / middling idea'. More actively, think around variations on 'I was surprised by . . . because . . .', 'I disagree with . . . because . . .', 'We all agreed that . . . because . . .'.

5 Now look at the *style* of the responses. What might you need to do as an editor to make these comments hang together?

6 Finally, get together and decide how you will organise your research and writing to maximise the opportunity to share resources and information.

Bigger documents

Imagine a report constructed by four people being edited and updated daily. How do you keep track of what is going on? There needs to be an agreed system. Adapting elements of the following might be a useful template for action:

● At the start the document needs a:

    ☺ header page with title and the outline plan

    ☺ section which everyone updates when they change the document, e.g. Andy modified sections 2.6 and 3.2 on Weds 1 April at 10.00.

    ☺ an agreed working order, e.g. John drafts section 2, then Anne revises it. All revisions circulated by —day

- Decide that citations will be added to the reference list in the agreed format.
- Agree to check e-mail and respond every X days.
- Use the 'revision editor' in your word-processing package. The person responsible for section X will not necessarily welcome five independent redrafts. A 'revisions editor' highlights revision suggestions for the sub-section editor to accept or reject as desired. By opening multiple copies of the document you can cut and paste between drafts.
- DO NOT USE PAGE NUMBERS TO REFER TO OTHER VERSIONS. These change with almost every version. Use section numbers and date each version carefully.
- Ensure that at least one or two people keep an archive of all drafts, so that you can revive an earlier version if disaster strikes.

Use e-mail to brainstorm ideas among friends, tutorial and seminar groups and old schoolfriends doing psychology at other universities. People like getting messages and usually respond. E-mail is a quick and cheap way of discussing points. There are a great many people you could brainstorm with: think more widely than just you and your lecturer.

14.4 ASSESSMENT OF TEAMWORK

Assessment tends to generate discussion about 'fairness'. There are dark hints about cheerful dossers getting good marks when their mates have done the work. How is this handled? Most staff will offer some variation on the following approaches for assigning marks, some of which involve team input. If the 'football factor' is in play, there may be an agreed penalty, say −10 per cent for a yellow card.

A The simple approach
Each member of the team gets the same mark, so it is up to everyone to play fair.

B The private bid
Each individual fills in a form privately, and the assessor tries to resolve discrepancies. This style:

Name ....
Names of other team members ....
I feel my contribution to this project is worth ....% of the team mark.
This is because ....
....
....
Signed ....

This approach may lead to discussion amongst your assessors, but it lets people with personal problems acquaint staff privately. It can require the wisdom of Solomon to resolve. Remember a marker will take note of what you say, but will not necessarily change the marks.

C Team effort

A form in this style asks everyone to comment on the contribution of each team member. Summing the totals constructs an index of activity, which is used to proportion the marks.

Estimate the effort made by each team member, 0 = no effort, 2 = did a bit, 3 = average, 4 = really useful, 5 = outstanding contribution.	X	Y	Z
Attended all meetings			
Contributed ideas			
Did a fair share of the writing			
Other – detail particular contributions:			
TOTAL			

14.5 COMMENTS ON TEAMWORK

Staff comments: 'Initially students are very democratic and give equal marks. With experience, they choose to raise the marks of those who have done more of the task.' 'The amount of chat was enormous, and between them they could tackle a more difficult problem than as individuals.' 'The team-writing exercise made everyone think about the order and quality of the material. The report was more extensive and detailed than one person could do in the time.' 'One team was happy to have this year's "mine's a third" candidate because s/he happily did the activities like data entry in the laboratory and making poster backgrounds, while cracking jokes and keeping the team cheerful.'

Figure 14.5 details reflections of second-year psychology students following a group research and report writing session. Overall, they see the exercise as positive and the disadvantages as surmountable with experience. Their reflections may be worth considering as you start team activities.

What were the advantages of team work?	What were the disadvantages of team work?
We organised the chairman early and managed the business of task delegation well. Between us we collected a great source of information which made for surprising breadth in the wide report. Other members of the group were relaxed and happy to talk about what we should be doing, and later to discuss how we should write up the joint report. Working as a group to produce a report gave us a diversity of style and opinions that strengthened the final piece. Ideas bounced around the group, which made it much more fun. We didn't run into problems in deciding on what to prioritise and how to move forward, which I thought we might have done. Groupwork added to my confidence. I realised I had things to contribute that helped us to get on.	Meeting together at the right time and place is a mountain to climb before work has even begun. Then there is illness, absences (alcohol-related or otherwise), and the inevitable lazy member of the group to deal with. The team decision may not be the one you wanted and argued for. Having to compromise on common topics and ideas. Recognising that other people have different ways of working, and having to find a way round it! Discovering that our team had three people with chairman qualities (Belbin, 1996) – but it helped us to know our team-playing strengths and weaknesses as it explained some reactions and interactions.

What will you do differently next time you work together?
Give meetings a definite structure, make sure the chairman keeps us on the focus of the meeting and that we come away knowing what to do next. Set criteria for action! Learn to bite my tongue and not try to take over. Use e-mail with attachments as well as the mobile phone to keep everyone up to speed. I discovered I have plant and company worker strengths (Belbin, 1996). Next time I will try to work on some of my less strong team-player characteristics.

Figure 14:5 Psychology students' opinions on teamwork, 2000

Team research and writing at university usually produces a better document than an individual response. This is not because the academic content is necessarily substantially better, but because team activities generate a series of drafts and more thinking about the topic and audience, so that the final product is more polished. Make the most of groupwork activities on your CV. It isn't the academic content that matters: highlight the skills you used in delivering a group product, such as negotiation, meeting deadlines, allocating tasks, collaborative writing, editing and co-ordinating research.

14.6 REFERENCES AND FURTHER READING

Anon. (1995). How to build effective teams. *People Management*, 23 February, 40–1.

Belbin, R.M. (1996). *Management Teams: Why they Succeed or Fail*. Oxford: Butterworth Heinemann.

Gibbs, G. (1994). *Learning in Teams: A Student Manual*. Oxford: Oxford Centre for Staff Development.

West, M.A. (1994*). Effective Teamwork*. Leicester: British Psychological Society.

Psycho-quick Crossword 2   Answers p. 266.

Across
1 Regard highly (6)
4 Listen to (4)
9 Belonging somewhere else (5)
10 It is not imaginary (7)
11 Attaching labels (7)
12 Put together (5)
13 Development in a regular pattern (6, 5)
17 Eighteenth Greek letter (5)
19 Gives an account, tells (7)
22 Go to pieces (5, 2)
23 Tease or trouble (5)
24 Reflect sound waves (4)
25 Protein that regulates cell processes (6)

Down
1 Spot on (5)
2 Initiate a specific response (7)
3 A feeling of weariness (5)
5 Be present, live (5)
6 Regular pattern or occurrence (6)
7 Treatment based on approved chemicals (4, 7)
8 Serenely (6)
14 Cheerfully crazy (6)
15 No sign of development, yet (7)
16 The spirit (6)
18 Symbolic diagram (5)
20 Gain knowledge (5)
21 Personal approach (5)

15 WRITING PRACTICAL REPORTS

Your report is concise, informative, and makes no sense. 70 per cent.

The test of a good report is that:

✔ The reader should be able to repeat the work without reference to additional sources.

✔ The reader should understand the significance of the outcomes of the work in the wider psychological context.

✔ It is short and to the point.

Skills involved in report writing include clear thinking, analysis, synthesis, written communication and persuasive writing.

Some practicals are truly *investigative*, where data are analysed to find an answer. You might take a series of tones and present them in pairs, dichotically, and use listeners' responses to work out whether listeners are left- or right-ear dominant. Here the emphasis is using the data to make particular judgements and evaluations. This type of practical is possible because you have also done 'developmental' practicals. *Developmental* practicals are designed to help you understand the *research process* at every step, by evaluating it as you progress and understanding where and how each step works. In this kind of investigation the report will place less emphasis on the final result than on the steps involved, and make statements about assumptions, validity of data, techniques, sources of error and bias, and alternative approaches used and discarded, or evaluated and rejected. There may be discussion of the choice of statistical test(s), the limits of the response-measuring technique, alternative approaches such as questionnaires versus interviews. This kind of practical calls on your analytical thinking as well as your problem-solving skills. Depending on the type of practical investigation involved, your report will change its focus and emphasis.

15.1 THE FORMAT

The normal expectation is that the writing is brief, direct, and follows the general format outlined in Figure 15.1.

Sections	Contents
Title	Short and precise title.
Author details	Author's name and contact address (e-mail).
Abstract	Short, precise summary – rarely longer than 200 words
Introduction	Background – the psychology context of the research and development of the rationale for the study, hypotheses/research questions.
Methodology	Sample, design, materials and equipment, procedures, ethical considerations.
Results	A summary of the findings using tables, graphs and figures.
Discussion and evaluation	Interpretation of results, relation to hypotheses/research questions; consideration of representativeness of findings and methodological limitations; consideration of the psychological relevance of the results and their implications for the broader context.
Conclusion	Brief summary of the outcomes. Suggestions for future research.
References	Vital! Include both psychological and methodological references.

Figure: 15.1 Outline for a report

Abstract or summary

You might write this in the style of an Executive Summary (Chapter 16). Describe the psychological context for the study, hypotheses tested, methodology, main findings and interpretation in brief sentences.

Introduction

Set the context by briefly reviewing the psychological literature most immediately relevant to the study, referring to other studies on this topic; this might involve a mini (one to five paragraph) literature review. Avoid the temptation to cover the whole of the lifespan when your practical is a study of people in Erikson's sixth stage of development. By the end of the introduction your reader should understand *why* you are doing this study and your hypotheses or research questions.

Methodology

This is the section in which you try to convince your reader that your study is reliable and valid, and provide them with enough information to be able to make a good stab at replicating your work.

The sample

A short description of your participants and the characteristics pertinent to this study (e.g., sex, age range, occupation, place of origin, student, professional). What is the size of your sample and how was it selected? Were they matched on any criteria?

Design

A short description, and reasons for choice, of techniques. Does the study involve naturalistic observation, correlational observation, experiment . . . ? If your study is experimental, did you use an independent (or between) groups, repeated measures (or within groups) or mixed design? Identify and define your dependent and independent variables. What controls are in operation? If your study is qualitative, what type of interview did you use and why? If you make up a new method, adapt a standard method or adopt a non-standard approach it must be explained in enough detail for the next researcher to evaluate and copy your technique. A full protocol might be put in an appendix. Explain, also, why it was necessary to create a new method – what was the problem with previous approaches?

Materials/apparatus and equipment

Which questionnaires did you use, and why? Give examples of representative items. Briefly describe any computer programme used. Many questionnaires, laboratory procedures and interview styles are standard. They should be cited but do not need to be explained in detail. You presented visual gratings tachistoscopically? Describe the stimuli accurately, report the rate of presentation and exposure timings. Remember, your reader ought to be able to replicate your study after reading this!

Procedure

Provide a brief description of the data-gathering process. Avoid listing every detail, minor deviation and exception. Statements like 'Questionnaire responses were coded and entered for analysis using SPSS' will do fine. You do not need to tell the readers about SPSS. Some students have a habit of correctly including laboratory procedures, interview schedules, apparatus details and sample size information, BUT omitting details of the subsequent qualitative, graphical or statistical analysis, which loses marks.

Ethics

What procedures did you have in place for obtaining participants' informed consent? What debriefing procedures did you employ? How did you ensure participant confidentiality? Check out **Try This 19.1 – Ethical implications** (p. 196) early on. Ask yourself the questions raised there and be clear about the answers, this will help your research and report writing. Are ethical issues reported fully?

Results

Summarise the results in prose, accompanied where appropriate with tables and graphs to show the main findings. Use tables, graphs, bar charts, scatter plots, etc., for clarification rather than decoration. Label them and refer to them in the text, or the reader will read through the whole section without using them. Think about how you order your materials – you might organise them according to type of analysis (descriptive, correlational, inferential) or in relation to your hypotheses. Consider putting the raw data in an appendix, or submit on disk. Don't clutter this section with it.

Discussion and evaluation

This section will cross-reference to the results section with the emphasis on explaining relationships, lack of relationships and patterns in the results. Consider how the results fit with previous psychological experience. Refer back to the introductory and literature sections to place these results in a wider context.

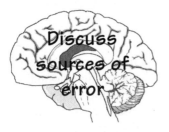

Caution

There is more than one explanation for most things. All measurements are prone to error and inaccuracy; if you have not worked out what might be a problem with the data, talk to people to develop some ideas. No self-respecting examiner will ever believe that you have a perfectly accurate data set (unless you happen to be a god, in which case our apologies for questioning your infallibility). Unless you are absolutely certain, it might be wise to use a cautious phrase like 'It appears, on the basis of this limited sample, that . . .', or 'Initially the conclusion that . . . appears to be justified, but further investigations are required to . . .'.

Conclusion

Resist at all costs the temptation to explain all the Wonders of the Known World from two measurements of anxiety before and after your anxiety management intervention. Ensure your conclusion is justified by the data, not by what you hoped to find. This is the place to suggest what research should be done to continue the investigation.

References

A report is a piece of academic work. Reference your sources and quotations fully (see Chapter 10).

Appendices

Some information is too detailed or tangential for the main sections (it would distract the reader from the exciting storyline) but may be included in appendices. Appendices are the home for questionnaires, details of laboratory protocols, example calculations, programmes, additional data that you want to include. Appendices are not 'dumping grounds' for scratty bits of paper with illegible workings-out, and copies of your 30 completed questionnaires. Limit appendices as far as possible.

15.2 WHERE THE MARKS GO!!

Most students hope most marks are awarded for all the time spent sweating over a steamy PC, talking to billions of clubbers to persuade them to complete questionnaires, trying to log into remote computers, and spending hours in the library chasing down esoteric research articles. Tragically, most academics see these efforts as worthy of some, minor, reward. A tutor has produced the handouts and briefing, explained what to do and how to go about it. The practical session will develop your skills and experience in handling data, samples and recalcitrant group members, and may be worthy of 50 per cent of the marks at the most generous. What your tutor really wants to know is:

- Have you understood what the results mean?

- Do you know why a psychologist would want to be doing this in the first place?

- Do you understand the flaws in the method and the limits of the results?

- Do you know what the intelligent research psychologist would do next?

Hence many marks go for the results and discussion sections of the report. So leave time to write these up, *and* redraft them so the writing is good, *and* add the references. Many reports lose marks because they stop at the results stage.

This next sentence concluded a student report: 'It can therefore be concluded that a fuller investigation is required, increasing the sample size.' This conclusion was on the right lines and showed that the author appreciated that sampling was an issue, BUT it is possible for the author to add value with a conclusion that is more information-rich. Something like: 'The restricted data set has limited the inferences that may be drawn. Follow-up research should widen the sample to include an equal number of southerners as northerners. Additionally, a third group, of people who consider themselves to be neither northerners nor southerners, should be added to increase confidence in the conclusions.' This is longer but no more difficult to write. The original author had discussed future experimental work informally, earlier in the project, but 'was shy of adding these sorts of ideas to the report'. Shy is nice in social situations but doesn't get marks. Forget 'shy' when reporting.

Use your departmental practical assessment sheets as a guide to self-assess and revise your reports, or use Figure 15.2. A 60/30/10 mark split is indicated here. What counts in your department?

15.3 FURTHER READING

Clark-Carter, D. (1997). *Doing Quantitative Research: From Design to Report*. Hove: Psychology Press.
Girden, E.R. (1996). *Evaluating Research Articles from Start to Finish*. London: Sage.

Name	Laboratory report title					
	1	2.1	2.2	3	Fail	
Structure and argument 60%						
Logical presentation						Discontinuous report
Topics covered in depth						Superficial report
Links to psychology clearly made						No links to psychological material
Clear, succinct writing style						Rambling, repetitious report
Technical content 30%						
Experiment appropriately described						Experiment poorly described
Graphs, tables and fully and correctly labelled						Incorrect/no labelling of graphs and tables
Appropriate inferences drawn from data						Inappropriate use of data
Sources fully acknowledged						Incorrect/absence of referencing
Presentation 10%						
Good graphics						Poor/no use of graphics
Good word processing						Poor/no use of word processing
Comments						

Figure: 15.2 Assessment criteria for a laboratory report

Howitt, D. & Cramer, D. (2000). *First Steps in Research and Statistics: A Practical Workbook for Psychology Students.* London: Routledge.

Kopala, M. & Suzuki, L.A. (Eds) (1999). *Using Qualitative Methods in Psychology.* Thousand Oaks, CA: Sage.

Lobban, C.S. & Schefter, M. (1992). *Successful Lab Reports: A Manual for Science Students.* Cambridge: Cambridge University Press.

Parrott III, L. (1999). *How to Write Psychology Papers*, 2nd edn. London: Longman.

Sides, C.H. (1992). *How to Write and Present Technical Information*, 2nd edn. Cambridge: Cambridge University Press.

Lab Prac Conundrum

Work out who did what on the laboratory practical, and what mark they got. Answers on p. 266.

Sam and Jake used the tachistoscope but didn't manipulate colour.

58%

Josh and Gabe got first-class marks, like Sam and Jake, but didn't measure reaction times.

63%

Juliet and Georgia didn't vary word length . . .

79%

. . . a task that kept Rees and Kim occupied.

72%

The word-length changers had an 8 in their mark.
Josh and Gabe didn't get 79% and the word-length changers didn't get 72%.

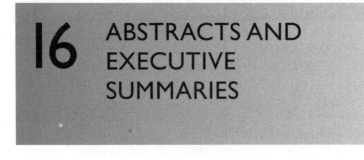

16 ABSTRACTS AND EXECUTIVE SUMMARIES

OK, OK, I started the report, I've done the abstract, just 6000 words to go.

Abstracts and Executive Summaries (ESs) inform readers about the contents of documents. While both approaches summarise longer documents, they have

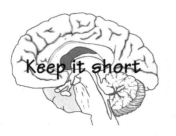

different formats and serve different purposes. Writing an abstract or an ES enhances your skills in reading, identifying key points and issues, structuring points in a logical sequence and writing concisely.

Most psychology journal articles include an abstract that summarises the contents. Abstracts appear in bibliographic databases to notify researchers of an article's content. Executive summaries are normally found at the start of reports and plans, particularly with business documents. An ES aims to describe the essential points within a document, usually in one or two pages. Depending on the context, the style may be more dynamic and less formal than an abstract.

16.1 ABSTRACTS

Look at some well-written abstracts before writing one. The *Quarterly Journal of Experimental Psychology, Cognition and Emotion, Perception* and the *British Journal of Psychology* contain many examples. Use **Try This 16.1** to look at the wider role of abstracts. An abstract should be a short, accurate, objective summary. It is not the place for interpretation and criticism. Abstracts should do the following:

☺ enable the reader to select documents for a particular research problem

☺ substitute, in a limited way, for the original document when accessing the original is impossible

TRY THIS 16.1 – Abstracts

Next time you read a journal article, read the paper first and make notes without looking at the abstract first. Then compare your notes with the abstract. Are there significant differences between them? Think about how you can use an abstract as a summary. (Remember, reading abstracts is not a substitute for reading the whole article.)

☺ access, in a limited way through translations, research papers in other languages.

Departments expect abstracts with practical reports and dissertations, but not with every tutorial essay. If you are asked to prepare an abstract of a paper or book, it might be useful to check off these points:

✔ Give the citation in full.

✔ Lay out the principal arguments following the order in the full text.

✔ Emphasise the important points; highlight new information, omit well-known material.

✔ Be as brief, but as complete, as possible.

✔ Avoid repetition and ambiguity. Use short sentences and appropriate technical terms.

✔ Include the author's principal interpretations and conclusions but do not add your own commentary. This is not a 'critical' essay.

Aim for about 120–250 words. The first draft will probably be too long and need editing.

16.2 EXECUTIVE SUMMARIES

An effective executive summary (ES) is a very much shortened version of a document and the style is generally less literary than an abstract. The format often involves bullet points or numbered sections. The general rule on length is one to two sides only, on the basis that really, really, really busy people will not read more. An ES can be part of an organisation's promotional material, in which case an upbeat, clear style with lots of impact is advantageous.

An ES written as part of a student exercise would normally be short, summarising a report or essay in one side. Longer ESs can be found on government websites, summarising longer documents. These may have a PR aim, for example to acquaint the reader with government policy in an accessible manner, rather than expecting a reader to tackle a draft Act of Parliament or Congress. See DoH (1999) for the Blair government's policy on adult mental health as an example.

The essential element when writing an ES is to eliminate all extraneous material. Do not include examples, analogous material, witticisms, pictures, diagrams, figures or appendices, or be repetitious or repetitious or repetitious. An ES will do the following:

✔ be brief

✔ be direct

✔ include all main issues

✔ indicate impacts, pros and cons

✔ place stress on results and conclusions

✔ include recommendations with costs and timescales if germane.

Chapter headings and subheadings may present a starting scheme for bullet points. Look at the discussion and conclusion sections for the main points the author is making. You can find examples of ESs through **Try This 16.2**.

On p. 106 the use of abbreviations was suggested as a way of speeding up writing, dealing with longer words or with phrases repeated regularly. How do you view the use of 'ES' rather than 'executive summary' in this chapter? Should this style be adopted? Note that when the phrase first appears, (ES) occurs afterwards to indicate that this abbreviation will be used thereafter.

TRY THIS 16.2 – Executive summaries

Have a look at some of these on-line sites and note the different styles of ES, or search for your own sites. Executive+summary will start a search; add *+government* or *+health* to refine your search area. As with all www-related exercises some sites may be defunct. Try to work when the system is not too slow.

APA (1999) *What practitioners should know about working with older adults: A summary* [on-line], American Psychological Association, US. http://www.apa.org/pi/aging/practitioners/executive.html. Accessed 27 March 2000.

Harrison, W.A. (1999). *Psychological disorders as consequences of involvement in motor vehicle accidents: A discussion and recommendations for a research program* [on-line], Monash University Accident Research Centre – Report #153, Monash University, Australia. http://www.general.monash.edu.au/MURAC/rptsum/es153.htm. Accessed 27 March 2000.

Hewison, J. (1999). *Genetic counselling for sex-linked and other disorders* [on-line] Project MCH 04-09, London: Department of Health. http://www.doh.gov.uk/research/mch/studies/execsum4-09.htm. Accessed 14 April 2000.

NHS Information Authority (1999). *An information strategy for the modern NHS 1998–2005* [on-line]. http://www.enablingpp.exec.nhs.uk/IMT/strategy.htm. Accessed 12 April 2000.

NHSiS (1999). *The National Health Service in Scotland Quarterly Bulletin No. 8* [on-line], National Health Service in Scotland. http://www.scotland.gov.uk/health/nhsqb/nhs8-01.asp. Accessed 27 March 2000. [The Scottish NHS's review of performance over the previous 3 months, against a set of previously published objectives. This document has a half-page abstract and a page-long list of bulleted summary points.]

Seymour, C.A., Thomason, M.J., Chalmers, R.A., Addison, G.M., Bain, M.D., Cockburn, F., Littlejohns, P., Lord, J. & Wilcox, A.H. (1997). Neonatal screening for inborn errors of metabolism: a systematic review. *Health Technology Assessment,* 1 (11) (ES) [on-line]. http://www.hta.nhsweb.nhs.uk/execsumm/SUMM111.HTM. Accessed 12 April 2000.

SSB-NRCASS (1997). *Report of the workshop on biology-based technology to enhance human well-being and function in extended space exploration* [on-line], Space Studies Board of the National Research Council at the Center for Advanced Space Studies, Houston, Texas, US. http://www.nas.edu/ssb/wbsees.htm. Accessed 27 March 2000.

UNDCP 1998 *World drug report* [on-line], United Nations General Assembly Special Session on the World Drug Problem, New York, 8–10 June 1998. http://www.odccp.org:80/adhoc/gass/wdr.htm. Accessed 12 April 2000.

US Department of Health and Human Services (1994). *Preventing tobacco use among young people* [on-line], Report of the Surgeon General, Atlanta, Georgia, US. http://www.cdc.gov/tobacco/sgryth2.htm. Accessed 27 March 2000. [This is an example of a long ES, eight and a half sides plus references. The headings directly mirror the reports' chapter titles and subheadings. There are one to three paragraphs under each subheading.]

16.3 REFERENCES

Asner, M. (1999). *A few pages may dictate your proposal's fate: Executive summary lays foundation for success* [on-line]. http://www.gtreseller.com/publications/may99/winningproposals/winningproposals.shtm. Accessed 10 April 2000.

DoH (Department of Health) (1999). *National Service Framework for Mental Health: Modern Standards and Service Models* (Sept. 1999) Department of Health [16576 COMMS 30k 1P].

Parrott III, L. (1999). *How to Write Psychology Papers*, 2nd edn. New York: Longman.

Psychograms 3

Try these psychological anagrams. Answers on p. 266.

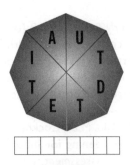

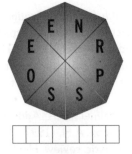

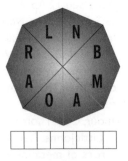

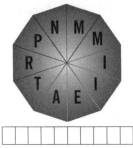

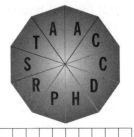

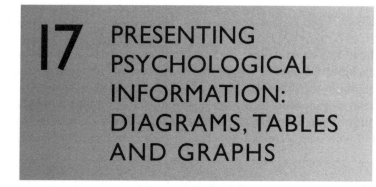

17 PRESENTING PSYCHOLOGICAL INFORMATION: DIAGRAMS, TABLES AND GRAPHS

To seek out new data, to boldly code where no one . . .

Diagrams, tables and graphs usually save lots of words, they are good value especially in exam answers where time is short and they give implicit evidence of psychological thinking. Presenting psychological information graphically exemplifies and clarifies relationships.

Throughout your student career someone has been hounding you about labelling, scales, legends, keys and titles because every figure must have them. So why stop adding them at university? No one will bother to chase you for them, or indeed mention it. Tutors will, however, deduct marks for their non-appearance. This is not because life is grossly unfair, which it is, but because all psychologists label figures correctly, don't they! The skill here is to give careful, consistent attention to detail and completeness. Don't forget to acknowledge sources with references, as in 'Figure n – My title for this figure (after Picture and Data 2010)'.

There are deliberate mistakes in most of the diagrams in this chapter, so exercise your critical skills. Look at each to see where you would do better.

17.1 TABLES

Most word-processing packages can import tables and graphs from spreadsheet, database and statistical packages to brighten up your report or essay. A smart graph is not a substitute for psychological analysis; but then it never did any harm either.

Things to avoid! avoid! avoid! Look critically at Table 17.1.

	1951	1961	1971	1981	1991	2001
85 + years	0.2	0.3	0.5	0.6	0.8	1.0
75–84	1.5	1.8	2.1	2.6	3.0	3.0
65–74	3.6	3.9	4.6	5.0	4.9	4.6
Total	5.3	6.0	7.2	8.2	8.7	8.6

Table 17:1 Older people in Britain (number in millions)

Table 17.1 contains correct data, but is awkward to read across the lines with this background, and is not properly referenced. It might be important to you to highlight the difference between the numbers in the different age groups, and the total population. Is the style in Table 17.2 better? Note the inclusion of the information source in the caption. This makes it clear to the reader that these are not your own, primary data, but are taken from another source.

	1951	1961	1971	1981	1991	2001
85 + years	0.2	0.3	0.5	0.6	0.8	1.0
75–84	1.5	1.8	2.1	2.6	3.0	3.0
65–74	3.6	3.9	4.6	5.0	4.9	4.6
Total	5.3	6.0	7.2	8.2	8.7	8.6

Table 17:2 Older people in Britain (number in millions). Source: Bond et al. (1993); OPCS (1993)

17.2 GRAPHS

Points about clarity of style and presentation are as true for graphs as for tables. Data should be plotted accurately and all the information should be clearly labelled – watch out that axis labels are full and explanatory. Predictor variables are usually plotted on the horizontal (x) axis, and criterion variables on the vertical (y) axis. See Bowen (1992) for good advice and lots of examples.

Figure 17.1 is an example of a graph with scales on both axes and a key but there is no title, the y-axis 0–40 scale is not labelled and has no units, and so the graph fails as an example of good practice.

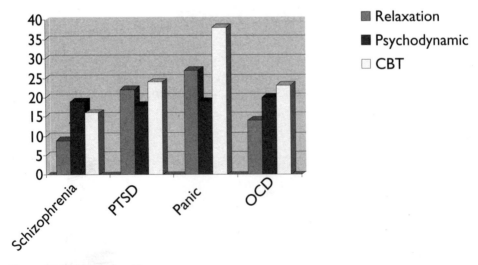

Figure 17:1 No title here!!

Is Figure 17.2 any more successful? There is a figure title, the y-axis scale is 0-100 but is still not labelled, are these numbers of people or per centages? Will your readers know what CBT, PTSD and OCD stand for? Provided that abbreviations are explained in the text there is no problem, it is worth double-checking.

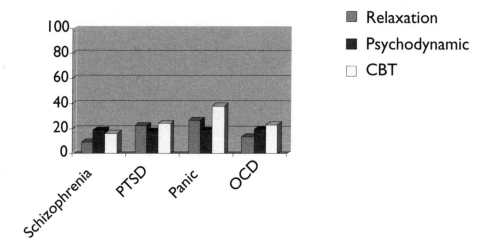

Figure 17:2 Effectiveness of different forms of therapy for different presenting problems

It is always a sound idea to indicate the error or bias in data; this is often crucial information when drawing inferences. Add error bars to graphs where the main plot is of mean, median or modal values. They indicate the range and therefore the precision of the data. Figure 17.3 illustrates the difference between a graph with and without the error bars. Graph B is more useful since it shows the considerable variability that is hidden by the mean. Is the y-axis appropriate? Why 0–150? Should it stop at 100?

Figure 17.4 shows a scatter plot with the regression equation for the line and r value added, but look at it carefully. Is this graph OK? It looks smart, and including the regression line and r value is the right thing to do, BUT:

✘ When x = 0, does y = 13.2? Extend the regression line to the y axis and check. Oh dear, where did this equation come from?

✘ Does the line fit the data? Is there a balanced distribution of points above and below the line? In fact the regression equation is right, it is the regression line that is incorrect. Oh dear.

✘ There is no citation in the title acknowledging the source of the data.

Good points:

✔ It looks smart.

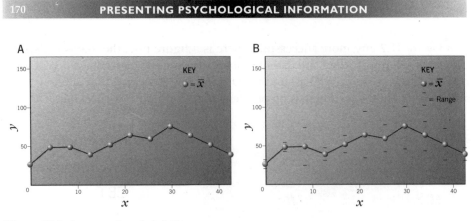

Figure 17:3 Are error bars helpful?

✔ There is an equation for the line and correlation coefficient, and it is correct.

✔ The line is in the same range as the data; it is not arbitrarily extended to the margins.

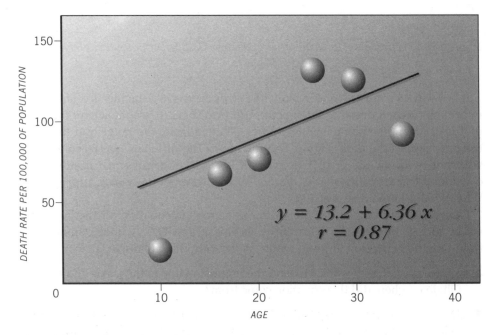

Figure 17:4 Death rates by age cohorts

17.3 TO TABLE OR TO GRAPH? THAT IS THE QUESTION (AS SOMEONE ONCE SAID)

Deciding whether to present data on a table or graph may mean experimenting to see which approach gets the message across clearly and without clutter. The following are examples of inappropriate tables and graphs. Try to avoid the errors they exemplify. What is the problem with Table 17.3?

The data in Table 17.3 are taken from the *Journal of Irreproducible Events*, **576**(3) (Sugar a & Cocoa, 2005). Generally you should reference the source as you viewed it (Sugar & Cocoa, 2005). BUT is this one you need to check before quoting any further? The UK, Eire and France can all be described as being in Northern Europe, but Greece? The Sugar & Cocoa (2005) table title is reproduced here exactly as in their text, but is it right? If you quote this as they did, might you be perpetuating an error? Should the total and per cent lines be highlighted differently for greater clarity?

Figure 17.5 is a classic example of how not to present a graph! Mixed variables, numbers and per centages on the x-axis, no y-axis legend, and there is no figure caption. This graphic FAILS.

Pie charts can be useful, but Figure 17.6 is unhelpful where percentage values for each segment are similar or where there are many fine slices. There is no figure caption. ANOTHER FAIL.

It is hard to imagine something worse than Figure 17.7, although rescaling has made the diagram more legible. Joining the data points implies there is a causal connection between the x-axis variables, the y-axis label has no units, there is no figure caption and, most disastrously, the whole numbers and percentages are presented in the same data set. FAIL WITH BLACK STARS.

Incidence of addiction to sweet products by country	UK	Eire	France	Greece
Number with addiction to chocolate	11	10	15	10
Number with addiction to all sweets	37	26	43	23
Total	49	35	58	33
Per cent	22	28	26	30

Table 17:3 Rates of addiction to chocolate and sweets in Northern Europe (from Sugar & Cocoa, 2050)

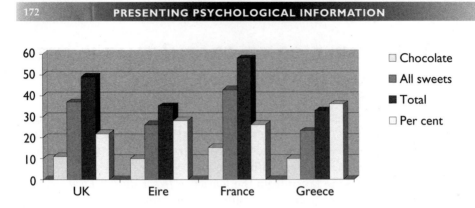

Figure 17:5

Figure 17:6

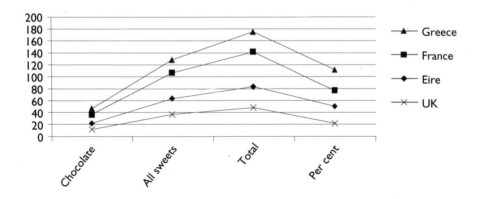

Figure 17:7

With the data in Figure 17.8, on the other hand, you can use the 'join-the-dots' technique; there is a logical day-to-day link; both axes are labelled; the full stress scale (0–100) is on the y-axis although the highest value is 80; this graph is a PASS.

Now pretend you are an examiner and interpret the graphs in Figure 17.9.

Have you really looked at Figure 17.9? . . . Then read on. The problems that arise with this figure appear in many dissertations and reports. Participants' scores on eight different tests on four different occasions are presented, or is it the same test on eight occasions and four different groups of people? Printing on four separate pages often compounds difficulties of comparison and interpretation. Problems are as follows:

✗ The y-axis label is there, but what is RT, in response to what, and what are the units?

✗ The x-axis changes from A–H in graph A to 1–8 in Graph B; were these different tests, and nothing to do with those in Graphs A, C and D?

✗ The x-axis label changes from test to sub-test and back again.

✗ Using A–D for the graph labels and A–H for the tests is not wrong, but is likely to lead to confusion.

HOWEVER, these are minor quibbles compared to the y-axis values: Graph C appears to have lots of high values, but they are the lowest of all. Graph B looks as if most of the values are low but they are the highest observations.

This presentation problem arises primarily because some computer packages scale the y-axis according to the range of the data. This is a potential disaster for 'compare and contrast' purposes. Graph C, where the highest value is less than 2, is scaled to fill the page – as is Graph B, where the highest value is 260. Avoid the problem by scaling the y-axis to a common height, or by exporting the data to a package which allows scaling of the y-axis to the values YOU want, or by hand-drawing the graphs (which will be perfectly acceptable). Where the reader needs to compare graphs, try to put them on the same page. Photo reduction and pasting a number of graphs on a page is often the efficient option, saving hours of unproductive, frustrating fiddling with printouts.

A value like the 260 in Graph B is so far outside the range of the rest of the data that it must prompt a check on its accuracy; it may be right or should it be 26 or 2.6? This may mean looking back at your raw data and takes time, BUT it is a job you have to take the time to do; if this is a mis-entry the psychological

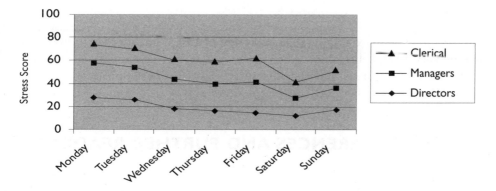

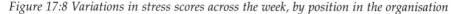

Figure 17:8 Variations in stress scores across the week, by position in the organisation

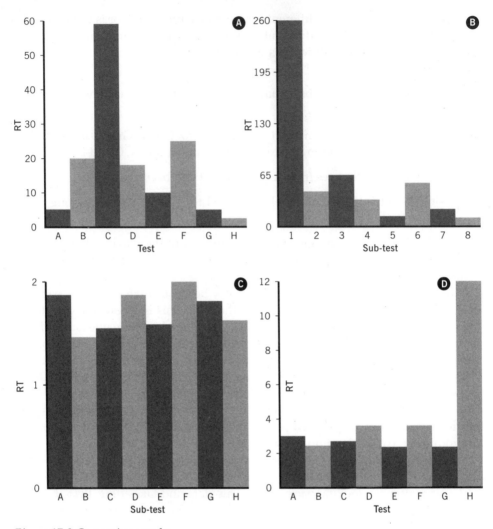

Figure 17:9 Comparing graphs

interpretation changes totally. Data entry errors are perilously easy to make and require very careful checking.

The advice in this chapter applies to all essays, reports, projects, slides for presentations and posters, etc., not just to dissertations.

17.4 REFERENCES AND FURTHER READING

Bond, J. Coleman, P. & Peace, S. (Eds) (1993). *Ageing in Society: An Introduction to Social Gerontology*, 2nd edn. London: Sage.

Bowen, R.W. (1992). *Graph It! How to Make, Read and Interpret Graphs*. New York: Prentice Hall.

Colman, A.M. (Ed.) (1995). *Psychological Research Methods and Statistics*. London: Longman.

Harris, P. (1986). *Designing and Reporting Experiments*. Oxford: Oxford University Press.

OPCS (Office of Population Censuses and Surveys) (1993). *The 1991 Census Persons Aged 60 and Over, Great Britain*. London: HMSO.

Parrott III, L. (1999). *How to Write Psychology Papers*, 2nd edn. London: Longman.

Psychologists aim to do it with 95 per cent confidence.

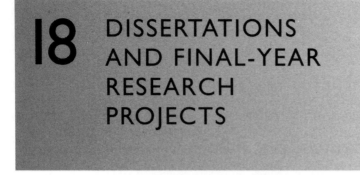

18 DISSERTATIONS AND FINAL-YEAR RESEARCH PROJECTS

Don't start vast dissertations with half vast ideas!

Dissertations and final-year research projects form a significant part of many psychology degree programmes. Each department has its own timing, style, expectations of length and monitoring procedures. Most departments run briefing sessions so everyone is aware of the rules. Missing such briefings is a BAD idea; one of your better ideas will be to reread the briefing material every six weeks or so to remind yourself of milestones and guidelines.

This chapter does not in any way attempt to replace or pre-empt departmental guidelines and advice. It does aim to answer some of the questions asked by students in the first two years of a degree when a dissertation is sometimes viewed as a kind of academic Everest, to be assaulted without aid of crampons or oxygen, and to say something about timescales for effective planning. More detailed information will be found in Parrott (1999) and Robson (1993). Skills addressed during dissertation and project research include autonomous working, setting and meeting personal targets in research, problem-solving and professional report production.

18.1 DISSERTATIONS ARE NOT ESSAYS; PROJECTS ARE NOT PRACTICALS. WHAT IS THE DIFFERENCE?

Getting a dissertation together is a very different activity from assembling an essay, requiring different skills. You look in detail at a particular topic, take stock of current knowledge of an issue, and offer some further, small, contribution to the discussion. The project is an opportunity, given a great deal of time, to explore material, develop an idea, design and conduct studies, analyse information and draw mature conclusions from the results. The results need not be mind-blowing (discovering an infallible cure for depression is unlikely!), and the world will not end if your research has a completely unexpected answer.

Essentially these are opportunities to enquire systematically into a topic or problem that interests you, and to report the findings for the benefit of the next person to explore that material. Dissertations and projects are sometimes published; aiming to produce a product that is a worthy of publication is wholly appropriate.

18.2 TIME MANAGEMENT

Typically you will explore a topic by yourself, making all the decisions about when, where, how and in what detail to work. While supervisors will advise and give clues as to what the department expects, basically it is down to you to plan and organise. Look at the handing-in date, say 1 May of final year; now work backwards:

(a) Allow three weeks for 'slippage', flu, visitors, Easter, career interviews, despondency (April).

(b) Writing-up time – allow 3–4 weeks – OK it should take 6–7 days but you have other things to do (March).

(c) Analysing the data, fighting the computer systems, getting printouts (February).

(d) Recovering from New Year, start-of-year exams, career interviews (January).

(e) End-of-term parties, PsychoSoc Balls, preparing for Christmas, end-of-term exhaustion, Christmas, (December).

(f) Gathering data from reluctant participants, local schools and hospitals, observational fieldwork, rescheduling interviews when your participants get the flu, have visitors, etc., . . . allow 6–8 weeks (October and November).

(g) Have an idea (no idea), check out the library, think about it, talk to supervisor, have more (too many) ideas, feel confused and worried, talk to supervisor . . . settle on a topic, allow 6–8 weeks (September and October).

A final-year project or dissertation, designed to be done between September and May, will consume chunks of time through the period. Even with an early start date (often meaning late September, because the first couple of weeks are needed for recovering from the vacation, starting new modules, catching up with friends and partying) a 1 May finish is very close. It is worth asking about planning in Year 2? Can data collection be done in advance? Can you check out potential participant organisations at Easter of Year 2? Summer vacation research, especially work abroad for cross-cultural comparisons, needs advanced planning, clear formulation of research questions and a workable, planned timetable.

This piece of work should not be rushed if it is to get a high mark. Most low marks go to those who start very late and those who leave the crucial thinking elements to the last week. You may have noticed useful thoughts occurring a couple of days after a discussion or meeting. You wake up thinking, 'Why didn't I say . . .'. High marks are awarded to dissertations in their third rather than their first draft. This means being organised so that there is thinking time at the end.

18.3 CHOOSING TOPICS

You need an idea to explore or hypothesis to test that is psychological in nature and, ideally, one that captures your imagination. If you are not interested, you are unlikely to be motivated to give it time and thought. If you fear your future might involve wearing a red cap and asking whether people want chips, consider a project that is relevant to future areas of employment, demonstrating your interest and skills to a future employer and giving you an insight into marketing, behavioural training, etc. A project may present an opportunity to indulge a hobby, like salsa dancing, or to visit someone, BUT must address a good question, as in 'the impact of regular salsa dancing on energy intake and expenditure balance', or 'the organisation of shift work rotas in a very large organisation in Madrid (because my boyfriend's doing his year abroad there)'.

Any piece of research involves exploring a topic, examining it from a number of perspectives and looking for solutions, interpretations or answers to issues or problems. The most awkward part of a dissertation is sorting out the questions to tackle. A good research topic will approach an interesting question in a way that can be addressed, to a reasonable extent, in the time and with the facilities available to you. Aim for a focused topic and avoid the 'splodge' approach where too huge a topic is discussed too generally, like 'a study of infant development/visual perception/gender'.

Questions that start *How . . .?, To what extent . . .?, How do factors X and Y affect . . ..?* will help to focus thinking. Trying to come to judgements may be more difficult, as in *Is Cognitive Behaviour Therapy more useful than . . .?* Topics that are both very big and largely unanswerable should be avoided, like *Will psychology have relevance in health-services planning in the second half of the twenty-first century?* Avoid too those where data are impossible to obtain, as in *A discussion of parapsychological phenomena in the West Indies,* or *The perceptual experience of the colour green among the Dani of New Guinea, using tachistoscopic presentation of Stroop-type stimuli.*

- Think small at the start.

Spotting gaps

Throughout the degree course make a note of thoughts like: 'Why is it like that?', 'Is it really like that in the people, groups, situations, adverts, workplaces that I know?', 'Is that really right?', 'But Professor Smart said . . .'. Also, note when lecturers say, 'But this area hasn't been explored yet', or 'This was studied in the 1940s by Long and Forgotten, but no developments since'. Another entry point is when an argument seems to have gone from alpha to gamma without benefit of beta. Now, it may be that the lecturer does not have time to explore beta on the way; there may be a great deal known. Alternatively, beta may be unexplored, may be a little black hole in search of a torch.

Having spotted an apparent 'hole' take a couple of hours in the library and on the www to see what is available. Many a tutor has sent a student to research a possible topic, to be met by the response, 'The topic is not on because there are no references available'. SUCCESS IS FINDING LITTLE OR NOTHING. This is what you want – a topic that is relatively unexplored so that you can say something about it. When researching for an essay you want lots of definitive documentary evidence to support arguments; for a project or dissertation you want to find little or contradictory material to support your contention that this is a topic worth exploring. If there is lots of literature, that's OK too; use it as a framework, a point to leap off from, to explore and extend. Check out areas where the published literature goes out of date very quickly. Can you cast twenty-first century ideas on an older topic?

Browsing

This is a primary dissertation research technique. Try to immerse yourself in materials that are both directly related and tangential to the topic. Wider reading adds to your perspectives, and should give insight into alternative approaches and techniques. You cannot use them all, but you can make the examiner aware that you know they exist.

There are still lots of questions to be answered; few of the lines of psychological enquiry have been sorted out, though one or two are done to death. Topics go in cycles. There are fads that relate to whatever is taught in the 2 weeks before dissertation briefings, and standard chestnuts often expressed as, 'I want to do something on children's understanding / attentional processes / the effects of stroke / crime in the city / parenting'. These are quite positive statements compared to the student who wants to do 'something social' or 'something to do with real people' or 'something while canyoning in France'. The choice of topic is your responsibility. There may be a list of suggested areas or particular questions that tutors are happy to supervise, and many departments make past dissertations available to read and consult. It can feel hard and confusing but thinking around possible topics and deciding on a valid research question is part of the dissertation activity.

Take care if you choose to investigate a personal interest. You might do an extremely good dissertation on 'maternal separation anxiety', 'the experience of carers of people with X syndrome' or 'drug use in youth and club culture'. You will get into deep water, and probably obtain lower marks, if you interpret all your respondents' comments as being guilt-ridden, present an entirely positive description of the altruism of carers or merely relate your 'clubbing till dawn' activities. Writing from any of these perspectives would be fine in a newspaper article that seeks to put across a single viewpoint. Researching is an objective academic exercise and requires objective reporting. If you feel extremely strongly about an issue you might write an excellent or a direly unbalanced report. Think about it.

18.4 DIFFERENT TYPES OF PROJECT

Once you've decided on your topic it's time to think about the research strategy that best fits your needs and interests. You will be familiar, from your courses on research design/methods and statistics, with the idea that psychologists employ different methods of collecting information. Broadly, the approaches taken are experimental, quasi-experimental, survey and case study, each of which has advantages and disadvantages.

Experimental studies

The experimental approach is characterised by assigning participants to treatment (e.g., giving them measured amounts of alcohol to drink) and control (e.g., giving them non-alcoholic, but otherwise equivalent drinks) conditions, and measuring the effect on a particular outcome (e.g., accuracy in dart-throwing). So, the researcher systematically manipulates an independent variable (alcohol–no alcohol) and measures the dependent variable (score on the darts board). If there is a substantial difference in the dependent variable between the treatment and control participants, then the researcher can make a causal inference that this difference is due to the manipulation – in this case, drinking alcohol improves darts playing. To be confident with this inference, you have to be confident that the conditions of the experiment were identical, but for the manipulation. This means you have to find some way of equating the groups. With a truly random assignment of people to different conditions, a whole host of other variables can be controlled for, and it becomes possible to generalise the effects from the sample to the population from which they were drawn. If your sample is large enough you might even be able to generalise to the population at large – whheeee, statistics time!

The main advantage of the experimental approach is the extent to which you have control over the situation, including the location and timing of events. Some researchers argue that the degree of control over the environment and participants' activities is crucial in obtaining accurate data about the phenomenon of interest. On the other hand, others argue that the experimental situation is simplified to the point where it becomes very unlike the 'real world'. What differences might you observe if you ran the darts experiment in a laboratory compared with in your local pub?

It is important to think about the internal validity of the study too. While you might be certain that something has happened (the alcohol has had an effect), can you explain *why*? We usually expect alcohol to have a negative impact on motor co-ordination, so it's odd that this particular set of results show fine motor co-ordinated activity has improved. Is there anything else about the experimental set-up that could have contributed to this effect? Maybe it's something to do with the anxiety-reducing effect of alcohol – perhaps the decreased level of anxiety about performing the task causes the elevation in performance. As soon as you move out of the lab into the field, your control over confounding variables, and thus the internal validity of the study, decreases. Be on the lookout for confounding variables.

Quasi-experimental studies

Sometimes variables are impossible, or at least extremely difficult, to manipulate. It's pretty unusual to be able to change someone's age, height, sex, country of birth, parents. When researchers are interested in such variables they employ quasi-experimental designs, in which participants are *not randomly assigned to conditions*. Instead they are assigned to different groups on the basis of differences in the variable(s) of interest.

Imagine researchers are interested in the influence of age on performance in the darts study. In order to test this experimentally the procedure is very similar to that described above, but instead of a randomised sample of participants, the researchers will find equal numbers of 20-year-olds and 70-year-olds to take part. Ideally, they will also include two control groups who would not consume any alcohol, one of the young people and one of the older people.

There's a distinct problem here though. Since the participants have not been randomly assigned to conditions, we can't make conclusive causal inferences; they may not be valid. Suppose our researchers found that the younger group performed better than the older – would it be OK for them to infer that the alcohol has a more powerful effect on younger adults? Could the difference be due simply to the age difference of the participants? NO. Older people, on average, have poorer eyesight and mobility and may have higher performance anxiety, along with many other differences. Any one of these differences could be responsible for the observed effects. The problem of the extraneous variable – keep it in mind.

Surveys (aka correlational methodology)

Quasi-experimental studies aren't the only way to deal with variables we cannot manipulate. The survey is frequently used in social science research, and comes disguised as market research, job reviews, service evaluations and opinion polls. They may appear in interview or questionnaire format. A researcher can gather information about several naturally occurring variables at the same time, and explore the relationships between them. This is why this approach is often called the correlational method.

Surveys provide a simple and straightforward means of collecting a lot of different data from people at one time, and can be administered almost anywhere. This contrasts with the experimental approach, which is usually restricted to looking at the effect of a limited number and type of variable. Postal surveys can be used to collect information from people in the population who might otherwise be difficult to get hold of, and can also be quite cost-effective. Some respondents find postal questionnaires with questions on sensitive areas, like sexual preference or eating habits, easier to respond to frankly. On the other hand face-to-face interviews give the interviewer opportunities to clarify understanding and encourage the interviewee's participation. Think about the type and level of detail you want in your data to help you decide which technique to adopt.

There are disadvantages too. Depending on the topic of enquiry, and the style of questions, respondents may try to show themselves in a good light, rather than be completely accurate about their feelings or attitudes. It is common to have very low response rates to postal questionnaires – perhaps 10–30 per cent. What might that mean about the representativeness of your sample? How will you able to spot whether respondents have understood your questions as you intended, or whether they have taken the exercise seriously?

Piloting your materials is important – get your housemates to check their understanding of your questions. Avoid the trap of an excess of closed questions or 'double-barrelled' constructions.

Do you think that the government was wrong to . . .?   Yes ——   No ——

Supposing they have a different idea about the government's action, or no opinion at all?

Do you think that Newcastle United should adopt a purple strip or
an orange strip?   Yes ——   No ——

How will you code a 'yes' response – as a vote for purple, for orange, or for any colour as long as it's purple or orange??

Additionally, in interviews, the responses may be affected by the skill, experience, personality and motivation of the interviewer. If you're tired or longing to get home to catch up with the latest S-Club7 video, this is likely to leak out non-verbally; your interviewee will feel that you're not really interested and will be much less forthcoming. Pilot your interview with members of your sample population – that way you can be confident that your questions generate the kind of information you need to explore your research question. Most people feel a little apprehensive when they start interviewing – like so many other things, your control over such feelings will improve with practice.

Case studies

The above approaches typically involve large numbers of participants. In case studies the focus turns to a different kind of sample, the individual, or in some cases a group, small, like the family, or perhaps larger and more varied like an occupational group. At one end of the continuum, researchers might track the cognitive performance of a single individual with a particular form of brain damage; at the other they might wish to explore how a community has responded to and dealt with a local tragedy.

A criticism levelled at the case-study approach is that the findings cannot be generalised to the population at large; they are specific to the particular case being studied. Of course, this isn't a problem if you are interested in this specific population. If you do wish your findings to be more generalisable, then replication is a good idea. Another issue is that such studies are based on the researcher's observations of behaviour and context. This means there is an opportunity to provide a very rich examination and description of a situation or behaviour, but it does not allow us to make any conclusive statements about the relationship, to define cause and effect. Nevertheless, as well as generating information to support a theory, a well-designed case study can generate the evidence to refute theories by demonstrating that a behaviour the theory predicts ought to happen, does not.

Beware

There is a temptation to feel you should show one thing or another, that there is a definitive answer to the question. In most psychological situations there are large areas of both subjective and objective disagreement. Much of what we know is an approximation. We hope to have the best information, given the information-gathering procedure, available at the time. Interview-based information is subjective, relying on people's openness, there being time to collect enough material and one's own subjectivity. It is particularly important to acknowledge this and consider the extent of it when you are interpreting qualitative material. Even objective data have their inaccuracies. Psychologists working with demographic information from a census are aware that even where the census is well regulated, individuals avoid the count for personal reasons and errors occur in collection and calculation procedures. Knowledge is partial: go for your best interpretation on what you know now, but keep looking for and recognise the areas of doubt in your arguments.

A tutor is especially important in warning against falling for trite arguments that can appear beguiling. Watch for moral arguments that are acceptable in one culture or time but inappropriate in another culture or time. Evaluating gender roles among the Azande using the standards and attitudes of a twenty-first-century Northern European will not work. Arguing that something 'is the best' is also fraught with danger. There is a good case to argue that Skinner is the greatest psychologist, but that accolade, we would argue, goes to either William James or Eddie Fitzgerald. Some less well-read persons might want to give this credit to Eric Berne, John Gray or . . . These last two sentences are extreme, unbalanced and unsupported as they stand. (They could keep a tutorial group going for some time! The answer, of course, is Fitz.) Avoid unsupported arguments and strong language unless there is overwhelming evidence.

18.5 PRE-PILOT THINKING

Resources

How accessible, and in what form, are the data you need? What are the implications for the numbers of participants in each cell, or the way in which you construct your interview questions? How long will it take to get your materials together? How will you organise the printing and copying of your questionnaire? Do you need to book the tachistoscope/tape recorder/polygraph? Are there enough electronic personal organisers for the size of sample you want? Do you need to do any programming? How many unemployed people do you need to get hold of, and what would be a good source? Finding out about the availability of resources is something you need to get done early on. Pilot work helps here.

Ethics

Think about ethical issues – what procedures does your department have in place? Are there any forms to complete? Will you have to apply to any external agency for ethical approval of your procedure? Think about what taking part in your research will involve for your participants. To what extent will they be inconvenienced or put at risk? How will you set up the research context? What opportunity will participants have to give informed consent? How will you debrief them? What means will you employ to ensure that the information you receive from them will be kept confidential? Again, these issues must be thought about early on, and some may be tested through pilot work.

Use **Try This 19.1 – Ethical implications** (p. 196) at an early stage of your deliberations. Asking yourself the questions raised there and being clear about the answers will help your research design.

18.6 PILOT WORK

Just about every lecturer nags every student to do a pilot; about 99 per cent of students do not bother and about 99 per cent regret it. PILOT WORK IS A GOOD IDEA. It allows you to work out your timings, try out a questionnaire or run a mini-programme, improve the presentation of your context to participants. Then you analyse the pilot dataset as if it were the entire set. Life is too complicated and the environment much too complex for anyone to get everything right first time. A pilot shows that there are other angles and other people to consult, suggests other variables to measure, demonstrates that your presence is essential, indicates other things you could do to enhance the research. More than one student has discovered that their testing space has been double-booked, or is right next door to where the barbershop quartet rehearses. Make sure you have all the right equipment, materials, information sheets and a complete procedural checklist.

At the end of the pilot ask yourself:

? Is this the best approach?

? Can I get all the data needed to address the hypothesis?

? Can the project be done in the time allowed?

? If not, revise the methodology.

18.7 THE FORMAT AND ASSESSMENT

A dissertation or thesis is a formal piece of writing. The reader expects the author to adhere to the 'rules', make the presentation consistent and tidy and observe the word-length requirements. If possible ensure the same typeface is used throughout, that there are page numbers on ALL pages, that all the figures and tables are included (with their titles or captions in consistent positions), and that you double-check the university guidelines and follow them, especially the WORD LENGTH. The general format is roughly along the lines given in Figure 18.1. Treat the page lengths as suggestions. There are plenty of high-quality dissertations submitted in different page combinations.

Find the marking guidelines your department adopts or see Figure 18.2. There are many variations. Some departments ask for an initial plan that counts, others do not. Remember the percentage distributions are only a guide; mark distributions vary considerably depending on the nature of the dissertation.

Section	Contents		Page length
0	Title page, Acknowledgements, Abstract, Table of contents, Table of figures.		
1	Introduction, Brief background, Research aims, Signpost thesis layout.		2–3
2	Literature review, summary of material relevant to this research. Links to psychology generally.		4–8
3	**Qualitative thesis**	**Quantitative thesis**	
	Methodology, a description of your research approach or discussion and evaluation of first theme/idea/concept.	Methodology – your research process, techniques used, criticism of techniques and evaluation of their accuracy and representativeness.	2 – Piece of string
4	Discussion and evaluation of second theme/idea/concept/	Results, with tabulations and graphs as required.	Piece of string
5	Discussion and evaluation of third theme/idea/concept, synthesis of themes and alternatives.	Interpretation of results, evaluation of accuracy and representativness, sensitivity analysis if relevant.	Another piece of string
6	Implications for future research. 'What I would have done if I had known at the start what I know now.' Conclusions.		1–2 1 1
Appendix	Datasets if required. Example copy of questionnaire. Computer program. Sample of interview transcripts.		Minimise

Figure: 18.1 Typical dissertation formats

Dissertation assessment	Please comment using following headings as appropriate
Planning phase *Clarity in formulation of project? Originality in formulation of project? Independent development of project?*	**10%**
Abstract	**5%**
Literature review *Relevance of literature selected? Comprehensive? Critical comments on literature?*	**15%**
Methodology *Appropriate to topic? Successful in execution? Followed plan and adapted it appropriately?*	**20%**
Analysis and interpretation *Planned? Appropriate? Extent to which aims were met? Consciousness of limitations?*	**25%**
Discussion and conclusions *Logical and thought through? Sustainability of conclusions? Suggestions for future research?*	**15%**
Presentation *Quality of figures, tables and photographs? References? Appendices? Page numbers? Appropriate length?*	**10%**
Degree of supervision required *Did the student take the initiative? Any illness or personal problems?*	
Further comments	

Figure: 18.2 Dissertation assessment criteria

18.8 WRITING AND WRITING UP

The term 'writing up' rather implies that it can be done in one go, and as a one-off activity. Developing ideas and seeing the implications of results takes time. Remember to write as you go. GET SOMETHING ON PAPER EVERY WEEK. Read a couple of things and then draft some paragraphs for the literature review. You can add to it when you read the next paper. Writing is part of the research activity: you read a bit, write a bit, think a bit; and the combination of these three activities tells you what you might do next. The project can also exemplify your time-management skills. Typical research patterns are mapped in Figure 18.3; the optimist's pattern is sadly misleading.

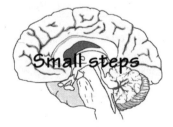

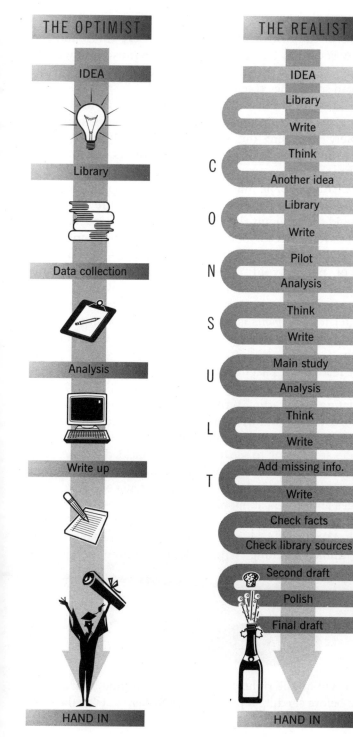

Figure 18:3 *The process of dissertation research*

Inclusive language

The publication guidelines of the British Psychological Society (BPS) and the American Psychological Association (APA) warn that all manuscripts will be edited for 'sexist language'. The idea is that even when we are trying to avoid stereotypes our language can sometimes convey bias of which we are unaware. A common example is the widespread use of the word 'man'. Consider the following: 'Man is making great strides in combating discrimination.' Clearly this isn't being achieved solely by men; the sentence could be changed to, 'Humankind is/People or Humans are making . . .'. It isn't always easy to avoid sexist language. Which pronoun do you choose in the sentence, 'When the researcher follows this procedure, she/he must . . .'? Many writers solve this one by writing in the plural – 'When researchers follow this procedure, they . . .'. Alternatively you could avoid the pronoun altogether – 'Researchers must always . . . when following this procedure'. Keep a lookout for the ways you describe men and women, boys and girls. Be consistent in the details you use – describe the physical characteristics of both; avoid consistently assigning women to subordinate roles. The idea is to be accurate and avoid bias in your writing.

Until relatively recently people who take part in research have been referred to as *subjects*. However, the term *participants* is recommended by major groups of psychologists, like the BPS and APA, because it is seen as being less demeaning to the people to whom it refers.

You cannot hope to have read all the past literature and to research all aspects of a topic. Much of dissertation management is about drawing a line, stopping reading, stopping investigating and starting writing. You are aiming to report on what you have read and discovered. Your opinions are based on cited material. If you took another year over your project, you would still be reporting on partial information. Your examiners are looking to see that you have tackled a reasonable topic in a relevant manner and drawn sensible inferences and conclusions from the findings. They do not expect you to explain why schizophrenia exists, account for all the different attitudes and beliefs about abortion or explain why surprises come in threes. Don't get overwhelmed by reading; keep it in balance. Use the checklist in **Try This 4.6** (p. 43) as a guide and remember to balance 30 minutes of www, or on-line bibliographic searching, with at least a couple of hours of reading.

Top Tips

- **Start writing**: the draft will not be right the first or second time. Ask a tutor how often they rewrite before sending a piece to a publisher. 'Lots' is the only answer worth believing.

- SPELL CHECK EVERYTHING.

- **References** matter; check that your references are properly quoted. It is miles easier to do this as you go along. Put them at the end of the document from the start. Getting to the last 3 days and then realising you have kept no record of references is like getting to within 6 inches of the summit of Everest and having to go back to base camp for flag and camera.

- **Proofread** what you have written, not what you think you wrote. Check for titles and keys on tables and figures, scale bars, units and data, and that the title page, abstract, acknowledgements and contents page are in the right format for your department. If you can leave a little time between writing and proofing, you spot more errors.

- **Proofreading is not easy**: get a flatmate to read through for grammar, spelling, bias and general understanding. If your friend understands your 'Effect of wearing pink on pulling' then so, probably, will your tutor. You can repay the favour by checking out your mate's dissertation on 'The personal habits of Compo'.

- **Abstract**: write this last.

18.9 REFERENCES AND FURTHER READING

Bell, J. (1993). *Doing Your Research Project*. Buckingham: Open University Press.

Foster, J.J. and Parker, I. (1995). *Carrying Out Investigations in Psychology*. Leicester: BPS Books.

Haslam, S.A. & McGarty, C. (1998). *Doing Psychology: An Introduction to Research Methodology and Statistics*. London: Sage Publications.

Marshall, C. & Rossman, G.B. (1995). *Designing Qualitative Research*, 2nd edn. London: Sage Publications.

Meltzoff, J. (1998). *Critical Thinking about Research: Psychology and Related Fields*. Washington, DC: American Psychological Association.

Parrott III, L. (1999). *How to Write Psychology Papers*, 2nd edn. London: Longman.

Robson, C. (1993). *Real World Research: A Resource for Social Scientists and Practitioner-Researchers*. Oxford: Blackwell.

Psycho-cryptic Crossword 2   Answers p. 267.

Across

1 I assist me in personal development (4-4)
6 See 3 down
9 Temperament distracts moose from Patty (10)
10 Adroit management of square but acrobatic troupe (4)
11 Overbearingly arbitary, a discovery of aerial dextrousness (4-8)
13 Teacher who weaves a fashionable rug (4)
14 Precedent-setting occasion recorded on cassette (4, 4)
17 Tissue shrouding amber men (8)
18 Invalid might wipe out, often with void (4)
20 Get four together and it all adds up (12)
23 Sounds like an older relative is against you (4)
24 Shorten letters, created from two with 22 and 23 (10)
25 Freud was right! – Beyond belief! (6)
26 Dodge wet tweed dog either way, but could be turned against you (3-5)

Down

2 Driving instincts to disfigure sore God (4)
3, 6 across Where were you when illumination reviewed history? (9, 6)
4 An ample sufficiency (6)
5 The analyst meanders along hypocrites' paths (15)
6 Ken seems bemused by humbled state (8)
7 A measure that is just needs time (5)
8 Kelly eats cress without regard for the consequences (10)
12 Downy, youths colour around black view (10)
15 Hidden within a shapes test perhaps? (9)
16 Full development of policy (8)
19 Vital urge to find backward pair in pool (6)
21 Marry off a French collar (5)
22 Half of the leisured tossed by water (4)

19 ETHICS

I passed the ethics exam, cheated of course.

OK, we agree, ethics is not a study skill issue BUT being aware of the associated ethical issues is a critical part of being a good psychologist, and keeping an eye out for ethical implications and nuances is part of learning to be a professional practising psychologist. Would you allow Stanley Milgram to run his obedience studies today? Many people would argue against it, on the grounds that he influenced ordinary people to behave in violent and oppressive ways towards others, and many of his participants experienced extreme distress during the course of the study. Others might argue that without Milgram's (1963) work we would not have been alerted to the possibility that lies within each of us to commit atrocities in particular circumstances. Do the behaviours revealed by this study justify the steps Milgram took to elicit them – what do you think?

The importance of research in psychology is demonstrated by the role that practicals, research methods and statistics classes have in all psychology degrees. If we want to increase our understanding of human behaviour then we need to carry out research with humans. This means we need to follow ethical, as well as scientific, guidelines. We need to be aware of the moral principles and rules of conduct that help to ensure we maintain high standards of work. It is very easy to cause hurt or harm when dealing with participants in research. Each researcher, beginner or expert, needs to consider very thoroughly the ethical implications of their projects and procedures before going ahead.

19.1 GUIDELINES FOR ETHICAL PRACTICE

Many institutions and organisations have documentation outlining recommendations for good practice. The BPS (1993) and APA (1990) have both formulated quite detailed principles and guidelines for research with human participants, and your department will have its own procedures, based on these; we strongly recommend that you familiarise yourself with them.

The BPS guidelines are organised around 10 areas of concern: general issues in research; obtaining consent from participants; the use of deception; the importance of debriefing participants; the right of participants to withdraw from the study; confidentiality of participant information; protection of the health and

> Cheerfulness may be the reason for ethics, but not the standard.

wellbeing of participants; considerations in observational research; giving advice to participants; and monitoring the research of colleagues. Many of the issues raised here will be relevant to the practicals you do in Years 1 and 2, and to your final-year research project.

19.2 FORMS TO FILL IN

Psychology research taking place in a hospital or university will almost certainly have been vetted by an ethics committee. There is one in your department. Talk to your tutor/supervisor about your project, and find out what procedures your department has for vetting undergraduate research. Many departments require you, together with your supervisor, to complete an ethics form and submit it to the committee, before you start collecting data. It might look something like Figure 19.1.

Consent

Wherever possible, you should inform the participant of the exact nature of the study. Once you have given this information and have answered all their questions, the participant will decide whether to consent to take part. Usually, researchers prepare written statements that make clear what the research will entail; it's a kind of contract between you and the participant. See Figure 19.2 for an example of a consent form. You need to consider the implications of consent for doing observational work too – unless you obtain consent to observe people, you should only observe in conditions where people would expect to be observed.

Deception

Imagine, as a favour to a mate, taking part in a study in which you simply had to sit in a room reading and listening to music. Then afterwards your mate tells you, 'Oh, by the way, we got this really neat camera and hid it in that ring-binder over there, so I've got a video of how you looked and behaved while you were in there'. How would you feel and what would you think?

Psychologists are required never to mislead participants or withhold information from them unnecessarily, particularly if participants are likely to feel uneasy or to object at debriefing. If in doubt about your procedure, check with a representative member of the target sample, and with your supervisor.

Debriefing

When people take part in your study, it is your responsibility to make sure that they have all the information they need to make sense of the nature of the study, and to answer any questions they may have. Check out people's experience of the study so that you can monitor any negative effects you hadn't thought of.

Ethics Form
Department of Psychology – Right-on University

1. **Project title**:

2. **Aims of study**:

3. **Investigator(s)**:

4. **Supervisor(s)**:

5. Will ethical approval for this project also be sought from another source (e.g., Home Office, local hospital)?   Yes / No

   If Yes, what is this source?

6. Are you aware that participants must give their <u>informed consent</u> to any investigation procedure?   Yes / No

   How will you ensure that participants have all the information they need in order to give you their informed consent?

   (Note – this is not required for studies that rely purely on questionnaires, as completion of these denotes consent)

7. What <u>inconvenience</u> might participants experience?

   What steps have you taken to minimise this?

8. Does your study involve <u>deception or the withholding of information</u>?   Yes / No

   If Yes, how will you conform to the BPS guidelines on deception?

9. How will you inform participants about their <u>right to withdraw</u>?

10. How will you ensure that personal information from your participants will be kept <u>confidential</u> and, if appropriate, anonymous?

11. <u>Protection of participants</u>

    a) Are you aware that your study should not expose participants to risks greater than those encountered in everyday life?

    b) If the procedures of your study may interact with a pre-existing medical condition in a participant, how will you find out whether participants have such a condition?

    c) If your study requires asking participants personal questions, how will you assure them that they do not have to respond?

    d) If you intend to work with children younger than 16, or with adults with impairments that may limit their understanding, how will you seek their consent? How will you seek permission from guardians?

    e) Will any researcher / investigator be exposed to any condition that may induce distress or risk (including research conducted outside the department, on sensitive topics, with certain kinds of participants)?   Yes / No

    If Yes, what steps have been taken to minimise such risks?

Figure 19:1 Example ethics form

Right-on University
Department of Psychology

Psychology of Attitudes to Ageing Study

I confirm that I agree to take part in this study. I understand that any information I provide will remain confidential, and that no one will be able to identify me from my responses.

a) I have had the opportunity to ask questions and discuss the study, and I am satisfied with the answers I have been given.
b) I have understood that the aim of the study is to explore the attitudes of young adults to older adults.
c) I have been informed that there are no disguised questions or procedures in this study.
d) I understand that I am free to choose not to answer a question without having to explain why.
e) I agree to being audio-recorded.
f) I agree to having extracts of my responses used in reports of this research.
g) I understand that I am free to withdraw at any point in the study.

Concerns about any aspect of this study may be referred to the Chair of the Ethics Committee, Department of Psychology, Right-on University.

Experimenter: Date:

Participant: Date:

Figure 19:2 Example consent form

Withdrawal

A participant comes to you a couple of days after your study and says, 'I've been thinking about your study, and I really wish I hadn't taken part now.' How do you respond?

You must make it clear to every participant that they have every right to withdraw from your study at any point. Participants have the right to withdraw their consent after the event – this means you are obliged to discard and/or destroy their data.

Confidentiality

Participants have the right to expect that any information they give you will be treated confidentially, and that they will not be identifiable from this information. You cannot publish these data without the participants' consent.

Protection

The risk that anyone takes in participating in a study should not be greater than any encountered in people's everyday routines. If your study involves physical exertion, you need to think about the risk that might pose to someone with a heart condition. If your area of interest is generally regarded as private and personal, such as sexual preferences and practices, then you need to make sure that participants will not suffer any stress, and to assure them of their right not to respond.

Work with animals

Not all psychology departments carry out work with animals, and there are many fewer opportunities for students to work with gerbils and mice than with humans. Nevertheless, ethical considerations apply here too. Wadeley (1991) recommends the following guidelines for animal research in psychology:

1 The researcher needs full knowledge of the law governing animal experimentation.

2 The researcher should have a thorough knowledge of the reactions of different species, in the interests of identifying and reducing distress.

3 Humane practices in breeding, capture, transport and care of animals, and the use of the smallest samples possible, should be observed.

4 All procedures must minimise pain and distress.

5 Invasive procedures should only be used by fully trained, competent and licensed individuals.

Top Tips

- Familiarise yourself with departmental and institutional ethical guidelines.

- Consider your study from all angles.

- Talk to your supervisor / tutor.

- Check your ideas out with someone who would 'qualify' to be in your study.

- Get rid of all ethical flaws before going any further.

- If in doubt, don't proceed.

TRY THIS 19.1 – Ethical implications

Either take a paper you are reading at present, or look at Carlson *et al.* (2000) p. 415 (Vitamin Supplements and Children's IQ) or p. 463 (Using Display Rules). Think around the ethical issues involved in doing this type of research. Make brief notes under the following headings:

? Who needs to be involved?

? Whose permission is required?

? How can consent be gained?

? How can we ensure debriefing is full and appropriate?

? How will confidentiality be ensured?

This is an area where discussion is a key skill: different individuals can have very different views.

Considering other people's perspectives is vital.

19.3 REFERENCES AND FURTHER READING

APA (American Psychological Association) (1990). Ethical principles of psychologists (amended 2 June 1989). *American Psychologist*, **45**, 390–5.

BPS (British Psychological Society) (1993). Ethical principles for conducting research with human participants. *The Psychologist*, **6**, 33–5.

Carlson, N.R., Buskit, W. & Martin, G.N. (2000). *Psychology: the Science of Behaviour*. London: Pearson Education.

Gale, A. (1995). Ethical issues in psychological research. In A.M. Colman (Ed.), *Psychological Research Methods and Statistics*. London: Longman.

Lindsay, G. (1996). Psychology as an ethical discipline and profession. *European Psychologist*, **1**(2), 79–88.

Milgram, S. (1963). The behavioral study of obedience. *Journal of Abnormal and Social Psychology*, **67**, 371–8.

Wadeley, A. (1991). *Ethics in Psychological Research and Practice*. Leicester: British Psychological Society.

Wadeley, A. (1992). Ethical considerations in carrying out psychological research. In R. McIlveen, L. Higgins & A. Wadeley (Eds), *BPS Manual of Psychology Practicals: Experiment, Observation and Correlation*. Leicester: British Psychological Society.

Whose brain is it anyway?

You are looking for 47 psychologists. Answers on p. 267.

Whose brain is it anyway?

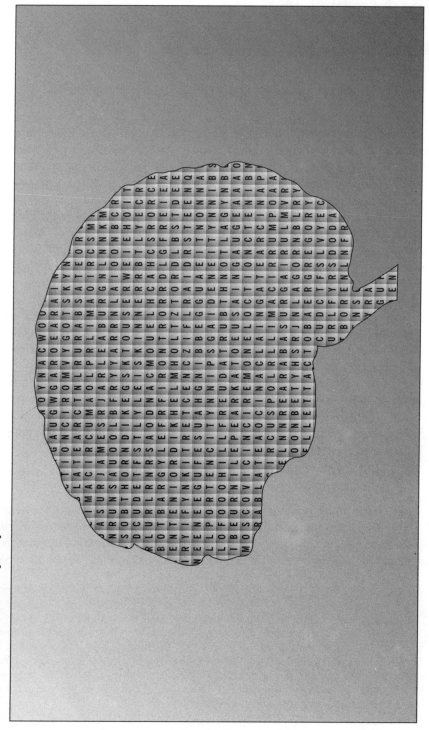

20 REVIEWING A BOOK

Authors love criticism, just so long as it is unadulterated praise.

At some point in your student career, a tutor will explore your skill in summarising and identifying the principal points in some aspect of psychology by asking for a book review. With luck it will involve a text of only 5 zillion pages and a 2-week deadline. This all adds to the fun (possibly), and admit it, given 6 weeks you would probably put off doing any preparation until 2 weeks in advance!

Before embarking on this exciting venture, read a couple of psychology book reviews. *British Journal of Educational Psychology*, *British Journal of Developmental Psychology*, *Perception* and *Discourse and Society* publish book reviews in most issues. Look for ideas of style and content. If you can find a copy of the book being reviewed, to compare the reviewers' comments with the original, then so much the better. The *British Journal of Educational Psychology* and *British Journal of Developmental Psychology* give authors the opportunity to respond to book reviews, and where they choose to do so there can be an interesting dialogue giving further insights into the authors' thoughts. Have a look at **Try This 20.1**; it gives an insight into the types of comments made by reviewers.

There is no right way to write a book review but there are some general guidelines. Book reviews are highly personal, reflecting the opinions of the reviewer, but think about the audience first. It will help you decide where to place the emphasis of the review, and guide the formality and style of the writing.

There are two general styles of review:

A **Descriptive** – an objective summary of the contents, scope, treatment and importance of a text.

B **Analytical or critical** – an objective appraisal of a text's contents, quality, limitations and applicability. It should discuss the text's relative merits and deficiencies and might compare it with alternative texts. This may require allocating time to browse through other material to place the book in context.

TRY THIS 20.1 – Book reviews

The following extracts are reproduced with permission from book reviews published in the *British Journal of Educational Psychology* (BJEP) and *British Journal of Developmental Psychology* (BJDP), © The British Psychological Society. The year, volume and page numbers are indicated. To get a feel for the approach and style of review writing, make a brief comment on each of the quotations. It is hard to make objective judgements without reading the original text and the whole review; aim here to distinguish style and content points. Some potential responses can be found on p. 267.

1. Barbara Koslowski's aim in writing *Theory and Evidence* is straightforward: to challenge the notion that scientific thinking is a problematic and therefore atypical aspect of human cognition. She pursues her aim on two fronts, theoretical and empirical. . . . Presents 16 mostly unpublished studies . . . (*BJDP*, 1998, **16**, 574)

2. *Critical Psychology* acknowledges the influence of related perspectives including feminism, critical theory, post-modernism, hermeneutics and discursive psychology. Fox and Prilleltensky do not set out to write an account of the history of critical psychology: other texts have come closer to that (e.g. Parker, 1989). Instead Fox and Prilleltensky's text introduces us to a particular strand of recent critical work in psychology. The book is also notable because it stands as a potential teaching text, which is relatively unusual in critical psychology (e.g. Stainton-Rogers *et al.*, 1995). (*BJEP*, 1998, **68**, 611)

3. Unfortunately, as I discuss below, the target article falls so far below the required standards of scholarship that the remainder of the book is devalued, despite the excellence of the individual commentaries. (*BJDP*, 1998, **16**, 573)

4. The book provides numerous and detailed examples of programme evaluations. These all clearly reveal the book's origin in the USA that will largely deny the British reader the sense of ownership and familiarity one assumes was intended. (*BJDP*, 1998, **16**, 571)

5. By and large, though, the monograph by Povinelli and Eddy stands as a model of excellence in how to conduct research in experimental psychology. They show considerable ingenuity in collecting informative data on a conceptually profound topic with non-linguistic participants. (*BJDP*, 1998, **16**, 570)

6. In certain of the chapters the references are not as up-to-date as one might have wished. For example, the most recent reference in the chapter by Fry is 1993 and in that by Stotsky is 1994. This may be due, in part, to the time taken in obtaining, editing and publishing the chapters. (*BJEP*, 1998, **68**, 622)

7. Moving on to more serious reservations about the book, the rationale behind the two sections is not entirely clear. Section 1 is entitled 'The scope of great ape intelligence', and includes a fascinating chapter by Matsuzawa and Yamakoshi on the distinct cultural traditions of two groups of chimps separated geographically. The second section is called 'Organisation of great ape intelligence: Development, culture and evolution', and includes a chapter by Boesch with content almost identical to that of Matsuzawa and Yamakoshi. Not only does Boesch talk about differences in cultural traditions according to geographic region, he even covers the same ground as the other authors by talking about . . . but there is a fair amount of evidence that generally (though not always) authors are oblivious to the contributions made by their colleagues. In consequence, there is little scope for a new perspective or understanding of ape intellect to emerge from the coming together of these contributing authors (because they do not come together). (*BJDP*, 1998, **16**, 569)

8. Editors Helena Helve and John Brynner have extensive research experience involving the study of youth transitions, attitudes and the economic and social arenas surrounding the developmental processes of young people. (*BJEP*, 1998, **68**, 617)

9. Finally, perhaps the most telling endorsement for any book is that I have already ordered copies for use in undergraduate psychology module on 'Gender Relations and Critical Social Psychology' during the next academic year. I welcome this thought-provoking and accessible text, and look forward to subsequent editions. (*BJEP*, 1998, **68**, 612)

To get a good perspective on a text, set aside time for reading well in advance. Leave time for your brain to develop opinions. The SQ3R technique (p. 49) is certainly valuable here, especially if you have a short time limit.

A *descriptive review* might include a combination of some of the following elements:

📖 an outline of the contents of the book

📖 a summary of the author's aims for the book and the intended audience

📖 an evaluation of the material included and comments

📖 quotations or references to new ideas to illustrate the review

📖 a brief summary of the author's qualifications and reference to his/her other texts

📖 citations of the psychology texts that this book will complement or replace, in order to place this text in its academic context

📖 a summary of any significant areas omitted.

Including long quotations is not a good idea unless they really illustrate a point. A reference list is required if you refer to other texts in the review.

A *critical review* both gives information about and expresses an opinion of a book. It should include a statement of what the author has tried to do, evaluate how well the author has succeeded and present independent evidence to support the evaluation. This type of review is considerably more time-consuming than a descriptive review. While reading, note passages that illustrate the book's purpose and style. Remember to balance the strengths with the weaknesses of the book and also consider how the author's ideas, opinions and judgements fit with our present knowledge of the subject. Be sure that where you are critical this is fair comment given the author's stated aims for the text. Reading the preface and introduction should give you a clear idea of the author's objectives.

A critical review might include:

📖 a description of the author's purpose for writing and qualifications

📖 the historical background of the work

📖 the main strengths and weaknesses of the book

📖 a description of the genre to which the work belongs, its academic context

📖 a commentary on the significance of the text for its intended audience.

- Read the book!

- Make notes on the principal themes and conclusions; look at the book again.

- Think about the content and decide on a theme for the review; look at the book again.

- Draft the outline to support the theme of the review and check that nothing vital is missed; look at the book again.

- Draft the review; look at the book again.

- Edit and revise the final version.

You must include a full reference (see Chapter 10) so a reader can locate the original text. You may also include the price and perhaps compare prices of competitive texts. Hardback and softback prices can be found through booksellers or the www.

You may want to comment on the style of the writing and the ease with which you think the intended audience will understand the contents. If it is well written or badly written then say so – 'this text is clearly written with case studies and examples illustrating key points' or 'although intended as an undergraduate text its style is turgid, the average undergraduate will find the detail difficult to absorb'. People read reviews to find out which books to read, and they like to know whether the material is written in an accessible manner. The real skill in reviewing involves giving yourself enough time to absorb the content of the text and then let your brain make the connections to other pieces of reading so that you offer valid links, complements and criticisms.

A Book Review Cannot Be Completed In One Draft On The Night Before A Tutorial!

20.1 REFERENCES AND FURTHER READING

International Journal of Psychoanalysis on-line at http://www.ijpa.org/ will give you access to some book reviews.
Psyche, an interdisciplinary journal of research on consciousness, publishes book reviews on-line at http://psyche.cs.monash.edu.au/
Psychology Book Reviews is a new site that intends to cover a wide range of psychology books. It can be found on-line at http://www.weyrich.com/ book_reviews/psychology_index.html
(All accessed 14 April 2000.)

HUGH & KRIY **CROWD BEHAVIOUR**

The Art of Illusion SEYMOUR CLERELEIGH

DRUG USE & ABUSE Val E. Omm & Hal Doll

Stages of Cognitive Development PRJ RAINES

THE CRIMINAL MIND HANS OFFMEISTERIO

Motivational Interviewing A. FREFFET

Ivor Brane INTELLIGENCE TESTING

Basic Colour Vision Vi O'Let

PSYCHOLOGIST'S BOOKSHELF

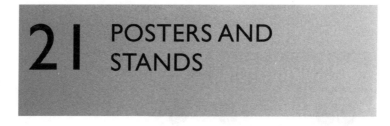

21 POSTERS AND STANDS

I like snappy, but concise does have its virtues.

Posters are one of the ways researchers share results at seminars and conferences. They may be part of a passive presentation, or more interactive, like stands, when the authors are available to answer questions. With both stand and poster presentations the key skill is communication, getting a message across clearly and concisely.

21.1 POSTERS

Posters have limited space, so the presenter is forced to concentrate on the essential elements and express them creatively through brief, concise statements and explanations. There is no room for flannel.

Most psychology departments display the posters produced by staff and postgraduates for conference presentations; corridor, office and laboratory walls are likely sites. Take a critical look at them. How effectively is the 'message' communicated? Can you read the main points at a distance of 1–2 m? Are you enticed into going closer and reading the detail? Do you like the colour combinations? Is there too much or too little material? Is there a good mix of pictures and text?

First check the presentation guidelines. There are often limits on size (which relate to the size of display boards and giving everyone a fair share of the space). Then find out about the audience. Whether it is children, fellow students or a presentation for a company, each would benefit from a tailored design and presentation, even though the basic information would be the same.

One of the fastest ways to lose marks is to overload with information. Printing an essay in 14pt font and sticking it on card will lead to instant failure, no matter how good the academic content. Soundbite messages are wanted. However, this is still an academic exercise, so a soundbite alone will not do. The academic argument and evidence is required on a poster, as in an essay. Figure 21.1 expresses visually some ideas about Piaget's stages of cognitive development. The academic argument or evidence needs to be added in text boxes to this poster. One test of the impact of a poster is that the message is almost carried by the visual items. Designing as here without text can help you produce a creative image.

Some attention should be paid to getting a 'grabbing' headline to encourage

Figure 21:1 Aim for visual messages

people to read further. The general advice is to go for simplicity and impact. Consider using a question-and-answer format to draw the reader into the topic.

Jolly-shaped posters, a brain for cognitive ideas, a stepped pyramid for Maslow's hierarchy of needs, a hamburger for eating issues or a big eyeball for perception studies will attract attention. Be careful not to let the background overwhelm the message: the background should complement and enhance, not dominate. It is also important when choosing a background not to bias the message with an inappropriate, stereotypical image. Amongst a gathering of 50 posters on depression there are likely to be 48 on black boards. Using a different background might make your poster stand out. Whatever the shape, ensure the maximum width and height is within the maximum-size guidelines.

Mount pictures and text onto contrasting coloured card or paper to highlight them. You could put primary information on one colour paper and supplementary information on another. Being consistent in design format assists the reader, for example by placing argument or background information to the left of an image, graph or picture, and the interpretation, result or consequence to the right. Using two different paper colours or textures to distinguish argument statements from consequence statements will reinforce the message. It may be effective to have a hierarchy of information with the main story in the largest type, and more detailed information in smaller types. By coding levels or hierarchies of information consistently, the reader can decide to read the main points for a general overview, or to read the whole in detail as desired.

Remember to acknowledge sources and add keys and titles to graphs and diagrams, and you must put your name somewhere.

Posters can be used for a 'compare and contrast' exercise. It may be advantageous to use creative visual coding to indicate examples of good and less good practice (Figure 21.2) but remember to include a key somewhere.

There are costs involved in poster production, including card, paper, photocopying, enlarging and printing photographic material. Colour printing is expensive so be certain everyone is happy with the size and shape of each diagram before printing. A rough draft or mock-up, in black and white, before a final colour print will save money. The first five to seven drafts are never right; font sizes that seem enormous on a computer screen look small on a poster board viewed from 2 m away. Any poster produced by a group will be the subject of much discussion and change before everyone is happy! SPELL CHECK ALL COPY BEFORE PRINTING.

Interactive posters with pop-up book effects, wheels to spin, hospital beds to wheel along a chart, or nests of overlays that slide away can be very effective. Take care that the structure is solid enough to cope with handling. Use a good glue, reinforce cut edges and ensure the poster is very safely attached to the wall or board. Multilayered card is heavy and likely to fall off.

Show your mock-up, pilot poster to a few people. Ask them what message it conveys. Is it what you intended? Are they following through the material in the order you wish? Can they distinguish major points from support material? What

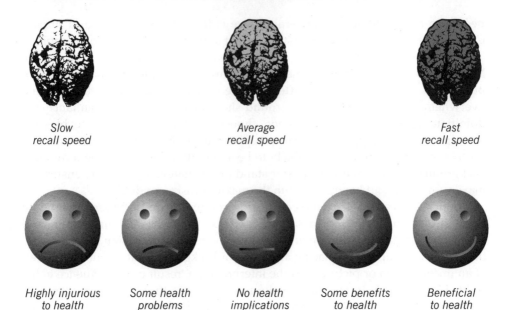

Slow
recall speed　　　　　*Average*
recall speed　　　　　*Fast*
recall speed

Highly injurious
to health　　*Some health*
problems　　*No health*
implications　　*Some benefits*
to health　　*Beneficial*
to health

Figure 21:2 Examples of visual codes or classifications

do they feel about the colour scheme? Are the font sizes large enough? Does the overall effect encourage them to read further? Are the main arguments supported by clear evidence? Decide whether the design promotes delivery of the message and then do the final version. If the poster is to be assessed, self-assess using your departmental assessment form or Figure 21.3. How are the marks are assigned? If the marks matter, change the design to meet the criteria for a higher grade.

21.2 VIRTUAL POSTERS

Virtual posters are designed electronically in word-processing or graphics packages. They have the advantages of being low-cost and easy to store and can be viewed via the www.

A virtual poster may be an electronic version of a physical poster and the guidelines above apply in the same way. Think about size: the maximum size will probably be defined as part of the project, probably one to three screens. Use a typeface and font size that is attractive and clear. Think about whether you find CAPITALS EASIER TO READ or a Mixed Case Style. Use different typefaces, colours and shading to highlight different types of information.

A virtual poster can be more fun IF it is possible to include electronic elements. Add HTML links to websites elsewhere, video, photographs, animated cartoons, short interactive computer programs to demonstrate a model in action . . . There are many possibilities. The facilities and the expense of scanning material into

	I	2:1	2:2	3	Fail	
Group names .... **Poster title**						
Poster structure (20%)						
Well organised						Disorganised
Single topic focus						No clear focus
Research and argument (60%)						
Main points included						No grasp of the main issues
Points supported by evidence						No corroborating evidence
Good use of relevant examples						Lack of examples
Ideas clearly expressed						Muddled presentation
Design and presentation (20%)						
Creative layout and design						Poor design
Good graphics						No/poor graphics
Good word processing						No/poor word processing
Key points readable at 2 m						Key points unreadable at 2 m
Comments						

Figure 21:3 Poster assessment criteria

digital form will govern your creativeness. Beware of limits on file size, which may be set as part of the exercise.

A www search in April 2000 found a range of posters from academic courses and conferences; different search engines located different sites. Search using posters+virtual+psychology or virtual+posters+university+psychology to view current examples.

21.3 ORGANISING AN EXHIBITION STAND

You may be asked to produce an exhibition stand as part of a module assessment, for a department or university open day or for a university society as part of

Freshers' Week. Given the effort and time required to produce a good stand it should be a team activity, and will benefit from the fusion of ideas. With five people on a team there will be five different, and all very reasonable, ideas and approaches. Leave time for discussion and consensus, so everyone gets involved and contributes fully. An exhibition involves verbal discussion of research findings with visitors. Conversations of this type require you to adapt the promotional 'blurb' to match visitors' interests and attitudes. This skill is different from an oral presentation for a tutorial or seminar: it develops the ability to think and adapt the message as you speak.

The nature and experience of the audience needs serious consideration. For a module exhibition the audience will include tutors, fellow students and . . . who else? Find out who is coming. Can you assume any background subject knowledge or not? It may be important to decide whether the exhibit will work at a variety of levels to suit all visitors. But remember if you devise a duck-hooking competition to attract the kids, the adults will be there too, and keen to hook those ducks. Anything that involves active participation, a quiz, a game, a short video or computer presentation will capture the interest and attention of a visitor.

Find out about the facilities and space available. What is the area and shape for posters? Are there power points for a video, computer, spotlights or other demonstrations? Will there be table and chairs available, so visitors can be encouraged to sit down and discuss issues in comfort?

If you have the chance, take a critical look at an exhibition. Careers-service fairs on campus are great opportunities; organisations are really trying to sell themselves so need to give clear messages. Consider what materials are used and how they are presented, and decide what you like and dislike, what works and does not work for you. Consider the size of photographs, font size on posters and literature, coloured and multicoloured backgrounds and the height of materials. What tempted you to certain stands? What encouraged you to talk with exhibitors? Was it the free tea or toffees? What could be adapted for your project?

Use pictures and demonstrations to entice visitors and draw them into the topic even when all the team members are talking to other visitors. Ensure that there is a logical arrangement to the material so that a visitor can follow through the exhibits in the order you wish. Put posters and the pictures to attract passers-by at eye-level, but pictures to attract younger children should be lower. If you intend people to sit down consider what they can see from that level.

The guidelines for poster production will assist with producing an exhibition stand. Co-ordinating colour and style themes through from posters to video to PC displays to promotional handouts will impress. If this is part of an assessment, the proportion of marks for the presentation is likely to be small; the quality of background research and the quality of discussion with stand visitors will get the bulk of the marks (Figure 21.4). Getting the 'storyline' right takes time. Practising your patter on a couple of people before an 'assessor' turns up is a good wheeze. Listening is important: watch for body and language clues and tailor your message to the visitor's interests and experience. The following reflective quotes

Stand title	
Group names	
Please grade on a 1–5 scale, where 1 is Useless, 3 is Average, 5 is Brilliant.	
1. How well did the group articulate the principle points and issues?	1 2 3 4 5
Comments	
2. How broad and effective was the evidence supplied to justify the claims?	1 2 3 4 5
Comments	
3. How well did individuals use personal illustration and anecdote to support the claims?	1 2 3 4 5
Comments	
4. How well did the stand materials support and enhance the points being made?	1 2 3 4 5
Comments	
5. How creative were the ideas? How much impact did they have? Which materials or approaches would you commend?	1 2 3 4 5
Comments	
Additional comments:	

Figure 21:4 Assessment criteria for an exhibition stand

are from Level 2 students who had just completed a 2-hour exhibition, talking to a range of people who were not subject specialists.

- The most important thing the stand exercise helped me to learn is . . . 'I found that each person I talked to gave me new ideas. I got better at really explaining as we went on.' 'I thought I had it well planned in advance, what I was going to say. Then as different people came you found they asked different questions so I had to keep re-organising my ideas and responses.' 'Being prepared in advance wasn't enough, I need this sort of practice so my message gets across clearly.' 'It was great interview practice even if some people did ask unreasonable questions.' 'I think it is easier to talk to one person but you really have to concentrate on them as well as the message you are trying to give.'

- I most enjoyed . . . 'Getting all the information together and making the stand.' 'Finding out what everyone else in the group thought about the project.' 'Trying being an interviewer with the other groups, I began to see a bit more about what the interviewer might see.' 'Being involved in something that worked well.'

- I least enjoyed . . . 'Being ignored by people and visitors who didn't seem too interested.' 'Dealing with some difficult questions, I don't like having to answer off the top of my head. I realise now that we needed some more background research to keep talking for more than about three minutes.' 'The first interview, I was too nervous, but once that was over the afternoon got better.'

Organising and running an exhibition stand is great fun and very exhausting. Have some chocolate handy!

Psychoceramics?

The study of crackpots.

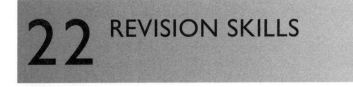

22 REVISION SKILLS

Time to stop writing, . . . and wait for more questions.

'I finish four modules this week, have three term papers and a project to hand in on Friday, and the first exam is on Monday. So when do I revise?' Well the answer is that you don't revise in this style. Revision, in the last-minute 'cramming' style, is really a school concept. It is part of a 'Get the facts ➜ Learn them ➜ Regurgitate in examination' process characteristic of surface learning. In 'real life', you don't revise, you have an accumulating body of knowledge and apply it continuously. University is a transition phase, but all your deep reading and learning activities should mean that revision as cramming becomes a small proportion of your activities.

Re-reading and reviewing material needs to be an ongoing process built into your weekly timetable, because it improves the amount of detail that you recall. So normal learning activities should reap rewards at exam time because they are also 'revision' activities that reinforce your learning, and you have been doing them all term. The following are a jolly wheeze:

✔ Getting your brain in gear before a lecture by reading last week's notes.

✔ Rereading notes from discussions.

✔ Using SQ3R (p. 49) in reading and making connections to other modules.

✔ Thinking actively around issues (see Chapter 7).

✔ Checking that you have good arguments (see Chapter 8), spotting gaps in the evidence and using that information to determine what you read, rather than just taking the next item on the reading list.

✔ Actively asking questions as you research (see Chapter 7).

Timetable 'revision slots' to continue these learning processes.

Tight deadlines are often a feature of university life. Most tutors will be blissfully unaware, and emphatically unsympathetic, when you have five essays due on the last day of term or semester and examinations 2 days later. Sorting out schedules is your problem not theirs, an opportunity to exercise your time-management skills.

22.1 REVISION AIMS

Exams test your understanding of interrelated psychology materials from coursework, personal research and reading. You will to have overview information on a large number of topics from detailed examples and case studies.

Understanding, relevance, analytical ability and expression are listed by Meredeen (1988) as the Holy Grail of examiners keen to donate marks. Reflect on where you can demonstrate these attributes to your nice, kind examiner:

1 UNDERSTANDING Have you shown you understood the question? Keep answers focused.

2 RELEVANCE There are no marks for irrelevant inclusion of material no matter how psychological. Stick to the issues and points the question raises. Don't let yourself be side-tracked.

3 ANALYTICAL ABILITY Aim for a well-reasoned, organised answer. Show that you understand the meaning of the question and can argue your way through points in a logical manner.

4 EXPRESSION Clear and concise writing and diagrams that make your ideas and arguments transparent to the examiner help enormously. The length of an answer is no guide to its effectiveness or relevance. A well-structured short answer will get better marks than a long answer padded out with irrelevant details.

22.2 GET ORGANISED – TIME MANAGEMENT AGAIN

If from the start you take 30 minutes each week for each module, to review and reflect, to think around issues and decide what to read next, you will also be revising. It is an ongoing process, and you will be well ahead of the majority! As exams get closer, sort out a work and learning timetable; say for the 5 weeks before exams. Put every essay, report and presentation deadline on it, add the exam times, lectures, tutorials and all your other commitments, and have a little panic. Then decide that panicking wastes time and sort out a plan to do six essays and revise 12 topics and include social and sporting activities to relax, and block the time in 2-hour slots, with breaks to cook and eat. Then organise group revision, discussion and sharing opportunities.

- Start earlier than you think you need to!
- Put revision time into your weekly plan; use it to think.

- Keep a revision record and attempt to allocate equal time to each paper.

- Speaking an idea aloud or writing it down lodges information in the brain more securely than reading.

Revising is not something you have to do alone. Think with friends and colleagues. Group revision assists:

☺ by generating comments on your ideas, adding the perceptions of others to your brain bank

☺ because it is easier for two or three brains to disentangle theories explaining children's understanding of home–school relations or the practicalities of attributional coding schemes

☺ because it's more fun (less depressing?)

☺ by making you feel less anxious about the exam, more self-confident

☺ because the challenge of explaining something to a group will help you understand the points and remember details more clearly

☺ by showing where you need to do extra study and where you are already confidently fluent with the material.

Don't be put off by someone claiming to know all because they have read something you have not. No one reads everything. If it is so good, ask for an explanation.

22.3 WHAT DO YOU DO NOW?

What were your thoughts as you left your most recent exams? Ignoring the obvious 'Where's the bar?', jot down a few thoughts and look at **Try This 22.1**.

TRY THIS 22.1 – Post-examination reflections

Write down your thoughts about your last examinations, and then look at the list below. These are random, post-examination thoughts of rather jaundiced first-year psychologists. Tick any points you empathise with. Make a plan.

☹ No practice at timed essays since A-level, I'd forgotten how after 12 months.

☹ Not enough time to write.

☹ My mind went blank, couldn't remember a thing.

☺ Too many specific places and dates to remember.

☹ Lack of revision.

☹ Missed the point of the last essay.

☺ Put in a load of things that were not relevant, cos I could remember them.

☹ Was thinking about going to the bar after, most of the time.

☹ Needed more direction towards the questions.

☺ You couldn't learn the whole course; I picked the bits that were missed off the exam paper.

☹ Had loads of facts in the lectures, but nothing to apply them to.

☹ Mostly relied on common sense and made something up.

☹ I had all this stuff about prejudice and discrimination and he asks about bargaining and negotiation.

☹ I think the detail in the lectures was confusing and the big handout added another layer of detail that wasn't in the lecture. I didn't really get started on it because there was too much to tackle.

22.4 GOOD REVISION PRACTICE

The rubrics for papers are usually displayed somewhere in a department, possibly in the course outline or on the examination noticeboard. Find out about the different styles of questions, how many questions you have to answer and what each question is worth. Plan your revision activities to match the pattern of the paper.

Revise actively

Sitting in a big armchair in a warm room reading old notes or a book is almost guaranteed to send you to sleep! **TRY** some of these ideas:

✔ Make summary notes, ideas maps, lists of main points and summaries of cases or examples.

✔ Sort out the general principles and learn them.

✔ Look for links, ask questions like:
  • Where does this fit into this course? – essay? – other modules?
  • How important is it? – a critical idea? – detailed example? – extra example to support the case?
  • Is this the main idea? – an irrelevance?

✔ Write outline answers to essays, then apply the criteria of Understanding, Relevance, Analysis and Expression. Ask yourself 'Does this essay work?' 'Where can it be improved?'

✔ Practise writing a full essay in the right time. Sunday morning is a good slot! Put all the books away, set the alarm clock and do a (timed) past paper. DON'T PANIC, the next time will be better. Examination writing skills get rusty; they need oiling before the first examination or your first answers will suffer.

✔ Remember you need a break of 5 minutes every hour or so. Plan exercise into your revision time, swimming, walking or going to the gym; the oxygen revitalises the brain cells (allegedly).

✔ Apply the ideas in the Active Reading SQ3R technique (p. 49) to your revision. Use the technique to condense notes to important points.

✔ Aim to review all your course notes a week before the exams! Then you will panic less, have time to be ill without getting behind, and feel more relaxed for having had time to look again at odd points and practise a couple of timed essays. (OK, OK, we said AIM!)

✘ Staying up all night to study at the last minute is not one of your best ideas in life.

Having a good understanding of your own behaviour, you will realise that reviewing the first four weeks of a module should, ideally!! (ho-hum), be completed by weeks 6-8, so that the ideas accumulate in your mind. The rest of the module will progress better because you understand the background and there is time to give attention to topics in the last sessions of the module. But then, who is ideal?

Outline essays

Outline answers are an efficient revision alternative to writing a full essay. Write the introduction and conclusion paragraphs in full, NO CHEATING. For the central section, do one-sentence summaries for each paragraph, with references. Add graphs and diagrams in full because practice makes them memorable. Then look carefully at the structure and balance of the essay; consider where more examples are needed and whether the argument is in the most logical order.

Keywords

Examiners tend to use a number of keywords to start or finish questions. Words like *Discuss*, *Evaluate*, *Assess*, *Compare* and *Illustrate*. They all require slightly different approaches in the answer. Use the **Try This 22.2** game to replace keywords and revise essay plans.

TRY THIS 22.2 – Replacing keywords in examination questions

Take a question, any question that has been set in an examination or tutorial in your department. Do an outline structure for your answer. Then replace the keyword with one or more of *Assess, Compare, Criticise, Explore, Illustrate, Justify, List, Outline, Trace, Verify*. Each word changes the emphasis of the answer, and the style and presentation of evidence.

Here is a list of keywords used in essay questions and 'possible' meanings (adapted from Lillis, 1997; Rowntree, 1988).

Analyse	Describe, examine and criticise all aspects of the question, and do it in detail.
Argue	Make the case using evidence, for and against a point of view.
Assess	Weigh up and make a judgement about the extent to which the conditions in the statement are fulfilled.
Comment	Express an opinion on, not necessarily a long one, BUT often used by examiners when they mean Describe, Analyse or Assess. (Cover your back.)
Compare	Examine the similarities and differences between two or more ideas, theories, objects, processes, etc.
Contrast	Point out the differences between . . . could add some similarities.
Criticise	Discuss the supporting and opposing arguments for, make a judgement about . . .; show where errors arise in . . . use examples.
Define	Give the precise meaning of . . ., or Show clearly the outlines of . . .
Describe	Give a detailed account of . . .
Discuss	Argue the case for and against the proposition, a detailed answer. Try to develop a definite conclusion or point of view. See Comment!
Evaluate	Appraise, again with supporting and opposing arguments to give a balanced view of . . . Look to find the value of . . .
Explain	Give a clear, intelligible explanation of . . ., Needs a detailed but precise answer
Identify	Pick out the important features of . . ., and explain why you picked this selection.
Illustrate	Make your points with examples, or expand on an idea with examples. Generally one detailed example and a number of briefly described, relevant supporting examples make the better argument.
Interpret	Using you own experience, explain what is meant by . . .
Justify	Give reasons why . . . Show why this is the case . . . Need to argue the case.

List	Make a list of (usually means a short/ brief response). Notes or bullets may be OK.
Outline	Give a general summary or description showing how elements interrelate.
Prove	Present the evidence that clearly makes an unarguable case.
Relate	Describe or tell a story, see Explain, Compare and Contrast.
Show	Reveal in a logical sequence why . . ., see Explain.
State	Explain in plain language and in detail the main points.
Summarise	Make a brief statement of the main points, ignore excess detail.
Trace	Explain stage by stage . . . A logical-sequence answer.
Verify	Show the statement to be true. The expectation is that you will provide justification to confirm the statement.

The quiz approach

Devising revision quizzes can be effective. You do not need to dream up multiple answers, but could play around with a format as in Figure 22.1. This is a short factual quiz based on a journal article by Willott and Griffin (1999) which discusses working-class male offenders' view of economic crime, but the answers in the second column are out of order. Can you sort them out?

1. What is the Robin Hood concept?	a. Women are generally less powerful than men, but women are not the dominant criminal group.
2. How were the data analysed?	b. Work is carried out for pay by individuals who also claim social security and unemployment benefits, benefits they would not be wholly entitled to if they declared this work.
3. What factors affect the unemployment–crime relationship?	c. Men provide for the basic needs of their families by the redistribution of wealth through activities that are legally classified as criminal.
4. What were the characteristics of the sample?	d. Constructivist grounded analysis (Henwood & Pigeon, 1992) and critical discourse analysis (Parker, 1990).
5. What is the informal economy?	e. Need to support a family (NAPO 1991); culture and context Crow et al., 1989; Hagen, 1993).
6. A traditional theory about crime is that those with less power are more predisposed to criminality. What counter-argument is offered to this view?	f. 66 working-class men, born and brought up in the West Midlands, UK, who had convictions for an economic crime.

Figure 22:1 Quiz questions for an article by Willott and Griffin (1999). (Answers on p. 219.)

Note the inclusion of references in the answers; they provide the evidence that increases your marks. The questions in Figure 22.1 cover facts, and are good for MCQ (multiple choice question) revision. Now consider the style of these questions:

? What are the theories that are considered in this article?

? Why was this research approach adopted?

? To what extent does this research support the idea that minor economic crime can fulfil a gender identity need?

? How is the 'lifeboat' concept constructed?

? What is the role of the state as envisaged by the respondents?

? Why might the respondents alter their stories if their wives were present at the interview?

These questions demand similar factual knowledge to those in Figure 22.1, but a more reasoned and extended response. They are useful for revising short-answer questions and essay paragraphs.

To get into the swing have a go at **Try This 22.3** *and* **Try This 22.4**. The first asks for quiz questions based on your notes from lectures and additional reading, and the second uses the same technique with a journal article.

TRY THIS 22.3 – Quiz questions from notes

Pick a set of notes and create a short quiz, 10 questions, in each of the two styles: first short factual questions then some more extended questions. Write the questions on one side of the page and answers on the reverse, so you can use them (without cheating too much) for revision.

TRY THIS 22.4 – Quiz questions from a journal article

Pick an article from any reading list and, rather than making notes, devise a set of five short and five extended questions that explore the topic. Again, write the questions on one side of the page and answers on the reverse, for revision purposes.

Revision is an opportunity to think about and continue to look for psychological explanations and insights. It is therefore a creative process, with ideas gelling and developing as you reread and reconsider. Note-making is an integral part of revision. Some general questions running in your head will encourage a questioning, active approach to revision. Have a go at **Try This 22.5** to explore this approach further.

TRY THIS 22.5 – Generic questions for revising psychology

Compile a list of questions that could be used in compiling a revision quiz. Some suggestions are on p. 269, but have a go at your own before looking.

22.5 REFERENCES AND FURTHER READING

Crow, I., Richardson, P., Riddington, C. & Simon, F. (1989). *Unemployment, Crime and Offenders*. London: Routledge.

Hagen, J. (1993). The social embeddedness of crime and unemployment. *Criminology*, **31**, 465–91.

Henwood, K.L. & Pidgeon, N.F. (1992). Qualitative research and psychological theorising. *British Journal of Psychology*, **83**, 97–111.

Lillis, T. (1997). Essay writing starter. In S. Drew & R. Bingham (Eds), *The Student Skills Guide*, Aldershot: Gower, 53–75.

Meredeen, S. (1988). *Study for Survival and Success*. London: Chapman.

National Association of Probation Officers (NAPO) (1991). *Working a Way Out of Crime*. Occasional Paper.

Parker, I. (1990). Discourse: definitions and contradictions. *Philosophical Psychology*, 3, 189–203.

Rowntree, D. (1988). *Learn How To Study: A Guide for Students of All Ag*es, 3rd edn. London: Warner Books.

Willott, S. & Griffin, C. (1999). Building your own lifeboat: Working-class male offenders talk about economic crime, *British Journal of Social Psychology*, **38**, 445–60.

Answers to Quiz, Figure 22.1: 1c, 2d, 3e, 4f, 5b, 6a

Psychograms 4

Try these psychological anagrams. Answers on p. 270.

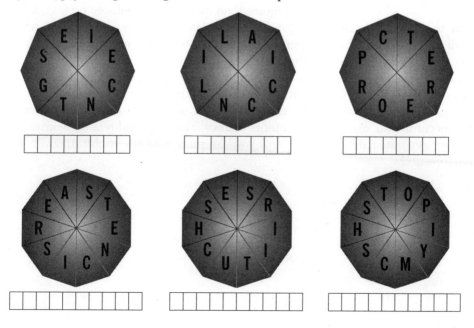

Support your psychology examiners – behave very strangely.

Relax – you did all that reflection and reviewing so the examinations will be a doddle. Check and double-check the examination timetable and room locations: they can change. Know where you are going, plan to be there 20 minutes early to find your seat or block number, visit the loo and relax. Check the student handbook so you know what to do if you are delayed. Make sure you have a pen, spare pens, pencils, eraser, correction fluid, highlighter pens, ruler and calculator if required. Make sure you read the information at the top of the exam paper, and take heed of anything the invigilator has to say. If you think there is a problem with the paper, tell an invigilator at once, so the psychology staff can be consulted.

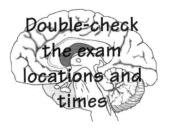

Double-check the exam locations and times

Find out in advance how the paper is structured and use the time in proportion. For example, on a 2-hour paper that has six short questions and one essay there will probably be 50 per cent for the essay and 50 per cent split equally between the six short questions. One hour on the essay and 9 minutes for each short question leaves 6 minutes to read the paper and plan the answers. Answer the number of questions required, no more and preferably no less. Leave time to do justice to each question, and don't leave your potentially best answer until the end. Equally, don't spend so much time on it that you have to skimp the remaining essays. Make sure there are no questions overleaf.

Should you be seized with anxiety and your brain freeze over, use the 'free association', red-and-blue-pen mode (p. 94) or brainstorming approach. Write out the question and then look at each word in turn, scribbling down the first words that occur to you, anything . . . authors' names, examples and related words. This should generate calm and facts, and you can plan from the spider diagram you have created.

23.1 EXAMINATION ESSAYS

Our advice here is reread the sections on argument (Chapter 8), revision (Chapter 22) and writing essays (Chapter 9), and write fast. Written exams are a test of your grasp of theory and your cognitive skills; they allow you to develop lines of argument, draw in diverse ideas and demonstrate your skills in argument, analysis, synthesis, evaluation and written communication. Remember to keep the psychology content high, use evidence to support your arguments wherever you can and cite supporting references.

Top Tips

- If all questions look impossible choose the one where you have the most examples to quote, or the longest question. Long questions usually give more clues to plan the answer. 'Discuss the role of behavioural choice with respect to sexual practices, smoking, food and drink choice and exercise routines in the maintenance of good health' is a question with loads of clues and parts to answer, whereas 'Discuss the role of behavioural choice in the psychology of health' is essentially the same question, which could be answered with the same information, but will be a minefield if you do not impose structure and facts.

- Plan your answer even if short of time. Underline keywords in the question, like <u>Discuss</u>, or <u>Compare and contrast</u>, and <u>contemporary research</u>. Don't restrict examples to one type of behaviour or context if the question asks about general issues. Do a quick list or spider diagram of the main points, and note ideas for the introduction and conclusion. Then rank the points to get a batting order for the sections.

- On a three-question paper plan questions 2 and 3 before writing the answer to question 2. Your brain can run in background mode on ideas for question 3 as you write the second answer.

- Watch the time. Leave a couple of minutes at the end of each answer to check through, amend spelling and grammar, and add extra points, references and tidy diagrams.

Some of the points examiners search for may be deduced from Figure 23.1, which lists comments from a random selection of examiners. They concentrate on the lower end of the marking scale and from it you may gather that examiners cannot give marks unless you tell them what you know: explain terms, answer all parts of the question, use lots of examples, remember you're a ~~Womble~~ psychologist. Everything needs setting in a psychological context. If you do not include psychological cases and examples, relating theory to the real world, you

Not a serious attempt   10 per cent
Does not address the question   20 per cent
Littered with factual errors   35 per cent
Fine answer to a question about social learning theory, pity the question was about development of play   38 per cent
Very weak effort – no attempt to define key terms or illustrate with examples   42 per cent
Confused but contains some relevant points   42 per cent
A scrappy answer with a couple of good points   45 per cent
Started well then ran out of steam, and no new material   49 per cent
Decent attempt, some relevant examples, <u>but</u> not fully focused on the question   50 per cent
Insufficient explanation/evaluation; listed some ideas at the end but these needed developing to raise the mark, only lecture materials (2 sides only)   52 per cent
Reasonable answer but misses out the crucial element of . . .   54 per cent
Reasonable effort as far as it goes, but does not define/explain technical terms – no examples   55 per cent
Accurate but generally descriptive, never got to the 'evaluate' section   55 per cent
Too much description – not enough critical evaluation   58 per cent
Has clearly understood lectures, but little evidence of reading beyond   58 per cent
Good discussion but needs to emphasise psychology more   60 per cent
Good intro. and well argued, with some evidence of reading. Good use of examples but unfortunately only from class material   64 per cent
Has done some reading and thinking. Limited number of recent refs.   65 per cent
Quite good – a general answer, omits outline of Theory of Planned Behaviour but lots of non-lecture examples   67 per cent
Excellent – focused, uses recent literature and well illustrated with examples   70 per cent
Outstanding   85 per cent

Figure 23:1 Comments on examination essays

are not going to hit the high marks. Organise your points, one per paragraph, in a structure that flows logically. Set the scene in your first paragraph and signpost the layout of the answer. Be precise rather than woolly, for example rather than saying 'Early on . . .' give the date. Try to keep an exciting, interesting point for the final paragraph. If you are going to cross things out, do it tidily.

Take-home examinations and seen papers

Essays written without the stress of the examination room can seem a walk-over, but still need revision and preparation. Get the notes together in advance, make sure you have found the library resources you require before the exam paper is published; at that point people are trampled underfoot in the race to the library. Think around possible essay topics to get your brain in gear. Don't leave it all to the last minute.

The questions may be more cognitively or theoretically challenging because the examiners assume that you will have more time to explore the issues, and more resources available. You can do all your preparation in the comfort of your usual working environment, but with a seen paper you still get to generate your final responses under examination conditions. Practise writing out your responses in the time allocated to the exam without using any of your notes. This is a good way of finding out how long you take to write the answer, and how quickly exam time passes!

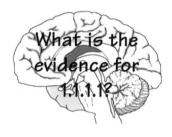

Open-book examinations

In an open-book examination you are allowed to take reference books and materials into the examination room. Make sure you find out beforehand exactly which materials are allowed, and remember to pack them in with your pens, pencils, etc. It can be tempting to think that you don't need to do much preparation for these exams since you will have all your materials with you – not so! Preparation and revision is still vital – just think how long it takes you to look up things in reference books, let alone find out about new topics. It's a good idea to test yourself on a sample question, using your reference materials, to give yourself an idea of how much extra time it takes looking things up. If you are taking your own notes into the exam get them organised and readable so you can find what you need fast.

23.2 SHORT-ANSWER QUESTIONS

Short-answer questions search for evidence of understanding through factual, knowledge-based answers and the ability to reason and draw inferences. There are usually clues to what is required in the question, e.g., list, describe, define, explain, etc. A reasoned paragraph answer is required to questions like 'Briefly describe habituation', ' Outline the difference between a psychology of women and a feminist psychology' or 'What was William James's contribution to our thinking about emotion?'. Questions like 'Outline Piaget's stages of cognitive development' or 'What are the consequences of visual cortex and association visual cortex damage?' require fact-rich answers, and can be answered as a set of points. Sometimes the length of answer is set in the question, e.g., 'Describe in not more than 30 words . . .'; make sure you don't exceed the word limit.

23.3 MCQs

MCQs (multiple-choice questions) test a wide range of topics in a short time. They may be used to help revision, in a module test where the marks do not count, or as a part of module assessment where the marks matter. A class test checks what you have understood, and should indicate where more research and revision is required. In a final assessment watch the rules. With on-line assessment once the answer is typed in and sent, *it cannot be changed*.

Look carefully at the instructions on MCQ papers. The instructions should remind you of the rules, such as:

There is/is not negative marking. (With negative marking you lose marks for getting it wrong). If there's no negative marking, it's always worth taking a guess if you're not sure of the answer. You have a one in four or five chance of success.

One or more answers may be correct, select all the correct answers. (This is how you can get 100 marks on a paper with 60 questions).

Go through the paper quickly, answering the all questions you can do easily, and then go back to tackle the rest; this will boost your confidence, and gain you a bit of extra time for the trickier questions. There are several types of questions.

The 'trivial pursuit' factual style
Questions like this test recall of facts, and understanding of theories. They are usually a small proportion of the exam paper.

Diffusion of responsibility leads to a(n) _____ probability of bystander intervention:

    (a) decreased
    (b) increased
    (c) neutral
    (d) it depends on the situation

Joe has a CA of 10 and an MA of 5. His IQ is:

    (a) 50
    (b) 100

(c) 150
(d) 200

Reasoning and application style

Reasoning from previous knowledge gives rise to questions like:

Dr N. Tuitive feels that people do what they do because of the situation they are in now or have been in previously. Dr N. Tuitive believes in the:

(a) behavioural approach
(b) psychodynamic approach
(c) humanistic approach
(d) trait approach

Some questions give a paragraph of information and possible responses. You apply theories or knowledge to choose the right response or combination of responses:

A set of scores has a mean of 10, a mode of 7, a median of 9, a range from 1 to 1000, and a standard deviation of 2.6. After completing these calculations, a psychologist notices that the highest score (1000) was really supposed to be 100. After the correction, this single score of 100 is still the highest value. Which of the following would be true of the recalculated statistics on this set of data?

(a) The mean decreases and the mode is unchanged.
(b) The median decreases and the standard deviation is unchanged.
(c) The mean decreases, the median decreases, the mode is unchanged, and the standard deviation is unchanged.
(d) The standard deviation is unchanged.

Appropriate revision techniques for MCQ papers include deriving quiz questions. Revisit **Try This 22.3** and **Try This 22.5**. Generating questions forces you to concentrate on details.

23.4 PRACTICAL EXAMINATIONS

Some laboratory courses have associated examinations. Taking laboratory notebooks or manuals into such exams may be allowed; if so, don't forget yours. Questions tend to be based on applying practical laboratory experience to psychological issues. Revising with past papers is always a good practice, or make up your own questions. Try variations on:

● If this reading experiment had been run with participants with dyslexia, how would you expect the results to change? Essentially a 'what will happen if the samples come from different populations' question, designed to see if you understand controlling principles.

- How might the responses change if (a) the stimulus pattern had been turned through 30°, (b) the thickness of lines was increased? Another 'what if we change the parameters' question that asks you to speculate logically about the outcome.

- Explain where errors can arise in measuring reaction times and the impact they have on data analysis and interpretation. A general question about where errors arise in your research.

- Describe the ethical implications involved in . . ., and explain how they can be minimised.

- Outline the observational approach you might use to explore . . . How accurate would you expect your results to be? A question that asks you to look creatively at how you would apply skills acquired in laboratory classes to address practical psychological hypotheses in the real world.

23.5 ORAL EXAMINATIONS

Vivas exist as part of some modules in some degree schemes, and in some universities as part of the final examination process. The thought of a viva has been known to spook candidates. Don't panic! Vivas are an opportunity to talk about a topic or subject in detail. It is a skill that should be more widely practised since in the workplace you are much more likely to 'explain an idea or project' than to write about it.

The finalists' viva voce exams are generally part of the degree classification process. After all the assessments and examinations, when the marks are sorted out some people are 'borderline specialists'; people so close to the boundary that another chance is given to cross a threshold. A viva may also be given to candidates who have had special circumstances, such as severe illness, during their studies. The viva is usually run by the external examiner, a nice professor from another psychology department. DO NOT PANIC. In all the departments we know vivas are used to raise candidates. You have what you have on paper, so things can only GET BETTER. If your name is on a viva list this is good news, sigh with relief, remember all that revision you did before and check out some answers to the questions below. Get a good night's sleep, avoid unusual stimulants (always sound advice) and wear something tidy. Examiners tend to appear in suits but are interested in your brain not your wardrobe. Celebrate later.

Typical viva topics

Projects and dissertations are a frequent opening topic. You are the expert; you did all the research and wrote it up. So the **Top Tip** is to glance through your work; it is on a disk somewhere (DON'T PANIC). Rehearse answers to questions, such as:

☞ What are the main strengths of your dissertation research?

☞ Outline any weaknesses you feel the research has.

☞ Can you explain why you adopted your research strategy?

☞ What do you feel were the main psychological issues you addressed?

☞ Since you started on this topic I see you did a module on . . . How might you have adapted your research in the light of what you learned in this module?

☞ Can you talk a bit about how your results relate to psychology generally?

☞ Obviously in a student dissertation there is limited time for data acquisition. How might you have expanded the data collection process?

☞ Would you like to expand on the literature review/results section / interpretation?

☞ Could you talk about sources of errors in the data?

Try to keep answers to the point and keep up the technical content. Any examiner recognises flannel. Waffle cannot reduce a mark, but you are trying to raise it. External examiners have supervised, marked and moderated thousands of dissertations during their career. They know every dissertation has strengths and weaknesses; they are impressed by people who have done the research and realise there were other things to do, other ways to tackle the issue, other techniques, more data to collect . . . so tell your examiner that you know too.

Use your 'psychology-speak' skills. Asked about the 'Lazarus's model of emotion' you could say:

> He said that people have primary appraisals about the environment, and secondary appraisals about how to cope. If you think you can cope then you treat what's going on in the environment as a challenge and you don't get stressed. But if you think you can't cope then you think of what's going on as a threat and that makes you feel stressed. Different people have different coping styles – problem-focused and emotion-focused – problem-focused is better because it's more directed at finding solutions.

It is a general answer but in the 2.2 class. You could say:

> Lazarus's original model was formulated in the 1960s and suggested that emotion arose from the individual's appraisal of the environment. Primary appraisal involves the initial appraisal of the environment – positive, negative or neutral. Secondary appraisal involves the individual's evaluation of how best to cope with the situation. Secondary appraisal comes in two main forms – emotion-focused and problem-focused. Emotion-focused coping refers to the defence mechanisms that an individual might adopt, like denial or avoiding the situation, while problem-focused coping involves finding solutions to the problems posed. But that model was formulated to explain

how people respond to stressors. Lazarus reformulated his ideas in 1991 to produce a more generalised model of emotion that he called the 'cognitive-motivational-relational' theory of emotion. Here primary appraisal encompasses goal relevance, goal congruence or incongruence and ego-involvement. Secondary appraisal assesses the environment in terms of how the individual might cope with it, and how this coping might affect future relations. He suggested that appraisals that situations might cause harm to the individual were innate, but that in some cases secondary appraisal could override decisions emerging from primary appraisal. I think this overcomes some of the earlier criticisms from people like Zajonc, for example, that he ignored the more automatic processes involved in emotional experiences.

A longer and more psychological answer. The candidate is aware not only of the original theory, but that it was stress-based and that the model has been updated to be more emotion-relevant. This answer cites other relevant work (Zajonc) and should get a First. So think a bit and try to answer with evidence, and examples, and references, just as in an essay.

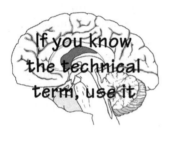

After thinking about your project you cannot do much more preparation. The examiner can ask about any paper and question, about the degree as a whole and psychology in general. If you missed a paper or question, or had a nightmare with a particular paper, and if you are still awake, think about some answers to the questions BUT the odds are they will not be mentioned.

After every exam try to review your answers as soon as you can. What did you learn from the exam process? University exams are a little different to school ones; a spot of reflection on your revision and exam technique might be useful before next time. Questions that might occur to you include:

- Had I done enough revision? Should the answer be no, ask 'Where could I have squeezed in a little more?'

- Would different revision activities be useful next time?

- Was there enough detail and evidence to support the answer?

23.6 REFERENCES AND FURTHER READING

Davies, D. (1986). *Maximising Examination Performance: A Psychological Approach.* London: Kogan Page.

Psychological links

Add two letters in the middle squares to complete the five-letter psychology-related words or abbreviations to left and right. When complete, an eight-letter psychological term can be read. Answers on p. 270.

A	N	O			L	U	E
P	E	T			G	I	D
H	U	M			G	E	R
N	O	N			A	S	E

24 'OF SHOES, AND SHIPS, AND SEALING WAX ...': A FEW ANSWERS TO THINGS PSYCHOLOGY STUDENTS ASK

Here is a potpourri of topics and lists addressing queries raised by students. Some items may seem bizarre and irrelevant, but check out the headings so that, should something become relevant during your degree, you know where to look.

24.1 TO JOIN OR NOT TO JOIN?

Get stuck in to your professional body – it can be helpful and fun. Check out the websites and see what they can do for you. Most countries where you find psychologists have an organisation that exists to promote their scientific and professional activities. These include the American Psychological Association (APA), the Australian Psychological Society (APS), the British Psychological Society (BPS) for the UK and Eire, and the Canadian Psychological Association (CPA). The societies share common aims of advancing the study of psychology, promoting the effective application of psychology to human welfare, ensuring quality education and training for budding psychologists and maintaining ethical and professional guidelines for practising psychologists.

The scope of psychology is so wide that the societies are typically arranged into different sections and divisions that focus on study or practice within a particular area. For example, the BPS has several divisions concerned with enhancing professional practice, such as the divisions of clinical and occupational psychologists, and sections in which members share interests and knowledge in particular areas, such as the social and developmental sections. There are also groups for members interested in more specialised or focused topics, like neuroscience, or older adults. All of these different groups organise meetings and conferences, which are a great way to expand your social and potential professional network, and give you the opportunity to put faces to 'big names' and perhaps realise that they too are still learning about the subject.

There are different levels of membership, and all have deals for student members. Generally students join at discounted rates, receive free monthly bulletins and newsletters; books and journals the society publishes are available at discounted prices; and there will be discounted rates for attendance at conferences. Many societies also have student-member pages on their websites. These are usually run for and by psychology students, and contain all manner of articles on coping with statistics or supervisors, recommended reading, how to get on to society committees, on-line discussion groups, links to other useful sites ... Check them out at:

http://www.apa.org The American Psychological Association site. Accessed 13 April 2000.

http://www.bps.org.uk The British Psychological Society site. Accessed 13 April 2000.

http://www.psychsociety.com.au The Australian Psychological Society site. Accessed 13 April 2000.

http://www.cpa.org.ca The Canadian Psychological Association site. Accessed 13 April 2000.

24.2 PROFESSIONAL PSYCHOLOGY

About a third of graduates in psychology go on to work in public services like education, health, public administration and the armed forces. Another third will probably work in industry or commerce, in human-resource management, marketing, public relations, consultancy, etc. Probably less than one tenth will carry out research or teach psychology. Altogether, up to a fifth of psychology graduates will become professional psychologists. While anyone can call themselves a psychologist, the professional bodies (see p. 230) usually have records of individuals who have achieved a sufficient level of training and experience to warrant being registered as professional psychologists. For example, since 1987 the BPS has kept a Register of Chartered Psychologists. It has very strict entry requirements (e.g. an accredited first degree, further training and x years supervised practice) and also maintains a very strict code of professional conduct. A chartered psychologist (C. Psychol.), then, is someone who is properly trained and qualified, and answerable to an independent professional body.

Accredited first degrees
Each society has guidelines for the knowledge and skills base they would expect to find in a graduate psychologist. They consider the qualifications of teaching staff, the syllabi, reading lists and course contents of undergraduate programmes of study in psychology. The institutions that provide programmes of study that

fulfil the society's requirements are approved, and the degree schemes are 'accredited'. Lists of recognised institutions and accredited programmes of study can be found on the appropriate webpages of each society. Holding an accredited degree qualifies you for graduate membership of the societies, and registration for further professional training, so it is often a prerequisite for enrolling on postgraduate training courses in the discipline.

See 'Leaving university' (p. 251) for careers information.

24.3 WE DIDN'T DO THIS AT SCHOOL/COLLEGE

Psychology is a big and diverse subject; no one gets to do all of it at A-level or any other stage. No problem. Psychology has a long tradition in drawing its experts from subjects other than psychology. Use your wider knowledge to look at 'psychology' issues from other angles.

Top Tips

- Don't panic.

- If faced with modules like adolescence or abnormal behaviour for the first time go to the lectures and get the general idea of the topic and material. Sort out the focus of the module.

- Doing background reading before a module starts can confuse, but it may be worth looking in local libraries for A-level texts, to pick out the background either before a course starts or during the first couple of weeks. An A-level text is likely to have the essentials with less detail than a university text, BUT you must move on to university-level texts. School texts are starting points not end points.

- Take your A-level notes to university: your attitudes notes may help someone who has helpful perception notes. People with a maths background can be very popular in statistics modules.

- If you are having difficulty with essay-writing, and especially if you have not written an essay in three years, find someone who did English, history or economics for A-level and pick their brains about writing. There are people who have excellent English-language skills, and can explain how to use semi-colons.

- Ask people which reading they find accessible and comprehensible.

24.4 STRESS

> It's hard to read
> the writing on the
> wall when you've got
> your back to it.

All students suffer from stress; it is normal, but needs management. Stress is a bodily reaction to the feeling that daily life's physical, emotional or psychological demands are getting too much. Some people view stress as a challenge and it is vital to them for getting jobs done; others hide a lot and eat vast quantities of comfort food. Trying to see stressful events as healthy challenges may help to avert some of the distress and unhappiness that tends to follow the interpretation of stress as threatening.

If you are feeling upset, or find yourself buttering the kettle and not the toast, try to analyse what's going on. Watch out for circumstances where you are stressed because of:

- Expectations you have for yourself. (*Are they reasonable at this time in these circumstances?*)

- Expectations of others, especially parents and tutors (*They have the best motives, but are these reasonable expectations at this time?*)

- Physical environment – noisy flatmates, people who don't wash up, wet weather, hot weather, dark evenings. (*What can be done to relieve these stresses?*)

- Academic pressures, too many deadlines, not enough time to read. (*Can you use friends to share study problems? Would it help to talk to someone about time management?*)

- Social pressures, partying all night. (*Are friends making unreasonable demands?*)

Serious stress needs proper professional attention (no text will substitute), but how do you recognise stress in yourself or friends? Watch out for signs like feeling tense, irritable, fatigued or depressed, lacking interest in your studies, having a reduced ability to concentrate, apathy and a tendency to get too stuck into stimulants like drink, drugs and nicotine. So that covers most of us! DO NOT GET PARANOID. *Please* do not wander into the health centre waving this page, and demand attention for what is really a hangover following a work-free term. Thank you.

Managing stress effectively is mostly about balancing demands and desires, getting a mixture of academic and jolly activities, taking time off if you tend to the 'workaholic' approach (the workaholic student spends nine hours a day in the library outside lectures, has read more papers than the lecturer and is still panicking). Get some exercise – aerobics, salsa, jogging, swimming, any sport, walk somewhere each day – and practise relaxation skills (Tai Chi classes are great fun). Study regularly and for sensible time periods. Break down big tasks into little chunks and tick them off as you do them. If you are stressed, TALK TO SOMEONE.

24.5 MATURE STUDENTS (NOT TO BE READ BY ANYONE UNDER 20, THANK YOU)

'They are all so young, and so bright, and I don't think I can do this.' Oh yes you can. You have had the bottle to get your act together and make massive arrangements for family and work, so handling a class of bright-faced 19-year-olds is easy. Just keep remembering that all those smart teenagers have developed loads of bad study habits at school, are out partying most nights, are fantasising about the bloke or girl they met last night/want to meet, and haven't got as many incentives for success as you. This degree is taking time from other activities, reducing the family income and pension contributions, which is great motivation for success. Most mature students work harder than students straight from school and do very well in finals.

'I really didn't want to say anything in the tutorial, I thought they would laugh when I got it wrong.' I'm nervous, you are nervous, he . . . (conjugate to gain confidence or get to sleep). At the start of a course everyone in the group is nervous. Your experience of talking with people at work, home, office, family, scout group, . . . means YOU CAN DO THIS. It is likely that your age gets you unexpected kudos; younger students equate age with experience and are likely to listen to and value your input.

'I hated the first week, all those 18-year-olds partying and I was trying to register and pick up the kids.' The first term is stressful, but having made lots of compromises to get to university give it a go, at least until the first set of examinations. If life is really dire you could switch to part-time for the first year, gaining time to get used to study and the complexities of coping with home and friends.

Mature students end up leading groupwork more often than the average. Your fellow students will be very, very, very happy to let you lead each time; it means they can work less hard. Make sure they support you too!

'It takes me ages to learn things, my brain is really slow.' OK, recognise that it does take more effort for older brains to absorb new ideas and concepts. The trick is to be organised and be ACTIVE in studying. This whole book should prompt useful ideas. The following suggestions are gleaned from a variety of texts and talking to mature students in Leeds. It is a case of finding the tips and routines that work for you. Like playing the cello, keep practising.

- Review notes the day after a lecture, and at the weekend.

- Check out your notes against the texts or papers; ask 'Do I understand this point?'

- Practise writing regularly – anything from a summary paragraph to an essay. Write short paragraphs, which summarise the main points from a lecture or reading, for use in revision. Devising quizzes is also fun (p. 217).

- Talk to people about psychology – your friends, partner, children, people you meet at bus stops, the dog or hamster. It gives great practice in summarising material, and in trying to explain in an interesting manner you will raise your own interest levels. Non-experts often ask useful questions.

- Try to visit the library on a regular basis, timetable part of a day or evening each week, and stick to the plan.

- Meet a fellow mature student once week or fortnight to chat about experiences and coursework over lunch, coffee or a drink.

- Have a study timetable, and a regular place to study, – the shed, attic, bedroom or a corner of the hall. Stick a notice on the door that says something like:

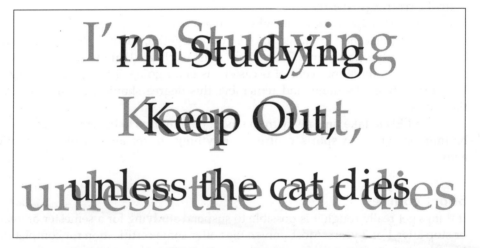

I'm Studying
Keep Out,
unless the cat dies

Be assured that once the family knows you are out of sight for a couple of hours they will find a series of devious things to do unsupervised.

- Remind yourself why you decided to do this degree, then ask whether this statistics or computer practical is really worse than anything else you have ever had to do. OK, so it is worse, but it will be over in X weeks.

- Some time management and a bit of organisation will get you through and by the second year you will know so much more about psychology and about how to manage than you did at the start.

- When you have finished and have your degree your family will be amazed and stunned, and you will have the qualifications you want.

- Make specific family fun time and stick to it: *'As a family we really tried to go out once a week for an hour, an evening, or all day. This made a real difference. We did walks, swimming, supper at the pub, visits to friends and family and loads of odd things. We took turns to choose where we went, which the kids thought was great.'*

- Don't feel guilty: lifelong learning is the way the world is going, and there is increasing awareness of and provision for mature students' needs.

Problems?

Check out the Students' Union. Most Union welfare offices have advice sheets for mature students, advisers for mature students and a mature students' society. If there is no mature students' society then start one. Generally, psychology staff are very experienced in student problems and in solving them. Most departments have a staff tutor or contact for mature students. Go and bother this nice person sooner rather than later. If you feel really guilty, buy him or her a drink sometime!

Family management

Even the most helpful family members have other things in their heads besides remembering that they promised to clean out the gerbil, vacuum the bathroom or buy bread on the way home. On balance, a list of chores that everyone agrees to and adheres to on 40 per cent of occasions is good going. Thank the kids regularly for getting jobs done, and remember this degree should not take over all their lives too.

YOU NEED to take time away from study: plan in trips to the cinema, games of badminton, visits to sports centre ... anything to get away from academic activities.

Short courses

If things get really rough it is possible to suspend studying for a semester or year, or stop after 1 or 2 years. Most universities offer some certification for completion of each whole or part year. Find out about your options.

Further reading

Rickards, T. (1992). *How to Win as a Mature Student*. London: Kogan Page.

Wade, S. (1996). *Studying for a Degree: How to Succeed as a Mature Student in Higher Education*. Plymouth: How To Books.

(Or do a library search using study, degree and mature as keywords, and check your university union website.)

24.6 EQUAL OPPORTUNITIES, HARASSMENT, GENDER AND RACIAL ISSUES

All universities have equal-opportunities policies; they aim to treat students and staff fairly and justly. Happily most of the time there are few problems, but if you feel you have one this section suggests some sources of advice.

Talk to someone sooner rather than later; there will be a departmental tutor who oversees these issues. Your problem is unlikely to be a new one, and there is normally a great deal of advice and experience available. It is really a matter of tapping into it. Check out your student union and your university or college handbook. There should be a contact name, someone who has a title like University Equal Opportunities Officer, or Adviser on Equal Opportunities.

Check out your own university websites, or visit these:

Loughborough University (1997). *Equal Opportunities.* University Handbook Online [on-line] http://www.lut.ac.uk/admin/central_admin/policy/student_handbook/section13.html. Accessed 14 April 2000.

Liverpool John Moores University (1997). *Equal Opportunities in LJMU.* University Policy [on-line] http://www.livjm.ac.uk/equal_op/opportun.htm. Accessed 14 April 2000.

Further reading
Adams, A. (1994). *Bullying at Work: How to Confront and Overcome It.* London: Virago Press.
Banton, M. (1994). *Discrimination.* Buckingham: Open University Press.
Carter, P. & Jeffs, A. (1995). *A Very Private Affair: Sexual Exploitation in Higher Education.* Ticknall, Derbyshire: Education Now Books.
Caplan, P.J. (1994). *Lifting a Ton of Feathers: A Woman's Guide for Surviving in the Academic World.* Toronto: University of Toronto Press.
Clarke, L. (1994). *Discrimination.* London: Institute of Personnel Management.
Davidson, M.J. & Cooper, C.L. (1992). *Shattering the Glass Ceiling: The Woman Manager.* London: Paul Chapman.

24.7 DROPPING OUT

'I've been here for a month, no one has spoken to me and I hate it. I'm off.' Happily this is a rare experience for psychology students, but every year there will be a few people amongst the thousands taking psychology degrees who are not happy. The main reasons seem to be 'Wrong subject choice, I should have done . . .', 'Everyone else is cleverer than me', 'The course was more scientific than

I expected', 'I was so shattered after A-level and school I really need a break and a rest' and 'I really felt I didn't fit in and it wasn't right'. There are big differences between school and university, homesickness is not unusual. All psychology departments lose students for these kinds of reasons – you will not be the first or last psychology student feeling unsettled. There are tutors to give advice and people in the union. Talk to someone as soon as you start to feel unhappy; waiting will probably make you feel worse.

The good news is that most people stick out the first few weeks, get involved with the work and social and sporting activities, and really enjoy themselves. Remember, there are 6000–22 000+ other people on your campus, 99.9 per cent are very nice, and at least 99.7 per cent feel as shy as you do. If you are really at odds with university life explore the options of suspending your studies, taking a year out in mid-degree or transferring to another university. Take the time to make this a real choice, not a rushed decision.

> **Question all unsupported statistics!**

24.8 DICTIONARIES – DO I NEED ONE?

Our tutees tend to agree that **you need a general dictionary** and a thesaurus. Not a dictionary of psychology; these are in the library and normally cannot be borrowed so they are always available for reference. Lecturers define technical terms as they go along, so your technical psycho-vocabulary expands rapidly as you discover new material. It is the non-technical words that are likely to catch you. You probably don't need a dictionary if you are familiar with:

actuate, adumbrate, antithesis, autonomic, biennial, bushmills, codex, commensurate, consensual, deduction, diurnal, emend, enigma, epitome, ergo, esoteric, exponential, extrinsic, facile, fallacious, fecund, genus, gestalt, harbinger, holistic, idiom, induction, intangible, intercalate, interface, interim, isotropic, juxtaposition, latent, leitmotif, lingua franca, locus, logical positivism, macula, mandatory, melange, milieu, minesapint, mutable, palimpsest, paradigm, plutocrat, postulate, protocol, quantum, quotient, refute, retsina, salient, schism, simulation, stigma, synergy, synthesis, temporal, tequila, transverse, trompe l'oeil, ubiquitous, Utopia, vis-à-vis, zeitgeist.

Addenda and corrigenda welcome!

Are you clear about the difference between amend and emend, affect and effect, ensure and insure, infer and imply, principle and principal, schema and schemata? Psychology dictionaries available in a library near you include:

Bruno, F.J. (1986). *Dictionary of Key Words in Psychology.* London: Routledge and Kegan Paul.

Everitt, B. & Wykes, T. (1999). *Dictionary of Statistics for Psychology.* London: Arnold.

Eysenck, M.W. (Ed.) (1990). *The Blackwell Dictionary of Cognitive Psychology.* Oxford: Blackwell Reference.

Grosser, G.S. & Spafford, C.S. (1995). *Physiological Psychology Dictionary: A Reference Guide for Students and Professionals.* New York: McGraw-Hill.

Harré, R. & Lamb, R. (1983). *The Encyclopedic Dictionary of Psychology.* Oxford: Blackwell.

Kalat, J.W. (1995). *Dictionary of Biological Psychology,* 5th edn. London: ITP.

Reber, A.S. (1995). *The Penguin Dictionary of Psychology,* 2nd edn. Harmondsworth: Penguin.

Statt, D.A. (1998) *The Concise Dictionary of Psychology,* 3rd edn. London: Routledge.

Stratton, P. & Hayes, N. (1988) *A Student's Dictionary of Psychology.* London: Arnold.

Stuart-Hamilton, I. (1996). *Dictionary of Developmental Psychology,* rev. edn. London: Jessica Kingsley.

Stuart-Hamilton, I. (1996). *Dictionary of Psychological Testing, Assessment and Treatment: Includes Key Terms in Statistics, Psychological Testing, Experimental Methods and Therapeutic Treatments,* rev. edn. London: Jessica Kingsley.

Sutherland, S. (1995). *The Macmillan Dictionary of Psychology,* 2nd edn. Basingstoke: Macmillan.

> Always use your spell checker,
> but spill chequers dOO knot awl
> weighs get tit write!

24.9 LATIN WORDS AND PHRASES

> Amos, amas, where is that lass?

Few people do Latin in school but there are many Latin phrases in normal, everyday usage. Understanding some of them will get you through university and assist in solving crosswords for life.

a priori	reasoning from cause to effect
ad hoc	for this unusual or exceptional case
ad hominem	to the man, used to describe the case where an argument is directed against the character of the author, rather than addressing the case itself
ad infinitum	to infinity (though not necessarily beyond)
ad interim	meanwhile
c.f.	confer, compare
CV	curriculum vitae, a short description of your life, suitable for employers
carpe diem	seize the day
de facto	in fact, or actual
e.g.	exempli gratia, for example
et al.	et alia, and other persons, appears in references to refer to multiple authors
et seq.	et sequens, that which follows
etc.	et cetera, and the rest, and never used in a good essay. It implies lazy thinking.
ex officio	by virtue of office
honoris causa	as an honour
ibid.	ibidem, the same, used when a reference is the same as the previous one
i.e.	id est, that is
inter alia	amongst other things
ipso facto	thereby or by the fact
loc. cit.	loco citato, in the place cited
mea culpa	it was my fault
n.b.	nota bene, note carefully, or take note
op. cit.	opere citato, in the work cited
post hoc	used to describe the type of argument where because x follows y, it is assumed y causes x
reductio ad absurdum	reduced to absurdity
(sic)	sic, which means so, is often printed in brackets to indicate that the preceding word or phrase has been reproduced verbatim, often to point up incorrect spelling
sic transit gloria mundi	nothing to do with Gloria being ill on Monday's bus, it means so passes earthly glory
tempus fugit	time flies
vi et armis	by force of arms
viva voce	by oral testimony, usually shortened to viva, meaning an oral examination

And finally the motto for the end of many a good seminar:

ergo bibamus	therefore let us drink.

24.10 GREEK ALPHABET

Psychologists, especially statistical types, will freely fling thetas and betas around in lectures. Duck. The highlighted items here are the basics. You can write faster using symbols, so it is worth knowing a few of the regular stars. ψ is often used as an abbreviation for psychology

He said eat a what? . . . This is about research, not nutrition!

A	α	Alpha	I	ι	Iota	P	ρ	Rho
B	β	Beta	K	κ	Kappa	Σ	σ	Sigma
Γ	γ	Gamma	Λ	λ	Lambda	T	τ	Tau
Δ	δ	Delta	M	μ	Mu	Y	υ	Upsilon
E	ε	Epsilon	N	ν	Nu	Φ	φ	Phi
Z	ζ	Zeta	Ξ	ξ	Xi	X	ψ	Chi
H	η	Eta	O	o	Omicron	Ψ	υ	Psi
Θ	θ	Theta	Π	π	Pi	Ω	ω	Omega

24.11 LAWS AND OTHER INTERESTING PHENOMENA

As you progress, other psychologists increasingly refer to things in shorthand, assuming quite rightly that you are familiar with the concept and no longer need the full explanation. This is fine so long as you don't confuse your doctrine of the association of ideas with the doctrine of specific nerve energies. The following list contains some of the more common ones; add others as you encounter them.

Should your patient cry **Eureka,** remember it means 'the bath water's too hot'.

ψ **Actor–observer effect** — the tendency to attribute our own behaviour to situational factors, and the behaviour of others to dispositional factors (*I didn't have time; he's so lazy*)

ψ **Availability heuristic** — a rule by which we make judgements of likelihood of an event on the basis of how easy it is to think of examples of that event

ψ **Barnum effect** — the acceptance of vague and generalised descriptions of personality that apply to most of us, as an accurate reflection of oneself

ψ **Belief in a just world** — the idea that people get what they deserve in life

ψ **Cognitive dissonance theory** — the theory that changes in people's attitudes to things can be motivated by an unpleasant state of tension that arises when there is disparity between a person's beliefs and their behaviour

ψ **Confirmation bias** — a tendency to seek for information that supports an idea, rather than looking for evidence to the contrary

ψ **Compliance** — engaging in behaviours for social reasons, rather than because you have an attitude or belief that would support that behaviour

ψ **Conformity** — the adoption of the standards and behaviours of the group as one's own standards

ψ **Diathesis-stress model** — the idea that mental illness develops when a person who is predisposed to develop that disorder encounters a level of stress that exceeds their ability to cope

ψ **Diffusion of responsibility** — an explanation of the phenomenon of bystander apathy – if there are several bystanders in an emergency situation, no one person assumes responsibility for helping ψ **Doctrine of association of ideas** — various associations are made between events and ideas, which allow meaningful thought to occur

ψ **Doctrine of specific nerve energies** — Müller's observation that different nerve fibres carry specific information from one part of the body to the brain, or from the brain to one part of the body

ψ **Dopamine hypothesis** — the idea that the positive symptoms of schizophrenia are caused by overactivity of the synapses in the brain that use dopamine

ψ **Drive reduction hypothesis** — the idea that a drive resulting from need or deprivation generates an unpleasant state that causes an organism to behave in particular ways. Reduction of drive is assumed to be reinforcing

ψ **Facial feedback hypothesis** — awareness of our facial expressions influences the way we feel

ψ **Five-factor theory** — the idea that personality is composed of the five primary dimensions: neuroticism; extroversion; openness; agreeableness; conscientiousness

ψ **Fundamental attribution error** — the tendency to overestimate the significance of dispositional factors and underestimate the influence of situational factors in explaining others' behaviour.

ψ **General adaptation syndrome** — the model proposed by Selye to describe the body's adaptation to chronic exposure to stress; it passes through the stages of alarm, resistance and exhaustion

ψ **Good continuation** — a Gestalt law of organisation that states that given two or more possible interpretations from the outline of a figure, the simplest interpretation will be preferred

ψ **Illusory correlation** — the impression that two events or ideas are related because they have occurred together, even though there is no connection between them ψ **Law of closure**

a Gestalt organisational principle that says we have a strong tendency to prefer complete or closed figures to fragmented or unconnected lines

ψ **Law of effect**

the tendency for a response to be strengthened if it is followed by a reward and weakened if it is not

ψ **Laws of Prägnanz**

a set of Gestalt principles of perception that show how we find meaning in even the most simple visual stimuli

ψ **Realistic conflict theory**

attitudes and behaviours between groups will depend on the goals of each group and whether or not these are compatible; if goals are incompatible competition will ensue

ψ **Representativeness heuristic**

a rule of thumb involving the assumption that typical (representative) members of any category occur more often that non-typical ones

ψ **Sapir–Whorf hypothesis**

the idea that language determines thought

ψ **Self-fulfilling prophecy**

the idea that expectations about a person can come about simply because the idea has been stated

ψ **Self-perception theory**

the theory that we can only know our own feelings and attitudes indirectly, by observing our own behaviour and then making attributions as we do when observing others

ψ **Self-serving bias**

the tendency to deny responsibility for failures and take credit for successes

ψ **Signal detection theory**

the act of perceiving or not perceiving a stimulus is actually a judgement of whether a brief sensory experience is due to background noise or background noise plus signal

ψ **Similarity principle**

a Gestalt organisation principle by which we tend to group similar figures, especially by colour and orientation

ψ Theory of mind	the ability to work out what other people think, know, feel and believe
ψ Weber's law	the observation that the size of the difference threshold is proportional to the intensity of the standard stimulus
ψ Yerkes–Dodson law	the principle that general performance is related to level of arousal; if arousal increases beyond an optimal point performance will decline
ψ Zipf's law	the fact that words that appear frequently in a language tend to be short

24.12 ACCURACY, PRECISION, DECIMAL PLACES, UNCERTAINTY, BIAS AND ERROR!

Most data collected for psychology studies involve human beings and as a consequence are noisy, imprecise and inconsistent and may also be biased. The trick is to recognise sources of error, acknowledge them and discuss their impact, for example in the methodology or discussion sections of a report. Discussing error is not a matter of mega *mea culpa*, 'it was his/her fault' statements. Unless exceptional care is taken, items, questions and variables are forgotten, data-collection methods influence the measurements and instruments may be inaccurate. The idea is to minimise all possible errors but only the infallible will succeed. Aim to be as objective as possible.

A true value, the absolutely accurate, correct value of something can be hard to determine, more often one has the best estimated value and one can describe it in terms of its accuracy and precision. An **accurate** value will be right or correct measurement. Data are **precise** when there is little uncertainty related to the measurement.

In experiments which record the reaction times of individuals, a test with a stopwatch will also include the time it takes for the stopwatch holder to react. In comparative tests, keeping the stopwatch operator the same should minimise error in the results: the error is consistent and the results precise. Where errors can be quantified it is good practice to quote a value with its associated resolution, for example with error bars and scatter plots (p. 170), so the reader has a feel for the precision and accuracy of the information.

Decimal places

A disadvantage of digital technology is that calculations can be reported to many decimal places. You need to decide what is relevant for a specific study or instrument. Avoid the apparent absurdity of 'a family with 2.45678 children', or 'Therefore we conclude the residents of Hobbiton make 3.21776 shopping trips per week to Buckland' or 'Survey results show the population of Stats-on-Sea are 26.3732 per cent Hindu and 56.4567 per cent Christian'.

So how many decimal places do you quote? Think about the accuracy you require and the application. A statistics package may calculate an average reaction time as 0.8765432 secs, but it is a spuriously accurate number. The stopwatch can only be read to milliseconds and a finer subdivision of time is meaningless. In practice, for most work, two decimal places will be appropriate.

Is the sample biased?

Bias is a consistent error in data. There should be plenty of information in statistics and laboratory sessions about taking samples in the right way and with enough replicates so that bias is minimised. Think about potential sources of bias when considering results. We think you would agree that when studying the attitudes of people to contraceptive use, giving a questionnaire to four girls from one church youth group is not going to provide results that are representative of the UK in the twenty-first century, and would leave the reader unimpressed. Such data are obviously inadequate and biased. Does your dataset have similar, albeit less blatant, drawbacks?

Data-entry errors

These are very, very, very common. Check carefully every time, against the original datasets. In statistics packages, use the command to show the smallest and largest datum: the commoner errors include forgetting a decimal or typing two items as a single entry.

Computational errors

Have all the formulae for calculations been entered correctly? Aside from cross-checking the equations look at the answers and make sure they are in the right 'ball park'. A quick, back-of-the-envelope calculation using whole numbers can give a feel for the range of answers to expect. If answers fall outside the expected range, check all the calculation steps carefully. Keep units the same as far as possible, or translate so that units are the same, and write down the units at each stage of a calculation.

24.13 EQUATIONS AND MATHS!

> The squaw on the hippopotamus is equal to the sum of the squaws on the other two hides.

Just a few points but if you have A-level maths ignore this section.

The sight of an equation tends to send perfectly normal psychologists into a state of total panic. **This is not necessary**. No one will ask you to rework Fermat's Last Theorem. You knew all about equations once; it is just a case of letting it flood back. The thing about university is that the education you were given from 5 to 16 gets to have some pay-off. Unfortunately some things, like mathematics and chemistry, went into a bit of memory that is currently dormant, so it is time to reopen your access routes. If in doubt ask someone with high-school maths or biology, or consult Van Der Molen and Holmes (1997).

An internationally renowned psychologist is talking to you about the latest excitements in perception or anxiety with delightful asides to lull you into a sense of security – and suddenly diverts to equations. DO NOT PANIC (well, only a little). Recall that scientific notation is just a shorthand. You can do the easy ones:

> The perceived size of an object and its retinal image can be calculated by multiplying the retinal size by the egocentric distance. (22 words) OR $S = sD$ (not 22 words!)

It is essential to define the elements of the equation, but having done it once, time and space are saved later by not having to write it all out again. Where appropriate, WHICH IS 99.9999 PER CENT OF THE TIME, the units of measurement should also be included.

Life gets to be more fun when data come in the form of tables and matrices. Thus a table that lists all the students in your class from Sheila to . . . n, and the local pubs, The Eysenck and Cattell to . . . n, can be referred to using matrix algebra. Yes, algebra. You can do it! What seems to cause confusion is making a distinction between the code used to refer to positions in a matrix and the actual data values themselves. Basically it works like map-reading with grid references. Suppose the data in the matrix refers to cash spent by individuals in the pub over a term, as here:

		The Phrenologist's Head	The Eysenck and Cattell	The Hammer and Anvil	The Shadow and Archetype	...n
		i_1	i_2	i_3	i_4	$...i_n$
Sam	j_1	£25.50	£16.75	£0.00	£3.00	
Jake	j_2	£45.70	£0.00	£16.80	£6.50	
Naomi	i_3	£52.80	£12.80	£36.45	£22.40	
Ollie	j_4	£28.67	£24.87	£16.85	£35.78	
Billy	j_5	£45.23	£12.60	£21.76	£0.00	
...n	j_n					

Each of the pubs is coded as $i_{1...n}$ and each member of the class as $j_{1...n}$. The total number of pubs is $\Sigma i = 1 - n$, and the total number in the class is $\Sigma j = 1 - n$. You can refer to a single cell: the shaded cell for Ollie in the Eysenck and Cattell is i2j4. The total amount spent by Sam is the sum of all the columns $i = 1 - n$ for row j_1. So that's the sum of Σ 25.50 + 16.75 + 3.00 = £45.25, and Ollie has spent £24.87 in the Eysenck and Cattell.

When you are faced with an equation, read it carefully and recall the rules (e.g. solve elements in brackets first). If you are feeling out of control verbalise the instructions as in the multiple choice below. Which of these verbal instructions are right?

$a + 15b - e$
   a) Multiply b by 15, then add a and subtract e.
   b) The sum of 15 times b and a, minus e.
   c) a plus 15, times b, and subtract e.

$6(x^3 + y^2)$
   d) Take the square of y and add it to the cube of x and multiply the total by 6.
   e) Multiply the cube value of x by 6, and then add the squared value of y.
   f) Cube x, then square y, add the two values together and multiply by 6.

$2x^2 - y^2$
   g) Two times the square of x, minus y squared.
   h) Square x and y, subtract and multiply by 2.
   i) Square x and multiply by 2, and then subtract the squared value of y.

See p. 252 for the answers.

Percentage problems?

50 per cent = ½ = 0.5   33.33 per cent = ⅓ = 0.333   25 per cent = ¼ = 0.25
20 per cent = ⅕ = 0.2   5 per cent = ¹⁄₂₀ = 0.05   1 per cent = ¹⁄₁₀₀ = 0.01

References and further reading

For further (and much more useful) memory jogging see:

Van Der Molen, F. & Holmes, H. (1997). Maths help. In A. Northedge, J. Thomas, A. Lane & A. Peasgood, *The Sciences Good Study Guide*. Buckingham: Open University.

24.14 AN ACRONYM STARTER LIST

Most psychologists compile a personal acronym list depending on their interests. Add acronyms to make a growing reference resource.

16PF	16 Personality Factor
AA	Alcoholics Anonymous
AA	Alzheimer Association
AABT	Association for the Advancement of Behaviour Therapy
AAC	Aids Action Council
ADHD	Attention-Deficit Hyperactivity Disorder
ADRDA	Alzheimer's Disease and Related Disorders Association
AI	Artificial Intelligence
ANS	Autonomic Nervous System
APA	American Psychological Association
APS	Australian Psychological Society
AQ	Achievement Quotient
ASCII	American Standard Code for Information Exchange
BIS	Behavioural Inhibition System
bpm	beats per minute
BPS	British Psychological Society
BRAC	Basic Rest-Activity Cycle
BTR	Baby Talk Register
CA	Chronological Age
CBT	Cognitive Behavioural Therapy
C. Psychol.	Chartered Psychologist
CHD	Coronary Heart Disease
CNS	Central Nervous System
CPA	Canadian Psychological Association
CR	Conditioned Response
CS	Conditioned Stimulus
CT	Computerised Tomography
DAT	Dementia of the Alzheimer Type
df	degrees of freedom
DNA	Deoxyribonucleic Acid
DSM	Diagnostic Symptoms Manual (I-IV)

DZ	Dizygotic (Twins)
ECR	Evoked Cortical Response
ECT	Electroconvulsive Therapy
EEG	Electroencephalogram
EMG	Electromyogram
EPI	Eysenck Personality Inventory
EPQ	Eysenck Personality Questionnaire
ERP	Event-Related Potential
ESB	Electrical Stimulation of the Brain
ESRC	Economic and Social Science Research Council
ESS	Evolutionarily Stable Strategy
FAPs	Fixed Action Patterns
GAD	Generalised Anxiety Disorder
GAS	General Adaption Syndrome
GPC	Grapheme-Phoneme Correspondence
HTML	Hypertext Markup Language
Hz	Herz
ICD-10	International Classification of Disorders – 10
INS	International Neuropsychological Society
IQ	Intelligence Quotient
jnd	just noticeable difference
LAD	Language Acquisition Device
LASS	Language Acquisition Support System
MA	Mental Age
MAOIs	Monoamine Oxidase Inhibitors
MMPI	Minnesota Multiphasic Personality Inventory
MRC	Medical Research Council
MRI	Magnetic Resonance Imaging
MZ	Monozygotic (twins)
NGOs	Non-Government Organisations
NIMBY	Not In My Back Yard
NIMH	National Institute of Mental Health
NLP	Neuro Linguistic Programming
NREM	Nonrapid Eye Movement
OCD	Obsessive Compulsive Disorder
PET	Positron Emission Tomography
PNS	Peripheral Nervous System
PTSD	Post-Traumatic Stress Disorder
r	correlation coefficient
REM	Rapid Eye Movement
RM	Raven's Matrices
ROC	Receiver Operating Characteristic Curve
SAS	Supervisory Attentional System
SD	Standard Deviation

SNS	Somatic Nervous System
SRRS	Social Readjustment Rating Scale
SSRI	Serotonin Specific Re-uptake Inhibitor(s)
TAT	Thematic Apperception Test
TPB	Theory of Planned Behaviour
TRA	Theory of Reasoned Action
UCR	Unconditional Response
UCS	Unconditional Stimulus
UNESCO	United Nations Educational, Scientific and Cultural Organization
UNHCR	United Nations Commission on Human Rights
WAIS	Weschler Adult Intelligence Scale
WHO	World Health Organization, part of United Nations
WISC	Weschler Intelligence Scale for Children
www	world wide web

24.15 LEAVING UNIVERSITY

Be a better psychologist and the world will beat a psychopath to your door.

Higher education changes people. Attitudes and values develop and perspectives evolve. It is worth reflecting on how you are altering as a person during your degree course, and thinking about how that might influence your choice of career. Ask yourself 'How does what I now know about myself, and my personal skills and attitudes, influence what I want to do after I graduate?' For a selection of ideas see http://www.udayton.edu/~psych/handbook/PSYCH-CAREERS.HTM, a series of psychologists' stories about their careers.

Knowing what you want to do when you graduate is difficult and there is an enormous choice of non-psychology careers available to you where your psychology degree is helpful but not essential. Your first advice point is your careers service. In the absence of a careers service do a www search for your local region using careers+service+university. UK students may be able to access http://www.prospects.csu.man.ac.uk/STUDENT/CIDD/startpts/casinfo.htm. Accessed 14 April 2000.

Career opportunities for psychology students are detailed at their professional bodies' sites, including

http://www.bps.org.uk/careers/careers.htm and
http://www.cpa.ca/aboutcareers.html; and at local university sites such as
http://www.york.ac.uk/depts/psych/www/etc/careers.html;
http://www.psych.bangor.ac.uk/deptpsych/services/Careers.html and
http://psyserver.pc.rhbnc.ac.uk/careers.html. (All accessed 14 April 2000.)

Make the most of your skills, the personal, transferable and academic. Look back at Figure 1.1 and check off your skills. Be upfront about them. Tell employers that you have given 20 presentations to groups of 5–50. You have used OHTs, slides and electronic display material. Practical skills are easy to list on a CV, but often seem so obvious that they are left out. Familiarity with different database and word-processing packages, modelling, statistics and hands-on laboratory and interview skills are all bonuses of psychology degrees. Tell employers you have these skills.

Building and updating a CV throughout your degree course will save time in the last year. There are plenty of texts on CV design: do a keyword library search or check out the careers service. There may be an on-line CV designer.

Top Tip

- Always write job applications in formal English, not a casual style. This may seem obvious, but as more applications are sent electronically via www site connections, it is easy to drop into a casual, e-mail writing style, which will not impress human-resources managers.

Think of yourself as a marketable product. You possess many skills that employers are seeking; it is a matter of articulating them clearly to maximise your assets.

Further reading
Hartley, J. & Branthwaite, A. (Eds) (2000). *The Applied Psychologist*, 2nd edn. Buckingham: Open University Press.

Marten, S. (1997). *Careers in Psychology: Your Questions and Answers*. Richmond: Trotman.

For websites check out http://www.ussc.alltheweb.com/ and search for psychology+careers.

Answers
The right answers in the exercise on p. 248 are a, b, d, f, g and i.

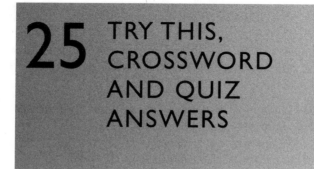

25 TRY THIS, CROSSWORD AND QUIZ ANSWERS

Psychograms I p. 12

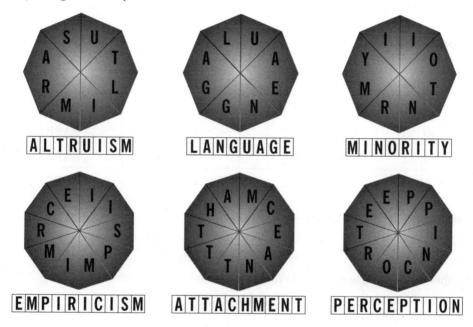

ALTRUISM LANGUAGE MINORITY

EMPIRICISM ATTACHMENT PERCEPTION

TRY THIS 2.3 – Reflecting on a class or module, p. 18

A selection of answers from Level 2 students:

What I want to get out of attending this module is . . . *I want to improve my skills on the computer. / I want to practise my communication skills, especially writing. / I want the module to give me a better idea of how to use arguments more effectively.*

What skills were lacking in me (the group) and caused things to go badly? *I wasn't happy being asked to work with people I don't know. / I prefer to rely on myself and to be able to get on with my work without having to discuss it with other people and have to compromise. / We didn't exchange contact details, telephone numbers and e-mail addresses which made co-ordinating meetings really difficult cos we all had different timetables. / We didn't have anyone in the group who was confident with the stats.*

What did I enjoy most about the session / module? ... *The content was really fresh and interesting, different from the rest of the course. / It was very hands-on and practical, with lots of time for practising skills. / The tutors were really friendly and helpful – a relaxed atmosphere that was easy to work in.*

What I enjoyed least about the module was ... *There was a huge amount of information to get down very quickly in the lectures, and not enough time to think about what was being said. / We learnt new skills every week, but didn't get a chance to practise them properly until the last 2 weeks. / Some aspects covered seemed really obvious and trivial.*

People links? p. 23

JUNG	WEST	BECK	GALE
RUNG	WELT	BACK	BALE
RUNE	WELL	BALK	BARE
RUSE	HELL	BALL	BART
ROSE	HULL	WALL	BURT

TRY THIS 4.2 – WWW addresses p. 39

Cog and Psy Sci	http://www-psych.stanford.edu/cogsci/journals
CNN Interactive	http://www.cnn.com/
Animal Bytes Database	SeaWorld Database http://www.seaworld.org.
Combined Health Information Database	http://chid.nih.gov/
Mental Health Net	http://mentalhelp.net/prof.htm
CyberPsychLink	http://cctr.umck.edu/user.dmartin/psych2.html
Online Dictionary of Mental Health	http://www.shef.ac.uk/~psyc/psychotherapy/
Links2Go: Psychology	http://www.links2go.com/topic/Psychology
PsycLIT	http://www.silverplatter.com/catalog/psyc.htm
Acoustical Society of America	http://boystown.org/asapp
AGELINE	http://www.library.unisa.edu.au/database/ageline
Wilson Social Science Abstracts	http://www.hwwilson.com/socsci.html

TRY THIS 5.3 – Where do you read? p. 50
Students' reflections:

> I've started reading on the bus on my way in, and find it's a really good time to get half an hour's worth of uninterrupted reading done. Good for thinking, not much good for note-taking obviously.

> I live with a bunch of Arts students who never seem to have as much reading as I do even though they're studying bloomin' literature. So I do my skimming for ideas in the house – no point in getting too heavily into it cos I know I'll get interrupted. And I tend to get my effective stuff done in the library. I've found myself a really quiet nook where I do all my note-taking, etc.

> I do it all at home so I don't get distracted.

TRY THIS 5.4 – Spotting reading cues p. 50
Example phrases:

> I will start with a description of what might be considered the basic requirements . . .; There will then follow a discussion of . . .; Recent publications highlight . . .; From these examples, it is clear that . . .; The present study comprised . . .; Consequently . . .; In all of the above, the focus was . . .; However . . .; Our study has revealed that . . .; A key feature of the model is . . .; Clearly there are some basic features of . . .; One such feature is . . .; One way to account for this is . . .; Immediately apparent from the figure is . . .; While the debate continues, I would argue . . .; Finally . . .

Psyco-quick crossword 1 p. 53
Across
3 Machismo; 7 Dilate; 8 Dryrot; 9 Milieu; 10 Dosser; 11 Body; 13 Value; 15 Drop; 17 Goitre; 18 Innate; 19 Thesis; 20 Trance; 21 Narcosis.

Down
1 Libido; 2 Family; 3 Medulla; 4 Hormone; 5 Stressor; 6 Outgroup; 11 Brighten; 12 Domineer; 13 Vertigo; 14 Uplifts; 15 Denial; 16 Optics.

What's my problem? Wordsearch 1 p. 63
Abnormal, Addict, Agnosia, Alexia, Amnesia, Anxiety, Aphasia, Bulimia, Complex, Conditioning, Delusion, Dementia, Dyslexic, Epilepsy, Fugue, Hysteria, Lunacy, Mania, Melancholic, Obesity, Oedipus complex, Panic, Paranoia, Phobia, Psychosis

TRY THIS 7.1 – Reasoned statements p. 70
Some responses, no right answers – can you do better?

1 *I have proved that girls are better at maths.* The scale to test the children's ability in maths had an alpha reliability of .85. There was a significant effect of gender on the test scores (F (2, 60) = 21.5, p < .01) showing that girls performed better on the test than boys (mean girl's score = 24.5, mean boy's score = 18.7). These results support the experimental hypothesis.

2 *Objective tests are the best way of measuring personality.* Objective tests contain items that can be answered and scored objectively, such as true/false or multiple-choice questions. Large numbers of items are tested on ethnically and geographically diverse samples to generate normative responses. Most objective tests use some form of validity scale to ensure that the respondents are answering the questions reasonably reliably and accurately (Testit, 2005). This type of test contrasts with projective tests in which questions are deliberately ambiguous, designed to elicit responses that reveal aspects of the respondents' personalities. These tests are very much more subject to interpretation by the tester, and have been found to be very low in validity and reliability (Rubbishit, 2007).

3 *People who see life events as threatening are less healthy.* According to Fusspot (2005) an individual's stress levels are affected by his or her cognitive appraisal, or perception, of the stressful situation. A study of coping with chronic stress in the workplace by Ulcer and Headache (2010) showed that some people treated the stressors in their lives as challenges and met them head-on, while those who treated them as threats became ill. Thus how we initially assess the stressor, how we tackle it and the extent to which we believe we can control it all seem to influence whether we become at risk of illness as result of being exposed to chronic stress.

4 *Working memory is vital to our everyday functioning.* In its broadest sense working memory can be thought of as the desktop of the brain. It is a cognitive function that helps us keep track of what we are currently doing; it holds information enough for us to dial a number, repeat a new name, or to answer a question that's just been posed. Thus, it encapsulates on-line cognition in both laboratory tasks and our daily lives (Logie, 1999).

Psychojumble p. 75
The top picture has a pear, skateboard, wellington and yacht. The lower one has an apple, bridge, monkey and trainer.

TRY THIS 8.1 – Logical arguments? p. 82
1 It is evident from the observation of children at play that boys are more aggressive than girls. [This is a statement that may be true, but is so general that it raises more questions than it answers. Is this a reference to published research or a recent study carried out in the practical class? What was the play scenario – structured or unstructured play? What kinds of behaviour were coded as being aggressive? – often girls are found to be less physically aggressive, but more

verbally aggressive. What age were the children? Were they in single-sex or mixed-sex groups?]

2 Motion sickness comes about when the vestibular organs receive information about movement that does not fit with the information about the relative motion between the person and the external visual field (e.g., Reason and Brand, 1975). Forward-facing seats lead to a lower incidence of motion sickness. [Sounds OK. Good to have the first idea referenced. What about the second statement – is it true? How does it fit with the first statement? What's important about facing forward? What about other factors, like the quality of the view, and the different visual conditions? A stronger link needs to be made between the two parts (see Turner and Griffin, 1999, if you're interested in following this one up).]

3 Burt's (1955) work with twins showed that the heritability of intelligence was 80 per cent, and this finding has been highly influential in the development of work in this area. [Yes, Burt's papers on this research make the claim reported here, and yes his work was very influential in the development of research. BUT the author appears to have missed out on the rather damning literature that says Burt's work should be seriously questioned on scientific and statistical grounds (e.g., Kamin, 1974). Getting the argument right requires confidence in the evidence.]

4 Categorisation is a cognitive mechanism that helps us categorise the world we live in. This helps us understand the world and simplify our perception of it. There are infinite numbers of social categories like Liberal Democrats and mothers. [An example of knowing what the writer is trying to say, but … The first sentence is circular. The second is fine. Plumping for merely two examples of social categories is a wasted opportunity to demonstrate their infinite variety. It is also more appropriate to use 'e.g.' rather than 'like' when giving specific examples.]

TRY THIS 8.2 – Logical linking phrases p. 82

Some examples:

> also; and; another example; but also; consequently; current discussions centre on; despite this; for example; for this reason; furthermore; however; if this is true; if … then …; in addition; in these cases; in this way; instead; interestingly; it also seems that; it remains to be established whether; one interpretation is; similarly; these ideas contrast with; these results confirm that; this research has shown; thus.

TRY THIS 8.3 – Fact or opinion? p. 83

Organisations provide the individual with an interpersonal arena in which, among other emotions, the experiences of love, companionship, betrayal and envy may influence performance and service delivery. Yet these experiences are barely represented in mainstream academic organisational literature. This omission is interesting. (Walsh, 1999, p. 20.) [The first sentence is factual – a generally recognised and accepted phenomenon. Is the second sentence fact or opinion? You might need to check a couple of databases to increase your confidence that this is the case and not simply a device for getting you to read on. The third sentence is Walsh's opinion; you might want to read the rest of the paper to decide whether or not you think she has identified an interesting omission.]

There is a growing interest in affect and organisation and management theory generally, yet it remains under-researched in the arena of strategic management processes. (Daniels, 1999, p. 24.) [This is tricky. Both parts of the sentence could be described as the author's opinion or something to be examined. You would have to read on in the text to decide. It is likely that some researchers would tend to agree with Daniels and others will disagree.]

Each stage also involves social activity. (Daniels, 1999, p. 24.) [Fact, but unsupported as it stands. Read on and you will find that the author develops supporting arguments over the course of the next three paragraphs.]

Even generating worry in others is sometimes necessary to promote behavioural change, as when a doctor issues a health warning to a patient. (Ostell, Baverstick and Wright, 1999, p. 30.) [An interesting sentence. The use of the word 'necessary' makes this a statement of opinion rather than fact. It is a fact that changes in behaviour can be associated with the generation of negative emotions? It isn't always necessary to use this approach. Is it ever necessary? What evidence do we have of its effectiveness? No evidence is cited here.]

It is important not to treat all emotional reactions in the same way, as different emotions tend to be provoked and sustained by different patterns of thinking. (Ostell, Baverstick and Wright, 1999, p. 32.) [The first half of the statement sounds like an opinion, but the second half provides ideas that show the sense of the first half. The whole is supported by the citation of two references.]

There are now Internet sites covering virtually every aspect of psychological research. (Johnson, 1999, p. 41.) [Fact, but unsupported as it stands. The author goes on to support the claim.]

Psych-ladders p. 89

T	E	S	T
T	E	N	T
P	E	N	T
P	E	N	S
P	O	N	S
P	A	N	S
P	A	N	E
W	A	N	E
W	A	V	E
W	A	D	E
B	A	D	E
B	O	D	E
B	O	D	Y
B	O	N	Y
B	O	N	G
L	O	N	G
L	U	N	G
L	U	N	E
L	A	N	E
L	A	Z	E
M	A	Z	E

M	O	D	E
M	O	L	E
H	O	L	E
H	A	L	E
H	A	L	O
H	A	L	T
H	O	L	T
H	O	O	T
F	O	O	T
C	O	O	T
C	O	L	T
C	E	L	T
C	E	L	L
M	E	L	L
M	E	L	D
M	E	N	D
M	I	N	D
M	I	N	E
L	I	N	E
L	O	N	E
L	O	B	E

TRY THIS 9.1 – Keywords in essay questions p. 93

1 Gives a quote in which the word *today* is used, and then asks you to discuss it – don't fall into the trap of thinking that you should be talking about the 1950s. Avoid trying to impress by covering a variety of different areas in applied, work and organisational psychology – it asks you to focus on *job design*. *Evaluate the extent to which you believe* means once you have discussed the contemporary work that demonstrates the relationship between applied and theoretical psychology, you need to commit yourself to a point of view about the quote.

2 You need to define terms and set limits on this one. What is a *simple* conditioning theory? Think about whether you include classical conditioning,

operant conditioning or just habituation. And what about the role of imitation and social learning? What are complex behaviours – make sure you use lots of examples; indicate the way(s) in which they may be considered complex. The main pitfall here is to define different types of conditioning, describe some research and ignore the word *explain*.

3 Stick to using one psychological measure since this is what it specifies. Don't forget there are various types of reliability and validity, respectively. Probably the most important keyword here is *relationship*. A common trap is to describe examples without showing how the concepts and forms are linked. How do different elements of reliability and validity affect each other?

4 Keywords here are *discuss* and *difficulties*. It would be very easy to *describe* lots of different definitions, and to suggest a compromise as a final position. The shopping-list approach won't do here, though. How did Simon, Binet, Weschler, Gardener and Sternberg get to their positions? What is missing from each approach? What are the limitations of each approach? These provide clues about the *difficulties*.

5 The main keyword is *discuss* – this implies that you cover all angles regardless of what your emotional response to the topic is. The secondary key phrases are *barbaric, damaging to the brain* and *therapeutically ineffective*. The biggest danger here is to be drawn by the use of emotive terms like these into second guessing what the examiner wants, and providing too biased a response. There should be a balance between the evidence to support this viewpoint and the evidence to refute it.

TRY THIS 9.2 – Evaluate an introduction pp. 95–6

We think that versions 1 and 3 are OK for university essays. Versions 2 and 4 have some interesting ideas and a couple of facts in them, but are curiously put together. Neither reads as though the author knows where they are going to go next. This is a big, age-old discussion in psychology and needs careful signposting and structuring. Version 2 starts with two generalised and overly stereotyped sentences that give an indirect idea of what is not going to be talked about. Sentences 3, 4 and 5 are much more relevant, though longwinded, as a definition of what the author will mean by personality – it is probably too all-encompassing to be helpful to the author in structuring what follows. Version 4 mentions genes and the environment, but not personality. It reads more like an introduction to an essay on nature–nurture issues in general. There are several unsupported and arguable assertions – what's the evidence that none of us value our biological roots, that we exist as experiments, or that we all find learning more interesting than heredity? This is a style to avoid.

Version 1 starts off reasonably enough, though the clause about our parents is unnecessary. It refers to Galton (no date), which is appropriate for setting some historical context to the debate. The final sentence gives a flavour of the nature of the debate but would be stronger if it used an illustrative example. Version 3 starts off indicating the possible breadth of definition and whips in a reference in the very first sentence. The reference might have been better placed in the third sentence, since Allport was better known in this area for his ideas about the nature of individuality. The second sentence includes the term 'important' which may be a signpost to a later discussion of the limits of categorising individuals through testing. The erudite bit about the word's Greek origins is nicely linked to a short but rich quote from Allport that sets up the subsequent discussion.

TRY THIS 9.3 – Good concluding paragraphs pp. 98–9

Version 1
A very nicely disguised 'the answer lies somewhere in between' conclusion. The author is clearly not happy about the reduction of the individual to a set of numbers or positions on a set of continua, and gives a reason for this disquiet; she makes her own position quite clear. The language is a bit general – a couple of cross-references back to previously used examples might have lent a bit more punch.

Version 2
A very much more clear 'it's a bit of both' response. Falls into the trap of using statistics to prove anything and everything. We hope the author was confident about the reliability and validity of his sources. Disappointing that such a rich and difficult debate is concluded with a bit of arithmetic.

Version 3
The first sentence does not sound like the beginning of a conclusion. Indeed it goes on to introduce new material – A BAD IDEA. A very abrupt ending – does the whole debate rely on the study of monozygotic twins separated at birth?

Version 4
This version draws together some of the previous discussion but then suddenly changes tack and offers what is described as a new hypothesis. This is a brave and worthy attempt to show the examiner that the author has been thinking hard nevertheless there are two problems here: (a) it's not new; it is another expression of a trait approach to personality; and (b) it could have been used as a resolution to earlier discussion, but instead fades into the last sentence, and it's not very clear where that came from!

TRY THIS 9.6 – Shorten these sentences p. 103

Wordy	Better
In addition to all the previous arguments there is the point that X.	Additionally, X.
One of several important factors in reading is phonological awareness.	Successful phonological awareness consistently predicts later reading ability.
The illusion of outgroup homogeneity refers to the fact that often people tend to assume that other people from different groups are much more similar than other people in the same group.	The illusion of outgroup homogeneity refers to people's tendency to assume greater similarity among members of other groups than within one's own group.
Being as how the brain is in charge of the release of glucocorticoids . . .	As the brain controls the release of glucocorticoids
Moving to another point in the debate . . .	Next; Additionally; Another point is
The reaction times were measured before and after eating, respectively.	The reaction times were measured before and after eating.
Chi-square is a kind of statistical test.	Chi-square is a statistical test.
One of the models that offers the best kind of explanations says that . . .	The most explanatory model suggests . . .
People who have suffered damage or trauma to the right side of the brain tend to have difficulty with spatial perception, and in particular with spatial tasks such as reading a map.	People with right parietal lobe damage often have difficulty with spatial tasks such as map-reading.
The nature of the problem . . .	The problem . . .
There are all sorts of problems with the way the experiment was run that mean these results may not be very reliable.	The reliability of the results is constrained by the procedural limitations of the study.
One prominent feature of the ear is the pinna, which serves the function of . . .	The pinna . . .
It is sort of understood that . . .	It is understood that . . .
There is such a huge amount of information covered by this title that it will be impossible to cover it all, so I have decided to only look at . . .	This essay will focus on . . .
The body of evidence is in favour of . . .	The evidence supports . . .

TRY THIS 9.8 – Synonyms for psychos? p. 105

1 reports. 2 main. 3 developed. 4 empirical. 5 consistent. 6 underlying.
7 effectiveness. 8 illustrated. 9 discrepancy. 10 resonates.

Psycho-cryptic crossword 1 p. 109

Across

1 Gametes; 5 Flicker; 9 Extremist; 10 Tools; 11 Visual signals; 13 Testable;
15 Diploe; 17 Triage; 19 Playmate; 22 Superstitious; 25 Islet; 26 Penetrate;
27 Stemmed; 28 Coroner.

Down

1 Grew; 2 Motives; 3 Trees; 4 Suitable; 5 Fetish; 6 Integrity; 7 Know-all; 8 Risk-
seeker; 12 Statistics; 14 Algorithm; 16 Platonic; 18 Impulse; 20 Abstain; 21 Stupid;
23 Outer; 24 Fear.

TRY THIS 10.1 – The Nightmare Reference List pp. 115–16

Errors included: missing authors, list was not alphabetical, missing dates,
incorrect use or absence of capitals, parentheses, publishers' names and locations,
title in italics . . . Never use *et al.* in reference lists.

The corrected list:

American Psychiatric Association (1994). *Diagnostic and Statistical Manual of Mental Disorders*, 4th edn. Washington, DC: American Psychiatric Association.

Hayes, N. (1998). *Foundations of Psychology: An Introductory Text*, 2nd edn. Surrey: Thomas Nelson.

Kline, P. (1993). *The Handbook of Psychological Testing*. London: Routledge.

Miura, I.T., Okamoto, Y., Kim, C.C., Chang, C.-M., Steere, M. & Fayol, M. (1994). Comparisons of children's cognitive representation of number: China, France, Japan, Korea, Sweden and United States. *International Journal of Behavioural Development*, **17**, 401–11.

Moscovici, S. & Hewstone, M. (1983). Social representations and social expectations: from the 'naïve' to the 'amateur' scientist. In M. Hewstone (Ed.), *Attribution Theory: Social and Functional Extensions*. Oxford: Blackwell.

Prichard, J.C. (1837). *Treatise on Insanity and Other Disorders Affecting the Mind*. Philadelphia, PA: Haswell, Barrington and Haswell.

Rick, J., Hillage, J., Honey, S. & Honeyman, S. (1997). *Stress: Big issues but what are the problems?* [on-line]. Institute for Employment Studies, Report 331. http://www.employment-studies.co.uk/summary/331sum.html. Accessed 31 October 1998.

Rosch, E.H., Mervis, C.B., Grey, W.D., Johnson, D.M. & Boyes-Braem, P. (1976). Basic objects in natural choice categories. *Cognitive Psychology*, **8**, 382–439.

Spearman, C.E. (1927). *The Abilities of Man: Their Nature and Measurement*. London: Macmillan.

Vallbo, A.B. (1995). Single-afferent neurons and somatic sensation in humans. In M.S. Gazzaniga (Ed.), *The Cognitive Neurosciences*. Cambridge, MA: MIT Press.

Wagner, H.L., MacDonald, C.J. & Manstead, A.S.R. (1986). Communication of individual emotions by spontaneous facial expression. *Journal of Personality and Social Psychology*, **50**, 737–43.

TRY THIS 12.1 – Brainstormed list p. 126

A possible structure, no right answers here.

Keywords

Eating; Anorexia nervosa; Eating disorder; Bulimia nervosa; Adolescent disorders; Low-calorie diet; Eating Disorders Association; Body dissatisfaction; Hunger; Hypertension, Transgenderism.

Fact or fiction?

Thinness is a desirable aim; Athletics – reduced performance by individuals; Do hormones control eating? Adolescent disorders; Young men are often ignored; Cultural influences – fact or fiction? Personal perception of your body: is it a visual or weight issue? Is it a positive, pleasurable state for some/in some situations? Who is observing – how do you know when you have a problem? Depression results from an individual's dissatisfaction with their body? Is it a first-world problem only? Altered sex drive – short- and long-term? A cause of distress in individuals? Cultural identity – thinness has different values in different cultures or communities?

Consequences/Controls for the body

Hormone release; Abuse of laxatives and diuretics.

External drivers

Social implications; Families are disrupted (or vice versa).

Care

High-calorie drink substitutes; Bone decay as a result – increased osteo problems?

Analytical approaches/methods

Eating Attitudes Test; Appropriate nursing care; Stunkard-Messick Eating Questionnaire; Twin studies might give insight into . . .?

Research Questions

Do hormones control eating? Gender differences in eating attitudes and behaviours; Personal perception of your body: is it a visual or weight issue? Is it a first-world problem only? Cultural identity – thinness has different values in different cultures or communities?

TRY THIS 12.3 – Discussant's role p. 131

Asks for examples. +	Seeks the sympathy vote. –
Asks for opinions. +	Keeps arguing for the same idea, although the discussion has moved on. –
Encourages others to speak. +	Asks for reactions. –
Helps to summarise the discussion. +	Is very defensive. –
Ignores a member's contribution. –	Gives examples. +
Is very (aggressively) confrontational. –	Offers opinions. +
Is very competitive. –	Summarises and moves discussion to next point. +
Keeps quiet. –	Diverts the discussion to other topics. –
Mucks about. –	Gives factual information. +
Offers factual information. +	Asks for examples. +
Speaks aggressively. –	

Psychograms 2 p. 135

HEREDITY

STRESSOR

MIDBRAIN

ARCHETYPAL

EXPERIMENT

SUBLIMINAL

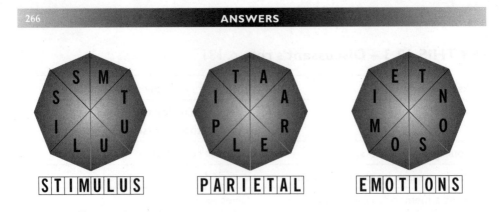

STIMULUS PARIETAL EMOTIONS

Psycho-quick crossword 2 p. 154

Across

1 Esteem; 4 Hear; 9 Alien; 10 Reality; 11 Tagging; 12 Match; 13 Growth cycle; 17 Sigma; 19 Relates; 22 Crack-up; 23 Annoy; 24 Echo; 25 Enzyme.

Down

1 Exact; 2 Trigger; 3 Ennui; 5 Exist; 6 Rhythm; 7 Drug therapy; 8 Calmly; 14 Whacky; 15 Latency; 16 Psyche; 18 Graph; 20 Learn; 21 Style.

Lab prac conundrum p. 161

Sam and Jake used the tachistoscope and got 79 per cent. Josh and Gabe manipulated colour and scored 72 per cent. Juliet and Georgia measured reaction time and got 58 per cent. Rees and Kim varied word length and scored 63 per cent.

Psychograms 3 p. 166

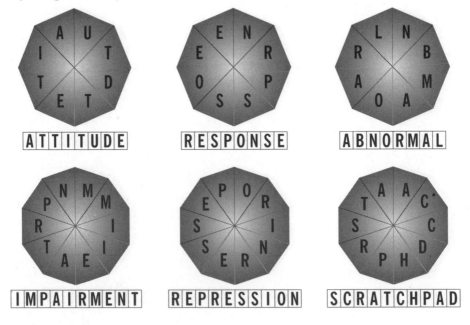

ATTITUDE RESPONSE ABNORMAL

IMPAIRMENT REPRESSION SCRATCHPAD

Psycho-cryptic crossword 2 p. 190

Across

1 Self-help; 6 See 3 down; 9 Somatotype; 10 Tact; 11 High-handedly; 13 Guru; 14 Test case; 17 Membrane; 18 Null; 20 Accumulative; 23 Anti; 24 Initialise; 25 Heresy; 26 Two-edged.

Down

2 Eros; 3, 6 across Flashbulb memory; 4 Enough; 5 Psychotherapist; 6 Meekness; 7 Metre; 8 Recklessly; 12 Pubescence; 15 Concealed; 16 Maturity; 19 Libido; 21 Unite; 22 Isle.

Whose brain is it anyway? p. 196

Adler, Allport, Argyle, Asch, Babbage, Bartlett, Bateson, Beck, Binet, Bruner, Cannon, Cattell, Charcot, Chomsky, Craik, Darwin, Ebbinghaus, Erickson, Eysenck, Fechner, Freud, Galton, Gibson, Gregory, Helmholtz, Hull, James, Jung, Klein, Kraepelin, Laing, Luria, Mandler, Miller, Moscovici, Neisser, Pavlov, Piaget, Rorschach, Sherrington, Skinner, Spearman, Tajfel, Thorndike, Vygotsky, Watson, Wolpe.

TRY THIS 20.1 – Book reviews p. 198

Comments on the extracts:

1. Barbara Koslowski's aim in writing *Theory and Evidence* is straightforward: to challenge the notion that scientific thinking is a problematic and therefore atypical aspect of human cognition. She pursues her aim on two fronts, theoretical and empirical. . . . Presents 16 mostly unpublished studies . . . (*BJDP*, 1998, **16**, 574) [A straightforward opening to a review that sets the scene in a factual manner.]

2. *Critical Psychology* acknowledges the influence of related perspectives including feminism, critical theory, post-modernism, hermeneutics and discursive psychology. Fox and Prilleltensky do not set out to write an account of the history of critical psychology: other texts have come closer to that (e.g. Parker, 1989). Instead Fox and Prilleltensky's text introduces us to a particular strand of recent critical work in psychology. The book is also notable because it stands as a potential teaching text, which is relatively unusual in critical psychology (e.g. Stainton-Rogers *et al.*, 1995). (*BJEP*, 1998, **68**, 611) [This is a useful paragraph that places the book in its general context, and in relation to other texts which are explicitly cited. It is unreasonable to expect in-depth treatment of all aspects of a subject as broad as critical psychology. The potential use with undergraduates has been flagged.]

3. Unfortunately, as I discuss below, the target article falls so far below the required standards of scholarship that the remainder of the book is devalued, despite the excellence of the individual commentaries. (*BJDP*, 1998, **16**, 573) [An unhappy reviewer, pointing out what is, for him, a fundamental flaw. He makes his main point in a single sentence and indicates that he will justify the point, giving his reasons and evidence, in the next paragraph.]

4. The book provides numerous and detailed examples of programme evaluations. These all clearly reveal the book's origin in the USA that will largely deny the British reader the sense of ownership and familiarity one assumes was intended. (*BJDP*, 1998, **16**, 571) [A book may reflect the background and cultural values of the author and it may be set in a particular context. This is not necessarily a disadvantage; it can be a strength. Many books are written to appeal to a world-wide readership – it helps the publisher's sales. You might consider whether an American reviewer would have thought to make this comment. It is the sort of statement that could reduce UK sales of this text.]

5. By and large, though, the monograph by Povinelli and Eddy stands as a model of excellence in how to conduct research in experimental psychology. They show considerable ingenuity in collecting informative data on a conceptually profound topic with non-linguistic participants. (*BJDP*, 1998, **16**, 570) [A positive response. There have been caveats earlier in the review but overall this is good work and the area of research is difficult.]

6. In certain of the chapters the references are not as up-to-date as one might have wished. For example, the most recent reference in the chapter by Fry is 1993 and in that by Stotsky is 1994. This may be due, in part, to the time taken in obtaining, editing and publishing the chapters. (*BJEP*, 1998, **68**, 622) [A fairly damning statement which points up a perennial problem with books; preparation and publication timescales can push contents out of date very quickly. Hence the emphasis on recent journal publications on reading lists. The statement is nicely exemplified. The reviewer is kind enough to offer an explanation for the dated contributions but only 'in part'.]

7. Moving onto more serious reservations about the book, the rationale behind the two sections is not entirely clear. Section 1 is entitled 'The scope of great ape intelligence', and includes a fascinating chapter by Matsuzawa and Yamakoshi on the distinct cultural traditions of two groups of chimps separated geographically. The second section is called 'Organisation of great ape intelligence: Development, culture and evolution', and includes a chapter by Boesch with content that is almost identical to that of Matsuzawa and Yamakoshi. Not only does Boesch talk about differences in cultural traditions according to geographic region, he even covers the same ground as the other authors by talking about . . . but there is a fair amount of evidence that generally (though not always) authors are oblivious to the contributions made by their colleagues. In consequence, there is little scope for a new perspective or understanding of ape intellect to emerge from the coming together of these contributing authors (because they do not come together). (*BJDP*, 1998, **16**, 569) [Most readers hope for considerable synthesis and good organisation in a text. This is a well expressed and exemplified way of saying that this element is missing.]

8. Editors Helena Helve and John Brynner have extensive research experience involving the study of youth transitions, attitudes and the economic and social

arenas surrounding the developmental processes of young people. (*BJEP*, 1998, **68**, 617) [A supportive statement that establishes that these editors are well qualified to edit this particular volume.]

9. Finally, perhaps the most telling endorsement for any book is that I have already ordered copies for use in undergraduate psychology module on 'Gender Relations and Critical Social Psychology' during the next academic year. I welcome this thought-provoking and accessible text, and look forward to subsequent editions. (*BJEP*, 1998, **68**, 612) [Clearly worth having; if you are on a module with a title like this it could be the book to buy.]

TRY THIS 22.5 – Generic questions for revising psychology, p. 218

- What is the purpose of . . .? (emotion, 'primitive' defence mechanisms)

- Why is . . . an inadequate explanation of . . .?

- Who are the three main authors to quote for this topic?

- Name two examples not in the course text or lectures for . . .?

- Explain the findings of . . .?

- What are the main characteristics of . . .? (Schachter's 2-factor theory of emotion)

- Outline the relationship between . . . and . . . (fear and surprise)

- What are the limitations of the . . . (methodological) approach? (judgemental heuristics, split-half tests of reliability, neural networks)

- Define . . .? / What does . . . mean? (anatomical coding, parametric, grapheme-phoneme correspondence)

- What are the limitations of . . .? (theory of planned behaviour, . . . feedback hypothesis)

- What methodology is employed to . . .?

- This is an unusual result. Why is this so?

- What is the purpose of . . .? (risk management, sexual behaviour)

- What was the main aim of . . .? (open-ended questions, expressive functions of consumption)

- What is the spatial scale involved here?

- How is . . . calculated? (population density, IQ, Weber fractions)

- Outline the sequence of events involved in . . .?

- If . . . did not occur, what would be the implications?

- How has . . . adapted to . . .? (primary school teaching changed in response to Piaget and Vygotsky's theories ?)

- Outline the different approaches that can be taken to the study of . . . (recall performance in the elderly)

- Will this work in the same way on a larger/smaller scale?

- How influential has . . . been? (leadership theory)

- What are the . . . (practical, social, ethical) . . . implications of this finding?

- What is meant by . . .? (serial and parallel processes in vision)

- Why is . . . important for . . .?

- Do I agree that . . .?

- Outline three types of . . .?

Psychograms 4 p. 219

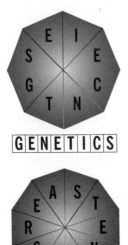

GENETICS

CLINICAL

RECEPTOR

RESISTANCE

HEURISTICS

PSYCHOTISM

Psychological links p. 229
Variance.

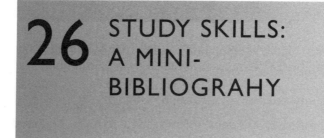

26 STUDY SKILLS: A MINI-BIBLIOGRAHY

This is a mini-bibliography of skills texts. A compilation of the references from each chapter is at http://www.geog.leeds.ac.uk/staff/p.kneale/psychologyskillbook.html. We will update the web links regularly please let us know of other sites to link with.

Try This 4.1 – WWW Resources for Psychologists (p. 38), has an extensive list of sites of subject interest.

Barnes, R. (1995). *Successful Study for Degrees*, 2nd edn. London: Routledge.

Bucknall, K. (1996). *Studying at University: How to Make a Success of your University Course*. Plymouth: How To Books.

Buzan, T. (1989). *Speed Reading*. Devon: David and Charles.

Drew, S. & Bingham, R. (Eds) (1997). *The Student Skills Guide*. Aldershot: Gower.

Fairbairn, G.J. & Winch, C. (1996). *Reading, Writing and Reasoning: A Guide for Students*, 2nd edn. Buckingham: Open University Press.

Hector-Taylor, M. and Bonsall, M. (1994). *Successful Study: A Practical Way to Get a Good Degree*, 2nd edn. Sheffield: Hallamshire Press.

Heffernan, T.M. (1997). *A Student's Guide to Studying Psychology*. Hove: Psychology Press.

Kirkman, J. (1993). *Full Marks: Advice on Punctuation for Scientific and Technical Writing*, 2nd edn. Malborough: Ramsbury Books.

Marshall, L.A. & Rowland, F. (1983). *A Guide to Learning Independently*. Buckingham: Open University Press.

Newby, M. (1989). *Writing: A Guide for Students*. Cambridge: Cambridge University Press.

Northedge, A., Thomas, J., Lane, A. & Peasgood, A. (1997). *The Sciences Good Study Guide*. Buckingham: Open University Press.

Rose, C. (1985). *Accelerated Learning*. Great Missenden, UK: Accelerated Learning Systems.

Rowntree, D. (1993). *Learn How to Study: A Guide for Students of All Ages*, 3rd edn. London: Warner Books.

Rudd, S. (1989). *Time Manage Your Reading*. Aldershot: Gower.

Russell, S. (1993). *Grammar, Structure and Style*. Oxford: Oxford University Press.

Saunders, D. (Ed.) (1994). *The Complete Student Handbook*. Oxford: Blackwell.

Van den Brink-Budgen, R. (1996). *Critical Thinking for Students: How to Use Your Recommended Texts on a University or College Course*. Plymouth: How To Books.

Weinstein, C.E. & Hume, L.M. (1998). *Study Strategies for Lifelong Learning*. Washington, DC: American Psychological Association.

Generic study skills www sites can be found at:

http://units.ox.ac.uk/departments/english/undergra/studysch.html.   The University of Oxford's English department: useful for essays and revision.

http://www.ucc.vt.edu/stdysk/stdyhlp.html. A series of study skills self-help information for Virginia Tech.

http://www.utexas.edu/student/lsc/. The Learning Skills Center at the University of Texas at Austin. Click on the 'Our Favorite Handouts' link.

http://www.adm.uwaterloo.ca/infocs/Study/study_skills.html. The study skills package at the University of Waterloo, Canada.

http://128.32.89.153/CalRENHP.html. The CalREN Project study tips.

http://www.yorku.ca/admin/cdc/lsp/handouts.htm. University of York, Ontario, Canada. Learning skills programme handouts.

http://www.campuslife.utoronto.ca/handbook/02-GettingGoodGrades.html. Getting good grades at the University of Toronto, Canada.

http://www.edinboro.edu/cwis/acaff/suppserv/tips/tipsmenu.html. Academic survival tips from Edinboro University, Pennsylvania.

INDEX